VEDANTA

OF

DHARMARĀJA ADHVARĪNDRA

Translated and Annotated by
SWĀMĪ MĀDHAVĀNANDA

WITH A FOREWORD BY
DR. S. N. DASGUPTA, C.I.E., M.A.,
PH.D. (*Cal. & Cantab.*), D. LITT. (*Hon. Rome*)

Advaita Ashrama
(Publication Department)
5 Dehi Entally Road
Kolkata 700 014

Published by
Swami Bodhasarananda
President, Advaita Ashrama
Mayavati, Champawat, Uttarakhand
from its Publication Department, Kolkata
Email: mail@advaitaashrama.org
Website: www.advaitaashrama.org

Eleventh Impression, May 2008
1M1C

ISBN 81-7505-113-2

Printed in India at
Gipidi Box Co.
Kolkata 700 014

FOREWORD

I congratulate most heartily Swāmī Mādhavānanda on his English translation of the Vedānta Paribhāṣā. I also appreciate the annotations that he has given. The Vedānta Paribhāṣā is an epistemologicial work on Śaṁkara Vedānta as interpreted in the Vivaraṇa school. The epistemological implications of the Pañca-pādikā of Padmapāda as interpreted in the Vivaraṇa, had alreday been collected and worked out by Rāmādvaya in his Vedānta Kaumudī. The work has not yet been published. When we compare the contents of the Vedānta Kaumudī with those of the Vedānta Paribhāṣā of Dharmarājādhvarīndra, the indebtedness of the latter appears to be so colossal that its claim to originality vanishes. There are also here and there traces of confusion which his son vainly tried to justify or to explain away in his commentary on the Vedānta Paribhāṣā. On the whole, this epistemological compendium on account of its brevity and lucidity of exposition has commended itself to the readers of Śaṁkara Vedānta. It is also interesting to notice that in accordance with the scheme of epistemology formulated in the Vivaraṇa, the perceptual situation is taken in a realistic manner. Parts of it, however, are not fully developed, and important questions which could be raised regarding it have not been anticipated. This may be regarded as a hypercriticism but it cannot be denied that there is much scope for elaborating the views of the Vivaraṇa school on epistemological matters.

This English translation of the Vedānta Paribhāṣā will introduce the epistemology of the Śaṁkara Vedānta to such readers as are not adepts in philosophical Sanskrit. The public owe a deep debt of gratitude for this work to Swāmī Mādhavānanda. It is also very gratifying to see that the Rāmakṛṣṇa Mission that has become so famous in the country for social service has also turned its attention towards intellectual service in such a significant work as the present one and many other translations that the learned author has done.

S. N. DASGUPTA

INTRODUCTION

The *Vedānta-Paribhāṣā* by Dharmarāja Adhvarīndra is a very important manual of the Vedānta philosophy, and is the most widely read book on the subject next to Sadānanda Yogīndra's *Vedānta-Sāra.* The author, who seems to have flourished in the seventeenth century, was a reputed scholar of Southern India, as we know from the introductory verses to the *Paribhāṣā,* as also from similar verses by his son and commentator. And we have ample evidence from the body of the book that, of the two main branches of the Śaṅkara school of Advaita Vedānta, founded by Padmapādācārya and Ācārya Vācaspati Miśra respectively, our author belonged to the former. In his discussions he has adopted the method and phraseology of Navya-Nyāya, introduced by Gaṅgeśa Upādhyāya in the fourteenth century.

The first six chapters of the *Paribhāṣā* are devoted to establishing the means of valid knowledge from the Vedāntic standpoint, and as such often contain refutations of other systems of philosophy, particularly Nyāya-Vaiśeṣika. Being to some extent of a polemical character, these chapters are rather abstruse for the beginner. But once he has ascended these rugged steps, he is ushered into the realm of Vedānta proper in the last two chapters of the book, where he will find a delightful compendium of the essential doctrines of the philosophy, embodying its subject-matter and aim.

As regards the means of knowledge there is great divergence among the different systems of philosophy. For instance, the Cārvākas, who are out and out materialists, believe only in perception; the Buddhists and the Vaiśṣikas in perception and inference; the Sāṅkhya and Yoga schools in perception, inference and verbal testimony (*śabda*); the Naiyāyikas add to these comparison as well; the Prābhākara school of Mīmāṁsakas include presumption; while the Vedāntists, along with the Bhāṭṭa school of Mīmāṁsakas believe in six means of knowledge, viz., perception, inference, comparison, verbal testimony, presumption and non-apprehension. As against the Naiyāyikas, the Vedāntins argue that presumption cannot be classed under inference, for it is based on negative invariable concomitance (*vyatireka-vyāpti*), which Vedānta does not admit; while non apprehension cannot come under perception, for, according to the logicians, it presupposes contact of the organ with the object, but non-existence cannot come in contact with the organ.

Again, with regard to the conception of knowledge, Nyāya holds that knowledge is a product of the contact of the mind with the self, while according to Vedānta it is eternal Pure Consciousness (*caitanya*); only it is manifested through mental states (*vṛtti*). The Vedāntin's theory of perception is in sharp contrast with the Naiyāyika's. Vedānta holds that Pure Consciousness has three forms—as associated with (that is, manifested as) the subject or knower or Consciousness limited by the mind as associated with the object, and as associated with the mental state, and perception of any external object (that is present and capable of being perceived) takes place when these three occupy the same space, by the mental state issuing through the organ and spreading over the object so as to assume the same form—like the water of a tank reaching a field through a channel and being shaped like the field. The mental state serves to remove the veil of nescience (*avidyā*) from the Consciousness associated with the object, which is revealed by a reflection of the Consciousness associated with the subject (that is, of the self, which is of the nature of intelligence). Some Vedāntists deny that the mind is an organ—which is a postulate of Nyāya—and according to them, the perception of internal objects like pleasure and pain is done by the witness—by which is meant that aspect of the self in which the mind, instead of being a qualifying attribute (*viśeṣana*), is a limiting adjunct (*upādhi*)—*directly*, that is, without the help of the mental state, as in the case of external objects. On this point, however, our author differs. The distinction between a qualifying attribute and a limiting adjunct is this, that the former affects (of course, speaking from the phenomenal standpoint) the self, while the latter only distinguishes it without affecting it in any way.

In Nyāya a cognition like, "The hill has

fire, because it has smoke," is inferential, whereas in Vedānta it is a composite experience, being perceptual in respect of the hill and inferential in respect of the fire. In Nyāya the validity of knowledge arises from particular favourable conditions, and is ascertained through a separate inference, while in Vedānta it arises spontaneously and is self-evident. Unlike Nyāya, Vedānta holds that *perceptual* knowledge may arise even from verbal testimony, as, for example, from a sentence like, "This is that Devadatta," or "Thou art That." While, according to Nyāya, a word primarily signifies an individual possessed of a generic attribute, in Vedānta it primarily signifies a generic attribute. In Nyāya, only words have implication (*lakṣaṇā*), but in Vedānta sentences also have it. Nyāya postulates *eternal* generic attributes (*jāti*), and inherence (*samavāya*), which is a special kind of intimate relation. Vedānta denies both, and substitutes *transitory* common features for the former, and essential identity for the latter. In Nyāya all error is taking one thing for another (*anyathā-khyāti*); in Vedānta, according to some, it is so only when the thing for which something else is mistaken is close enough to the latter to be in contact with the organ, as when we see a crystal beside a ruby as red; in other cases we have a cognition of something which is logically indefinable (*anirvacanīya-khyāti*)—which is the general view. In inference, Nyāya, like Vedānta, admits an intermediate cause (*vyāpāra*), but it is consideration (*parāmarśa*), or the knowledge that the reason, or ground from which we infer, is present in the thing in or about which something is inferred; but in Vedānta it is the latest impression of the knowledge of invariable concomitance between the reason and the thing inferred. In Nyāya the effect is something quite different from the cause; in Vedānta they are essentially the same, which accords with the Sāṅkhya view also. The above list is by no means exhaustive. The reader will come across other differences as he goes through the book.

A glance at the table of contents will give an idea of the nature and variety of the topics discussed in the book. We refrain from adverting to them here. It will be noticed that the author has bestowed a good deal of attention on the accuracy and comprehensiveness of the definitions, inserting one qualifying epithet after another into them for this purpose—to which not a little of the stiffness of books of this kind is due. He has faithfully presented in a nutshell the traditional views on important questions relating to Vedānta, and it is seldom that he has put forward any views of his own, as he has once done while discussing the perception of internal objects, and again under IMPLICATION (*lakṣaṇā*). He has often referred to great authorities like Padmapāda, Prakāśātma-yati and Vācaspati Miśra in his book, and his debt to these masters is indubitable. As to how far the contributions of our author are original, or the question of his close indebtedness to any antecedent author, for example, Rāmādvaya, as Dr. Dasgupta asserts, can be decided only when the works in question have been published. We leave the issue open, and trust that future research scholars will be in a position to settle the matter conclusively. That he has eminently succeeded in producing a handy volume for the general reader, is a fact that will be evident to all who study the book.

Of all the systems of philosophy, Pūrva-Mīmāṁsā and Vedānta follow the Vedas as closely as possible, the latter relying on Śruti confirmed by reason and realisation. But there is this outstanding difference between the two that, while Pūrva-Mīmāṁsā is a staunch believer in the ceremonial portion of the Vedas (*karma-kāṇḍa*), Vedānta lays the emphasis, and justly so, on the philosophical portion (*jñāna-kāṇḍa*), consisting of the Upaniṣads. Another point of difference between the two systems is that Vedānta believes in the Vedas having emanated from God, while Mīmāṁsā holds that they are eternal and do not depend on any agent, either for emanation or for creation.

Although Vedānta has three main phases, viz., Dualism, Qualified Monism and Monism, represented by Madhvācārya, Rāmānujācārya and Śaṅkarācārya respectively, it is Monism or Advaita that is the culmination of the philosophy. Its theme, the essential identity of the individual self and Brahman and the unreality of the universe, has been ably dealt with in the *Paribhāṣā*, and the steps to its realisation, viz., hearing, reflection and meditation, by the qualified aspirant have been clearly shown. Incidentally, the place of contemplation (*upāsanā*) and rites, as preparing the ground for the higher form of practice, has been indicated. No difficulty will be experienced in harmonising these apparently conflicting standpoints, if we remember that the scriptures provide different ways of approach to the highest Truth according to the temperament and capacity of the aspirant. Since the one indivisible Brahman *appears*, through the veil of *māyā* or the cosmic illusion, as the manifold universe, the whole phantasm with its attendant evils will disappear the moment a person realises his identity with Brahman—an identity that has never been lost, but only forgotten.

The popularity of the *Vedānta-Paribhāṣā* is testified by the number of commentaries written on it and available in print, beginning with the *Vedānta-śikhāmaṇi* by the author's son, Rāmakṛṣṇa Adhvarin, which again has got a gloss named the *Vedānta-maṇiprabhā* by Amaradāsa. Other published commentaries on the book are the *Arthadīpikā* by Śivadatta, the *Vedānta-paribhāṣā-prakāśikā* by Pedda Dīkṣita, the *Āśubodhinī* by Paṇḍita Kṛṣṇanātha Nyāyapañcānana, the *Paribhāṣā-prakāśikā* by M. M. Anantakṛṣṇa Śāstri, as well as one by Paṇḍita Jīvānanda Vidyāsāgara, B.A. All these have been consulted with profit in preparing this translation.

The only English rendering so far made of the book was that by Principal Arthur Venis, M.A., of the Sanskrit College, Benares, which appeared, with notes, serially in *The Pandit* in 1882-1885, but never came out in book form. Accordingly the present book is, I think, imperative, which leaves little room for considering the fitness of its author. Advantage has been taken of the above edition as well as of the Bengali version of the book by Śrī Śaraccandra Ghoṣāla, M.A., B.L.

I have also received considerable help from Paṇḍita Upendracandra Tarkācārya, Kāvya-Vyākarana-Purāṇa-Sāṅkhya-Vedānta-Tarka-Ṣaḍdarśana-tīrtha, of the Belur Math *Catuṣpāṭhī*, with whom I read the book. I am much indebted to Mahāmahopādhyāya Yogendranātha Tarkatīrtha, Professor of Vedānta and Mīmāṁsā, Sanskrit College, Calcutta, and to Dr. Satkari Mookerjee, M.A., Ph.D., Lecturer in Sanskrit, Pāli and Philosophy in the University of Calcutta, for valuable help during the revision. Last but not least, my thanks are due to Dr. S. N. Dasgupta, C.I.E., M.A., Ph.D., D.Litt., King George V Professor of Mental and Moral Philosophy in the University of Calcutta, and lately Principal, Sanskrit College, Calcutta, for his learned Foreword to the book.

The text has been prepared by comparing the above-named editions. An attempt has been made to make the translation faithful, and as literal as practicable. Notes have been added wherever they were deemed necessary, without, however, making them lengthy. References have been given to most of the quotations. The Sanskrit Glossary and the Index are other features that should prove useful. The book in its present form will, it is hoped, popularise the study of Vedānta among the English-knowing people in all parts of the world.

Belur Math, April, 1942 MADHAVANANDA

PREFACE TO THE SECOND EDITION

The first edition of the book having long run out, a second edition was urgently called for. In this edition the book has undergone substantial revision, for which I am deeply indebted to Pāṇḍita Dīneśa Candra Śāstrī, Tarka-Vedāntatīrtha, Adhyāpaka at the Ramakrishna Mission Institute of Culture, Calcutta. It is hoped that this revised edition will be equally acceptable to the English-knowing students of Vedānta. Aug., 1953

A WORD ABOUT THE FOURTH EDITION

The third edition of this reputed book having long been run out, we are now bringing out the fourth edition. We are sorry, it could not be printed earlier due to some unavoidable circumstances. We are, however, glad to place the book at the disposal of reading public.

Buddha Jayanti : May, 1972 PUBLISHER

KEY TO TRANSLITERATION AND PRONUNCIATION

		Sounds like			Sounds like
अ	a	o in *son*	ड	ḍ	d
आ	ā	ah	ढ	ḍh	dh in *godhood*
इ	i	i short	ण	ṇ	n
ई	ī	ee	त	t	French t
उ	u	u in *full*	थ	th	th in *thumb*
ऊ	ū	oo in *boot*	द	d	th in *then*
ऋ	ṛ	ri	ध	dh	theh in *breathe here*
ए	e	e in *bed*	न	n	n
ऐ	ai	y in *my*	प	p	p
ओ	o	oh	फ	ph	ph in *loop-hole*
औ	au	ow in *now*	ब	b	b
क	k	k	भ	bh	bh in *abhor*
ख	kh	ckh in *blockhead*	म	m	m
ग	g	g hard	य	y	y
घ	gh	gh in *log-hut*	र	r	r
ङ	ṅ	ng	ल	l	l
च	c	ch (not k)	व	v	w
छ	ch	chh in *catch him*	श	ś	sh
ज	j	j	ष	ṣ	sh (almost)
झ	jh	dgeh in *hedgehog*	स	S	s
ञ	ñ	n (somewhat)	ह	h	h
ट	ṭ	t	ं	ṁ	ng
ठ	ṭh	in *ant-hill*	ः	ḥ	half h

CONTENTS

CHAPTER I

CHAPTER II

INFERENCE

CHAPTER III

CHAPTER IV

VERBAL TESTIMONY

CHAPTER V

RESUMPTION

CHAPTER VIII

THE AIM OF VEDĀNTA

(xix)

ABBREVIATIONS

Ait. Br.	...	Aitareya Brāhmaṇa
Bṛ	...	Bṛhadāraṇyaka Upaniṣad
Bṛhannār.	...	Bṛhannāradīya Purāṇa
Br. S.	...	Brahma-Sūtras
Bṛ. Vā.	...	Bṛhadāraṇyaka-Upaniṣad-Vārtika
Chā.	...	Chāndogya Upaniṣad
f. or ff.	...	and following
G.	...	Bhagavad-Gītā
Ka.	...	Kaṭha Upaniṣad
Kū.	...	Kūrma Purāṇa
Kau.	...	Kauṣītakī Upaniṣad
Mā.	...	Māṇḍūkya Upaniṣad
Mār.	...	Mārkaṇḍeya Purāṇa
Mbh.	...	Mahābhārata
Mu.	...	Muṇḍaka Upaniṣad
n.	...	note
N. S. Ed.	...	Nirṇaya Sāgara Edition
Pū. Mī. Sū.	...	Pūrva-Mīmāṁsā-Sūtras
Ṛ	...	Ṛg-Veda
Śiv.	...	Śiva-Purāṇa
Śv.	...	Śvestāśvatara Upaniṣad
Tai.	...	Taittirīya Upaniṣad
Tai. Br.	...	Taittirīya Brāhmaṇa
Tai. S.	...	Taittirīya Saṁhitā
Up.	...	Upaniṣad
Vāj. S.	...	Vājasaneya Saṁhitā
Viṣ.	...	Viṣṇu Purāṇa
V. S. S.	...	Vizianagram Sanskrit Series

CHAPTER I

PERCEPTION

Introduction

यदविद्याविलासेन भूतभौतिकसृष्टयः ।
तं नौमि परमात्मानं सच्चिदानन्दविग्रहम् ॥ १ ॥

1. To that Supreme Self, the embodiment of Existence, Knowledge and Bliss (Absolute),[1] by the manifestation of the nescience (*avidyā*)[2] relating[3] to which the projection[4] of the (simple) elements[5] and things[6] made up of these elements takes place, I bow.

[[1] These are not qualities of the Supreme Self, in which case they would be transitory, thereby making the Self changeful, but the latter *is* Existence-Knowledge-Bliss Absolute.

[2] An inscrutable entity without a beginning, to which are attributed the projection, maintenance and dissolution of the whole universe. It explains how the one indivisible Brahman is cognised as the multiple universe. It is not a mere absence of knowledge, but a positive entity. It is not real, because it ceases with the realisation of one's identity with Brahman: not unreal, because we perceive its effects, the subjective and the objective universe. It is neither identical with Brahman nor different from It.

[3] According to Prakāśātma-yati, the author of the *pañcapādikā-vivaraṇa*, a gloss on Padmapādācārya's commentary, *Pañcapādikā*, on Śaṅkara's *Śarīraka-Bhāṣya* on the *Brahma-Sūtras*, nescience is in Brahman as well as about Brahman. But according to Vācaspati Miśra (9th century), the author of the famous commentary *Bhāmatī* on the same *Bhāṣya*, it

is in the individual self (*jīva*), although it is about Brahman.

[4] This includes maintenance and dissolution as well.

[5] The original or uncompounded (*apañcīkṛta*) forms of the five elements—earth, water, fire, air and ether—are meant.

[6] In fact, the whole universe of name and form.]

यदन्तेवासिपञ्चास्यैर्निरस्ता भेदिवारणाः ।
तं प्रणौमि नृसिंहाख्यं यतीन्द्रं परमं गुरुम् ॥ २ ॥

2. I salute that prince of monks, my teacher's teacher, named Nṛsiṁha, whose pupils have routed dualists, as lions do elephants.

श्रीमद्वेङ्कटनाथाख्यान् वेलाङ्गुडिनिवासिनः ।
जगद्गुरूनहं वन्दे सर्वतन्त्रप्रवर्तकान् ॥ ३ ॥

3. I salute the world-teacher named Śrīmat Veṅkaṭanātha,[1] resident of Velāṅguḍi,[2] who was an expounder of all[3] systems of philosophy.

[[1] This was his own teacher.

[2] Probably the cultured village called Vidaṅguḍi lying to the south of the Cauvery and east of Kumbakonam.

[3] Not Vedānta alone.]

येन चिन्तामणौ टीका दशटीकाविभञ्जिनी ।
तर्कचूडामणिर्नाम कृता विद्वन्मनोरमा ॥ ४ ॥

4. He who has written a commentary on the *Cintāmaṇi*,[1] called *Tarkacūḍāmaṇi*, in which he has smashed ten commentaries, and which has been appreciated by scholars—

[[1] *Tattva-cintāmaṇi* by Gaṅgeśa Upādhyāya, the founder of the new school of Hindu logic.]

टीका शशधरस्यापि बालव्युत्पत्तिदायिनी ।
पदयोजनया पञ्चपादिका व्याकृता तथा ॥ ५ ॥

5. Who has also written an illuminating commentary[1] for the students on Śaśadhara,[2] and has besides expounded the *Pañcapādikā*[3] by construing its words[4]—

[[1] Called *Nyayaratna.*

[2] Author of the *Nyāya-siddhānta-dīpa.*

[3] See note 3 on verse 1. Padmapāda was a favourite disciple of Śaṅkara.

[4] This verse does not occur in many of the printed editions.]

तेन बोधाय मन्दानां वेदान्तार्थावलम्बिनी ।
धर्मराजाध्वरीन्द्रेण परिभाषा वितन्यते ॥ ६ ॥

6. That Dharmarāja Adhvarīndra[1] is composing this Paribhāṣā[2] based on Vedāntic teachings, for the enlightenment of backward students.

[[1] Literally, 'Prince of adepts in performing sacrifies.'

[2] The word generally means terminology. Here, however, it means a lucid exposition of the accepted principles of the philosophy.]

Liberation the Supreme End of Life

इह खलु धर्मार्थकाममोक्षाख्येषु चतुर्विधपुरुषार्थेषु मोक्ष एव परमपुरुषार्थः, "न स पुनरावर्तते" इत्यादिश्रुत्या तस्यैव नित्यत्वावगमात्, इतरेषां त्रयाणां प्रत्यक्षेण, "तद्यथेह कर्मजितो लोकः क्षीयते, एवमेवामुत्र पुण्यजितो लोकः क्षीयते" इत्यादिश्रुत्या च अनित्यत्वावगमाच्च। स च ब्रह्मज्ञानादिति ब्रह्म तज्ज्ञानं तत्प्रमाणञ्च सप्रपञ्चं निरूप्यते ।

Among the four kinds of human ends in this world, called righteousness (*dharma*),[1] wealth, objects of desire and liberation, it is liberation that is the supreme human end, for that alone is known to be eternal from such Śruti texts as, "(And) he (the qualified aspirant) does not return[2]" (*Chā*, VII. xv. i, adapted), while the other three are known to be transitory by perception or[3] from such Śruti texts as, "Now, as in this world the comforts gained through one's labours are exhausted, exactly so in the other world the comforts achieved through one's good deeds are exhausted" (*Chā*. VIII. i. 6). And that liberation comes through the knowledge of Brahman. Hence Brahman, the knowledge of It, and the means (*pramāṇa*) of that knowledge are being described in detail.

[[1] Strictly speaking, its results, viz., heaven etc.
[2] To this earth, to take up a fresh body.
[3] As the case may be. Righteousness being imperceptible, anything about it is known only through the scriptures.]

Valid Knowledge and its Means

तत्र प्रमाकरणं प्रमाणम् । तत्र स्मृतिव्यावृत्तं प्रमात्वमनधिगताबाधितार्थविषयकज्ञानत्वम् । स्मृतिसाधारणन्तु अबाधितार्थविषयकज्ञानत्वम् । नीरूपस्यापि कालस्येन्द्रियवेद्यत्वाभ्युपगमेन, धारावाहिकबुद्धेरपि पूर्वपूर्वज्ञानाविषय-तत्तत्क्षणविशेषविषयकत्वेन न तत्राव्याप्तिः । किञ्च सिद्धान्ते धारावाहिकबुद्धिस्थले न ज्ञानभेदः, किन्तु यावद्-

घटस्फुरणं तावद्घटाकारान्तःकरणवृत्तिरेकैव, न तु नाना, वृत्तेः स्वविरोधिवृत्त्युत्पत्तिपर्यन्तं स्थायित्वाभ्युपगमात् ; तथाच तत्प्रतिफलितचैतन्यरूपं घटादिज्ञानमपि तत्र तावत्-कालीनमेकमेव, इति नाव्याप्तिशङ्कापि ।

Now the word 'means' stands here for the instrument[1] of valid knowledge (*pramā*).[2] Here,[3] if recollection is excluded from it, then valid knowledge would mean that knowledge which has for its object something that is not already known and is uncontradicted[4]; while if recollection is included in it, it would mean that knowledge which has for its object something that is uncontradicted. Since time, although it is colourless, is admitted to be cognised through the organs,[5] even a continuous cognition[6] has for its object particular moments that are not the objects of the preceding cognition; hence the definition does not fail to apply there. Moreover,[7] according to the tenets of Vedānta, in the case of a continuous cognition there is no break in knowledge, but so long as there is the cognition of a jar, the mental state[8] that assumes the form of the jar is just one, and not multiple, for a mental state is admitted to last till another state opposed to it has arisen. Hence, in this case, the knowledge of the jar etc., which is but Pure Consciousness[9] reflected in the mental state in question, also being just one throughout that time, there is not the least suspicion about the definition being too narrow.

[[1] A thing is produced by a number of causes. Only the extraordinary cause is called the instrument (*karaṇa*).

[2] As opposed to illusion or error, as when we mistake a rope for a snake.

[3] Opinion is divided as to whether recollection, say of a jar that has been seen on the previous day, is valid knowledge or not. Two definitions are being given to suit these differing views.

[4] By an experience of a diametrically opposite nature.

[5] By the Mimāṁsakas. When we say, "The jar exists now," we not only see the jar but also the present moment. Here time is cognised by the eye.

[6] For example, when we see a jar for some length of time, in each successive moment we see the same jar no doubt, but the cognition in each case is different, because it also takes note of the particular moment in which it takes place and which belongs to no preceding cognition. Hence the object not being already known, the definition is quite applicable.

[7] The reply not being according to Vedānta, the objection is being answered in another way.

[8] This will be dealt with on p. 15.

[9] The unconditioned Brahman, free from attributes.]

ननु सिद्धान्ते घटादेर्मिथ्यात्वेन बाधितत्वात् कथं तज्ज्ञानं प्रमाणम्? उच्यते। ब्रह्मसाक्षात्कारानन्तरं हि घटादीनां बाधः, "यत्र त्वस्य सर्वमात्मैवाभूत् तत् केन कं पश्येत्" इति श्रुतेः। न तु संसारदशायां बाधः, "यत्र हि द्वैतमिव भवति तदितर इतरं पश्यति" इति श्रुतेः। तथाच 'अबाधित'-पदेन संसारदशायामबाधितत्वं विवक्षितम्, इति न घटादिप्रमायमव्याप्तिः। तदुक्तम्—

"देहात्मप्रत्ययो यद्वत् प्रमाणत्वेन कल्पितः।
लौकिकं तद्वदेवेदं प्रमाणान्त्वाऽऽत्मनिश्चयात्॥"

इति। 'आ आत्मनिश्चयात्'—ब्रह्मसाक्षात्कारपर्यन्तमित्यर्थः।
'लौकिकम्' इति घटादिज्ञानमित्यर्थः।

Objection: According to the tenets of Vedānta, a jar etc. are contradicted as being unreal.[1] So how can the knowledge of it be valid knowledge?

Reply: The answer is this. It is only after the realisation of Brahman that a jar etc. are contradicted, for the Śruti says, "But when to the knower of Brahman everything has become the Self, then what should one see and through what?" (*Bṛ.* IV. v. 15); but they are not contradicted in the transmigratory state,[2] for the Śruti says, "Because when there is duality, as it were, then one sees something" (*Ibid.*). Hence the word 'uncontradicted' means 'not contradicted during the transmigratory state,' and therefore the definition is not too narrow to include the valid knowledge of a jar etc. So it has been said, "Just as the notion of one's identity[3] with the body is assumed to be valid knowledge, exactly so is this ordinary knowledge—till the self is truly known.[4]" The last clause means, "Till Brahman is realised." By 'ordinary knowledge' is meant the knowledge of a jar etc.

[[1] Brahman alone being real.

[2] The state of relative existence, when one thinks oneself to be different from Brahman and passes from one body to another, being subject to birth and death.

[3] As when one says, "I am stout," or "I have come here."

[4] As identical with the Supreme Self.]

Perception as a Means of Knowledge: the Mental State

तानि च प्रमाणानि षट्—प्रत्यक्षानुमानोपमानागमार्थापत्त्यनुपलब्धिभेदात्। तत्र प्रत्यक्षप्रमायाः करणं प्रत्यक्षप्रमाणम्। प्रत्यक्षप्रमा चात्र चैतन्यमेव, "यत् साक्षादपरोक्षाद् ब्रह्म" इति श्रुतेः। 'अपरोक्षादि'त्यस्य अपरोक्षमित्यर्थः।

Those means of knowledge are six in number, their divisions being perception, inference, comparison, verbal testimony, presumption and non-apprehension.[1] Of these, the means known as perception refers to the instrument of valid perceptual knowledge, which knowledge, according to Vedānta, is nothing but Pure Consciousness,[2] for the Śruti, says, "The Brahman that is immediate[3] and intuitive[4] (*Bṛ* III. iv. 1.). '*Aparokṣāt*' (intuitive) in the text stands for '*aparokṣam.*'

[[1] These will be taken up one by one in the following six chapters.

[2] For the sake of convenience, this epithet will henceforth be dropped, the word 'Consciousness' in this connection beginning with a capital.

[3] Not obstructed from the seer or subject by anything.

[4] Of the essence of intuited knowledge.]

ननु चैतन्यमनादि, तत् कथं चक्षुरादेस्तत्करणत्वेन प्रमाणत्वमिति? उच्यते। चैतन्यस्यानादित्वेऽपि तदभिव्यञ्जकान्तःकरणवृत्तिरिन्द्रियसन्निकर्षादिना जायते, इति वृत्तिविशिष्टं चैतन्यमादिमदित्युच्यते, ज्ञानावच्छेदकत्वाच्च वृत्तौ ज्ञानत्वोपचारः। तदुक्तं विवरणे, "अन्तःकरणवृत्तौ ज्ञानत्वोपचारात्।"

Objection: Is not Consciousness without a beginning? So how can the eye etc., as instruments of that, be the means of knowledge[1]?

Reply: The answer is this. Although Consciousness is without a beginning, yet that mental state which reveals it arises through the contact of the organs, etc. Hence Consciousness qualified[2] by the mental state is spoken of as having a beginning. And as the mental state limits the (resulting) knowledge, it is figuratively[3] designated as knowledge. So it has been said in the *Vivaraṇa*, "On account of the mental state being figuratively spoken of as knowledge."[4]

[[1] The contention is that knowledge should not need any instrument.

[2] That is, reflected in it; not Pure or Absolute Consciousness as It is, for It is identical with Brahman. Of course, according to the Advaita school of Vedānta, any such qualification or limitation is but apparent.

[3] Because, being insentient, it cannot properly be called knowledge.

[4] An adaptation of line 17, p. 41, Vizianagram Sanskrit Series, to which edition the subsequent references to the *Vivaraṇa* will also be made. See note 3 on p. 1.]

ननु निरवयवस्यान्तःकरणस्य परिणामात्मिका वृत्तिः कथम्? इत्थम्। न तावदन्तःकरणं निरवयवम्, सादिद्रव्यत्वेन सावयवत्वात्। सादित्वञ्च "तन्मनोऽसृजत" इत्यादिश्रुतेः। वृत्तिरूपज्ञानस्य मनोधर्मत्वे च "कामः सङ्कल्पो विचिकित्सा श्रद्धाऽश्रद्धा धृतिरधृतिर्ह्रीर्धीर्भीरित्येतत् सर्वं मन एव" इति श्रुतिर्मानम्, 'धी'-शब्देन वृत्तिरूपज्ञानाभिधानात्। अत एव कामादेरपि मनोधर्मत्वम्।

Objection: The mind being devoid of parts, how can there be a mental state, which is a modification?

Reply: In this way: In the first place, the mind is not devoid of parts, for, being a substance with a beginning, it must have parts. And that it has a beginning is proved by such Śruti texts as, "It projected the mind" (*Bṛ.* I. ii. 1, adapted). That the knowledge which is a mental state is an attribute of the mind is borne out by the Sruti text, "Desire, resolve, doubt, faith, want of faith, steadiness, unsteadiness, shame, intelligence and fear—all these are but the mind" (*Bṛ.* I. v. 3); for the word 'intelligence' refers to the knowledge that is a mental state. For this very reason desire etc. are also attributes of the mind.

ननु कामादेरन्तःकरणधर्मत्वे, "अहमिच्छामि" "अहं जानामि," "अहं बिभेमि" इत्याद्यनुभव आत्मधर्मत्वमवगाहमानः कथमुपपद्यते ? उच्यते। अयःपिण्डस्य दग्धृत्वाभावेऽपि दग्धृत्वाश्रयवह्नितादात्म्याध्यासाद् यथा "अयो दहति" इति व्यवहारः, तथा सुखाद्याकारपरिणाम्यन्तःकरणैक्याध्यासात् "अहं सुखी," "अहं दुःखी" इत्यादिव्यवहारः।

Objection: If desire etc. be attributes of the mind, how can experiences such as "I wish," "I know," "I fear," which apprehend them as attributes of the self, be explained?

Reply: The answer is this. Just as a lump of iron has not the property of burning, yet, on account of the false identification with fire, which is the substratum of the burning property, we use the expression, "The iron burns," similarly the use of expressions such as, "I am happy," "I am miserable," is due to the false identification[1] (of the self) with the mind, which is modified in the form of happiness etc.

[[1] Produced by nescience.]

ननु अन्तःकरणस्येन्द्रियतयाऽतीन्द्रियत्वात् कथं प्रत्यक्ष-विषयतेति ? उच्यते। न तावदन्तःकरणमिन्द्रियमित्यत्र मानमस्ति। "मनःषष्ठानीन्द्रियाणि" इति भगवद्गीतावचनं प्रमाणमिति चेत्, न, अनिन्द्रियेणापि मनसा षट्त्वसंख्या-पूरणाविरोधात्। नहीन्द्रियगतसंख्यापूरणमिन्द्रियेणैवेति नियमः, "यजमानपञ्चमा इडां भक्षयन्ति" इत्यत्र ऋत्विग्गत-पञ्चत्वसंख्याया अनृत्विजाऽपि यजमानेन, "वेदानध्यापयामास महाभारतपञ्चमान्" इत्यादौ च वेदगतपञ्चत्वसंख्याया अवेदेनापि भारतेन पूरणदर्शनात्; "इन्द्रियेभ्यः परा ह्यर्था अर्थेभ्यश्च परं मनः" इत्यादिश्रुत्या मनसोऽनिन्द्रियत्वाव-गमाच्च।

न चैवं मनसोऽनिन्द्रियत्वे सुखादिप्रत्यक्षस्य साक्षात्त्वं न स्यात्, इन्द्रियाजन्यत्वादिति वाच्यम्। नहीन्द्रियजन्यत्वेन ज्ञानस्य साक्षात्त्वम्, अनुमित्यादेरपिमनोजन्यतया साक्षात्त्वा-पत्तेः, ईश्वरज्ञानस्यानिन्द्रियजन्यस्य साक्षात्त्वानापत्तेश्च।

Objection: The mind, being an organ, is imperceptible. So how can it be an object of perception?

Reply: The answer is that in the first place there is nothing to prove that the mind is an organ.

Objection: The statement of the *Bhagavad-Gītā*, "(The *jīva* draws) the organs, with the mind as the sixth" (XV. 7), is a proof.

Reply: No, for there is nothing contradictory in making up the number six by the mind, although it is not an organ. There is no hard and fast rule that the making up of a number relating to the organs must be done by an organ alone; for in the passage, "They, with the sacrificer as the fifth one, eat the *iḍā*,"[1] we find that the number five relating to the priests is made up by sacrificer, who is not a priest, and in the passage, "He taught the Vedas, with the *Mahābhārata* as the fifth" (*Mbh.* I. lxiv. 131, XII. cccil. 20), the number five is made up by the *Mahābhārata*, which is not a Veda. And that the mind is not an organ is evident from such Śruti texts as, "Higher than the organs are the objects; higher than the objects is the mind" (*Ka.* III. 10).

It cannot be urged that if the mind thus be not an organ, the perception of happiness etc. will not be immediate[2] (*sākṣāt*); because the immediacy of knowledge does not lie in its being due to an organ; for in that case inference etc.[3] also, being due to the mind,[4] would be immediate,[5] and God's knowledge, which is not due to any organ, would not be immediate.[6]

[[1] A special portion of the sacrificial offerings, which at a certain stage of the sacrifice used to be eaten by the priests and the person performing the sacrifice. The deity connected with it was also named Iḍā, and is identified with the goddess of speech.

[2] But would be mediate, not being produced by any organ.

[3] That is, inference, comparison and verbal testimony.

[4] Which, according to the logicians, is an organ.

[5] And hence would be classed as perception.

[6] So that God will never have any perceptual knowledge.]

The Criterion of the Perceptuality of Cognition: Three Kinds of Consciousness

सिद्धान्ते प्रत्यक्षत्वप्रयोजकं किमिति चेत्, किं ज्ञानगतस्य प्रत्यक्षत्वस्य प्रयोजकं पृच्छसि, किंवा विषयगतस्य ? आद्ये प्रमाणचैतन्यस्य विषयावच्छिन्नचैतन्याभेद इति ब्रूमः।

तथाहि त्रिविधं चैतन्यम्—विषयचैतन्यं प्रमाणचैतन्यं प्रमातृचैतन्यञ्चेति। तत्र घटाद्यवच्छिन्नं चैतन्यं विषयचैतन्यम्, अन्तःकरणवृत्त्यवच्छिन्नं चैतन्यं प्रमाणचैतन्यम्, अन्तःकरणावच्छिन्नं चैतन्यं प्रमातृचैतन्यम्।

Objection: What, then, is the criterion[1] (*prayojaka*) of perceptuality according to the tenets of Vedānta?

Reply: Do you inquire about the criterion of the perceptuality of knowledge or of objects[2]? If it be the former, we say it is the unity of the Consciousness reflected in the means of knowledge with the Conciousness limited by the object. To be explicit: Consciousness is threefold—as associated with the object (*viṣaya*), with the means of knowledge (*pramāṇa*) and with the subject or knower (*pramātṛ*). Of these, Consciousness limited by a jar etc, is the Consciousness associated with the object; that limited by the mental state is the Consciousness associated with the means of knowledge; and that limited by the mind is the Consciousness associated with the subject.

[[1] The condition or circumstances under which the term may be used.

[2] When we say, "This jar," the knowledge is perceptual. The jar also is said to be perceptual, as being an object of perception. Of course the criteria of knowledge being perceptual and an object being perceived are different. That of the perception of objects will be dealt with on p. 25.]

तत्र यथा तड़ागोदकं छिद्रान्निर्गत्य कुल्यात्मना केदारान् प्रविश्य तद्वदेव चतुष्कोणाद्याकारं भवति, तथा तैजसमन्तःकरणमपि चक्षुरादिद्वारा निर्गत्य घटादिविषयदेशं गत्वा घटादिविषयाकारेण परिणमते। स एव परिणामो वृत्तिरित्युच्यते। अनुमित्यादिस्थले तु अन्तःकरणस्य न वह्न्यादिदेशगमनम्, वह्न्यादेश्चक्षुराद्यसन्निकर्षात्। तथाच "अयं घटः" इत्यादिप्रत्यक्षस्थले घटादेस्तदाकारवृत्तेश्च बहिरेकत्र देशे समवधानात् तदुभयावच्छिन्नं चैतन्यमेकमेव, विभाजकयोरप्यन्तःकरणवृत्तिघटादिविषययोः एकदेशस्थत्वेन भेदाजनकत्वात्। अत एव मठान्तर्वर्तिघटावच्छिन्नाकाशो न मठावच्छिन्नाकाशाद्भिद्यते। तथाच "अयं घटः" इति

घटप्रत्यक्षस्थले घटाकारवृत्तेर्घटसंयोगितया घटावच्छिन्न-चैतन्यस्य तद्वृत्त्यवच्छिन्नचैतन्यस्य चाभिन्नतया तत्र घट-ज्ञानस्य घटांशे प्रत्यक्षत्वम्। सुखाद्यवच्छिन्नचैतन्यस्य तद्वृत्त्यवच्छिन्नचैतन्यस्य च नियमेनैकदेशस्थितोपाधिद्वया-वच्छिन्नत्वात् नियमेन "अहं सुखी" इत्यादिज्ञानस्य प्रत्यक्षत्वम्।

Now, as the water of a tank, issuing through a hole, enters in the form of a channel a number of fields, and just like them assumes a rectangular or any other shape, so also the luminous[1] mind, issuing[2] through the eye etc., goes to the space occupied by objects such as a jar, and is modified into the form of a jar or any other object. That very modification is called a state (*vṛtti*). But in the case of inference[3] etc. the mind does not go to the space occupied by fire etc., for the latter are not in contact with the eye etc. Thus in cases of perception such as, "This jar," the jar etc. and the mental state in the form of those combine in the same space outside the body, and hence the Consciousness limited by both is one and the same; for the mental state and objects such as a jar, although (usually) they are dividing factors, do not (here) produce any difference, since they occupy the same space. For this very reason the ether limited by a jar that is within a monastery is not different from the ether limited by the monastery.[4] Similarly, in the case of the perception of a jar as, "This jar," the mental state in the form of the jar being in contact with the jar, the Consciousness limited by that mental state is not different from the Consciousness limited by the jar, and hence the knowledge of the jar there[5] is a perception so far as the jar is concerned.[6] Again,[7] since the Consciousness limited by happiness etc. and the Consciousness limited by the mental state relating to them are invariably limited by the two limiting adjuncts[8] that occupy the same space,[9] the knowledge, "I am happy," is invariably a perception.[10]

[[1] Transparent, light and mobile. This explains its power to reach and take the form of objects and reveal them.

[2] This is essential to the perception of external objects only, happiness etc. being perceived inwardly.

[3] When, for instance, we infer the presence of fire in a distant hill by seeing smoke in it.

[4] The entity is one and the same; only the limiting adjuncts (*upādhis*) vary. The ether (*ākāśa*) is the subtlest of the elements and pervades everything. It is one and indivisible.

[5] In the case cited.

[6] But not in respect of the qualities or actions in the jar. For the perception of these, the mental state should be of that particular form.

[7] In the perception of internal objects.

[8] Viz., happiness etc. and the mental state in the form of those.

[9] Viz., that occupied by the mind.

[10] In respect of the happiness only.

Objections to the Definition of Subjective Perception Answered

नन्वेवं स्ववृत्तिसुखादिस्मरणस्यापि सुखाद्यंशे प्रत्यक्षत्वापत्तिरिति चेत्, न, तत्र स्मर्यमाणसुखस्यातीतत्वेन स्मृतिरूपान्तःकरणवृत्तेर्वर्तमानत्वेन तत्रोपाध्योर्भिन्नकालीनतया तत्तदवच्छिन्नचैतन्ययोर्भेदात्; उपाध्योरेकदेशस्थत्वे सति एककालीनत्वस्यैवोपाधेयाभेदप्रयोजकत्वात्। यदि चैकदेशस्थत्वमात्रमुपधेयाभेदप्रयोजकम्, तदा "अहं पूर्वं सुखी" इत्यादिस्मृतावतिव्याप्तिवारणाय वर्तमातत्वं विषयविशेषणं देयम्।

Objection: In that case the recollection of the happiness etc. abiding in oneself would also be a perception in respect of the happiness etc.[1]

Reply: No, for there the happiness that is being recollected being a past event, and the mental state in the form of recollection being a present event, the two limiting adjuncts[2] in the mind belong to different times, and hence the two Consciousnesses limited by them are different; for the criterion of the unity of the substratum having the limiting adjuncts is that the two limiting adjuncts must occupy the same space at the same time. If, however, the criterion of that unity be occupation of the same space alone, then in order to prevent (the definition of perception) from unduly extending to a recollection[3] such as, "I was happy before," the object must be qualified by the idea of presence.[4]

[[1] Though not in respect of the time, place, etc., related to them.

[2] Viz., the happiness that is being recollected and the mental state in the form of the recollection.

[3] Which is not a perception.

[4] That is, the concluding portion of the definition given in the first paragraph of p. 14 should read: "Limited by the object, which must be present."]

नन्वेवमपि स्वकीयधर्माधर्मौ वर्तमानौ यदा शब्दादिना ज्ञायते तदा तादृशशाब्दज्ञानादावतिव्याप्तिः, तत्र धर्माद्यवच्छिन्न-तद्वृत्त्यवच्छिन्नचैतन्ययोरेकत्वादिति चेत्, न। योग्यत्वस्यापि विषयविशेषणत्वात्। अन्तःकरणधर्मत्वाविशेषेऽपि किञ्चिदयोग्यं किञ्चिद्योग्यमित्यत्र फलबलकल्प्यः स्वभाव एव शरणम्। अन्यथा न्यायमतेऽप्यात्मधर्मत्वाविशेषात् सुखादिवत् धर्मादेरपि प्रत्यक्षत्वापत्तिर्दुर्वारा।

Objection: Even then, when the present righteousness and unrighteousness relating to oneself are known through verbal testimony[1] and so forth,[2] the definition unduly extends[3] to such verbal comprehension etc., because there the Consciousness limited by righteousness and unrighteousness and the Consciousness limited by the mental state in the form of those are one.[4]

Reply: No, for capability of perception also must form a qualifying attribute of the object. That in spite of their being equally attributes of the mind, some are capable of being perceived while others are not, can be explained only by a reference to the inherent nature of things, which we must assume on the basis of the actual result.[5] Otherwise, even in the Nyāya system, righteousness and unrighteousness would inevitably be matters of perception like happiness etc., because they are equally attributes of the self.[6]

[[1] By somebody saying, "You are righteous," or "You are unrighteous."

[2] Refers to inference such as, "I possess righteousness and unrighteousness, for I experience happiness and misery."

[3] For the conditions of perception are satisfied here, though it is not a case of perception.

[4] For these two limiting adjuncts occupy the same space, viz., that covered by the mind, at the same time.

[5] To make the effect, viz., perception, possible.

[6] So the logician should not raise this objection.]

न चैवमपि सुखस्य वर्तमानतादशायां, "त्वं सुखी" इत्यादिवाक्यजन्यज्ञानस्य प्रत्यक्षता स्यादिति वाच्यम्, इष्टत्वात्। "दशमस्त्वमसि" इत्यादौ सन्निकृष्टविषये शब्दादप्यपरोक्षज्ञानाभ्युपगमात्।

It cannot be urged that even then, while happiness is present, the knowledge arising from sentences such as, "You are happy," would be a perception; for we accept this view, inasmuch as in sentences like, "You are the tenth man,"[1] which refer to objects that are in contact (with the organ[2]), we admit immediate or perceptual knowledge even from verbal testimony.

[[1] Ten rustics swam across a stream, and one of them counted their number to see if all had crossed. To their dismay, one was found missing. Then everyone took his turn at counting, but the result was the same. So they began to lament, when a kind passer-by inquired what it was all about. On being told what had happened, he readily understood the situation, and asked one of them to count again. When the man stopped at nine, the new-comer said to him, "You are the tenth man." This he repeated with the rest of them. Then they saw their mistake and went away happy. Everyone had left himself out in the counting!

[2] This is with regard to external objects. In the case of internal objects, the contact is with the mind.]

अत एव "पर्वतो वह्निमान्" इत्यादिज्ञानमपि वह्न्यंशे परोक्षम्, पर्वतांशेऽपरोक्षम् पर्वताद्यवच्छिन्नचैतन्यस्य बहिर्निःसृतान्तःकरणवृत्त्यवच्छिन्नचैतन्याभेदात्; वह्न्यंशे तु अन्तःकरणवृत्तिनिर्गमनाभावेन वह्न्यवच्छिन्नचैतन्यस्य प्रमाणचैतन्स्य च परस्परं भेदात्। तथाचानुभवः "पर्वतं पश्यामि," "वह्निमनुमिनोमि" इति। न्यायमते तु "पर्वतं-मनुमिनोमि" इत्युनुव्यवसायापत्तिः।

Therefore knowledge such as, "The hill has fire," is also mediate[1] so far as the fire is concerned, and immediate[2] in respect of the hill; for the Consciousness limited by the hill etc. is not different from that limited by the state of the mind that has gone out, but in respect of the fire, since the mind does not go out to form a state, the Consciousness limited by the fire and the Consciousness[3] associated with the means of knowledge are different from each other. Thus the experience[4] takes the form, "I see the hill," and "I infer the fire." But in the system of logic[5] the apperception (*anuvyavasāya*)[6] would be of the form, "I infer the hill."[7]

[[1] That is, not a perception.

[2] That is, a perception.

[3] Or Consciousness limited by the mental state.

[4] It is a composite experience, partly perceptual and partly inferential.

[5] Which does not admit this twofold character of the cognition.

[6] Perception of a cognition. The cognition, "This jar," is a perception, while the perception, "I know the jar," is an apperception. Similarly with inference.

[7] Instead of, "I infer fire in the hill." The hill is perceived, not inferred.]

असन्निकृष्टपक्षकानुमितौ तु सर्वांशेऽपि ज्ञानं परोक्षम्; "सुरभि चन्दनम्" इत्यादिज्ञानमपि चन्दनखण्डांशेऽपरोक्षम्, सौरभांशे च परोक्षम्, सौरभस्य चक्षुरिन्द्रियायोग्यतया योग्यत्वघटितस्य निरुक्तलक्षणस्याभावात्।

In an inferential knowledge, however, in which the subject[1] is not in contact with the organ,[2] the knowledge is wholly mediate. Knowledge[3] such as, "A fragrant piece of sandal," is also immediate in respect of the piece of sandal,[4] and mediate in respect of the fragrance, because the latter being incapable of apprehension by the eye,[5] the definition, mentioned before,[6] based on capability of being perceived cannot apply here.

[[1] *Pakṣa*: that in or about which something is inferred.

[2] For example, in the inference, "An atom of earth has smell, because it is earth, as is the case with a jar." Here the atom, being an imperceptible substance, can never come in contact with the eye or skin, which are the only two

organs that can perceive substances. Therefore the knowledge is not perceptual, but inferential, both in respect of the thing to be inferred, viz., smell, and in respect of the subject, viz., the atom.

[3] Ocular knowledge is meant, as when on seeing a piece of sandal from a distance we make the statement.

[4] Because it is actually in contact with the eye.

[5] Because smell is an object, not of the eye, but of the nose, which owing to its distance is not in contact with the fragrance.

[6] See p. 19.]

न चैवमेकत्र ज्ञाने परोक्षत्वापरोक्षत्वयोरभ्युपगमे तयोर्जातित्वं न स्यादिति वाच्यम्, इष्टत्वात्। जातित्वोपाधित्वपरिभाषायाः सकलप्रमाणागोचरतयाऽप्रामाणिकत्वात्। "घटोऽयम्" इत्यादिप्रत्यक्षं हि घटत्वादिसद्भावे मानम्, न तु तस्य जातित्वेऽपि जातित्वरूपसाध्याप्रसिद्धौ तत्साधकानुमानस्याप्यनवकाशात्। समवायासिद्ध्या ब्रह्मभिन्ननिखिलप्रपञ्चस्यानित्यतया च नित्यत्वसमवेतत्वघटितजातित्वस्य घटत्वादावसिद्धेश्च। एवमेवोपाधित्वं निरसनीयम्।

It cannot be urged that if we thus admit both mediacy and immediacy in the same knowledge, they would not be generic attributes (*jāti*)[1]; for we accept this objection, because technical terms regarding something being a generic attribute or a characteristic other than that (*upādhi*) are unsupported by any means of knowledge, and as such are unauthorised. Perceptions such as, 'This jar,' are a proof of the existence of the attribute 'jarhood,' for instance, but not of its being a generic attribute as well; for since the thing to be established, viz., generic attribute, is something fictitious, the inference that establishes it also has no room. Moreover, since inherence (*samavāya*)[2] is unfounded, and the whole universe, which is other than Brahman, is transitory, the definition of a generic attribute, which is based on its being eternal and inherent in many things, cannot apply to jarhood etc. Exactly in a similar way, the fact of being a characteristic other than a generic attribute may (also) be refuted.

[[1] A generic attribute (*jāti*) is a distinct category in the Nyāya philosophy, and is defined as "that which is eternal and inherent in many things," for example, jarhood (*ghaṭatva*). It is present in all jars, and would persist as an entity even if all jars were gone. That is, it is eternal. Vedānta denies such generic attributes. According to it, jarhood is the sum total of the characteristics of a jar, which distinguishes it from other things. It is not eternal. Now, according to the old school of Nyāya, cross division (*saṅkara*) is one of the impediments to a generic attribute. It consists in two things being mutually exclusive and also coexistent. For example, materiality (*bhūtatva*) and limitedness (*mūrtatva*) thwart each other's being a generic attribute, for materiality is in earth, water, fire, air and ether, but not in mind, while limitedness is in the first four and mind, but not in ether. Hence if mediacy and immediacy, which exclude each other, co-exist in knowledge, they lead to a cross division, and therefore they cannot be generic attributes. This is the contention. The Vedāntin replies that it is a welcome objection, because he does not admit such generic attributes. Examples of characteristics other than generic attributes are: the state of being a blue jar (*nīla-ghaṭatva*) and etherhood (*ākāśatva*). These also, according to the Vedāntist, should not be put in a separate class. They are just attributes.

[2] According to Nyāya, inherence is eternal relation. It is the relation between the whole and parts, generic attributes and individuals, qualities or actions and the substances possessing them, and ultimate difference (*viśeṣa*) and the eternal substances—atoms, ether, time, space, etc. Vedānta denies inherence and substitutes essential identity (*tādātmya*) for it.]

"पर्वतो वह्निमान्" इत्यादौ च पर्वतांशे वह्न्यंशे चान्तःकरणवृत्तिभेदाङ्गीकारेण तत्तद्वृत्त्यवच्छेदकभेदेन परोक्षत्वापरोक्षत्वयोरेकत्र चैतन्ये वृत्तौ न कश्चित् विरोधः। तथाच तत्तदिन्द्रिययोग्यवर्तमानविषयावच्छिन्नचैतन्याभिन्नत्वं तत्तदाकारवृत्त्यवच्छिन्नज्ञानस्य तत्तदंशे प्रत्यक्षत्वम।

In sentences like, "The hill has fire," since the mental states are admitted to be different in respect of the hill and the fire, their distinguishing characteristic (*avacchedaka*) also are different, and hence there is no contradiction in mediacy and immediacy being together in the same Consciousness. So[1] knowledge that is limited by mental states in the form of particular objects, is a perception in respect of such knowledge, when it is not different from the Consciousness limited by objects that are present and are capable of being apprehended by particular organs.

[[1] Here a comprehensive statement about the criterion of the perceptuality of knowledge is given, summing up the points discussed in the preceding pages.]

The Perceptuality of Objects: its Definition Vindicated

घटादेर्विषयस्य प्रत्यक्षत्वन्तु प्रमात्रभिन्नत्वम्। ननु कथं घटादेरन्तःकरणावच्छिन्नचैतन्याभेदः, "अहमिदं पश्यमि" इति भेदानुभवविरोधादिति चेत्, उच्यते। प्रमात्रभेदो नाम न तावदैक्यम्, किन्तु प्रमातृसत्तातिरिक्तसत्ताकत्वाभावः। तथाच घटादेः स्वावच्छिन्नचैतन्येऽध्यस्ततया विषयचैतन्य-सत्तैव घटादिसत्ता, अधिष्ठानसत्तातिरिक्ताया आरोपित-सत्ताया अनङ्गीकारात्। विषयचैतन्यञ्च पूर्वोक्तप्रकारेण प्रमातृचैतन्यमेवेति प्रमातृचैतन्यस्यैव घटाद्यधिष्ठानतया प्रमातृसत्तैव घटादिसत्ता, नान्येति सिद्धं घटादेरपरोक्षत्वम्, अनुमित्यादिस्थले त्वन्तःकरणस्य वह्न्यादिदेशनिर्गमना-भावेन वह्न्यवच्छिन्नचैतन्यस्य प्रमातृचैतन्यात्मकतया वह्न्यादिसत्ता प्रमातृसत्तातो भिन्ना इति नातिव्याप्तिः।

The perceptuality of objects[1] such as a jar, however, consists in their not being different from the (Consciousness associated with the) subject.

Objection: How can a jar etc. be one with the Consciousnss limited by the mind, since it contradicts our experience of difference, as when we say, "I see this"?

Reply: The answer is this. The absence of difference from the subject does not indeed mean identity; it means having no existence apart from that of the subject. To be explicit, since a jar etc.

are superimposed on the Consciousness limited by them, their existence is but the existence of the Consciousness associated with the object, for the existence of what is superimposed is not admitted to be something over and above that of its substratum. And since the Consciousness associated with the object is, in the manner described above,[2] but the Consciousness associated with the subject, the latter Consciousness alone is the substratum of a jar etc., and hence their existence is but[3] that of the subject, and not somethirg else. So the immediacy[4] of a jar etc. (in knowledge) is proved. But in cases of inference etc., since the mind does not go out to the space covered by the fire etc., the Consciousness limited by the fire is not one with the Consciousness associated with the subject, and therefore the existence of the fire etc. is distinct from that of the subject. So (the definition of perception) does not wrongly extend to such cases.

[[1] This is the answer to the second part of the question mentioned on page 13, viz., the criterion of the perceptuality of objects.

[2] In the illustration of the water of a tank. See p. 15.

[3] That is, nothing over and above the existence of the Consciousness associated with the subject.

[4] The fact of their being objects of perception.]

नन्वेवमपि धर्माधर्मादिगोचरानुमित्यादिस्थले धर्माधर्मयोः प्रत्यक्षत्वापत्तिः, धर्माद्यवच्छिन्नचैतन्यस्य प्रमातृचैतन्याभिन्नतया धर्मादिसत्तायाः प्रमातृसत्तानतिरेकादिति चेत्, न, योग्यत्वस्यापि विषयविशेषणत्वात्।

Objection: Even then, in the case of an inference

regarding righteousness and unrighteousness, the latter would be objects of perception, because the Consciousness limited by them not being distinct from the Consciousness associated with the subject, the existence of righteousness etc. is not apart from that of the subject.

Reply: No, for capability of perception is also a qualifying attribute of the object.

नन्वेवमपि "रूपी घटः" इति प्रत्यक्षस्थले घटगतपरिमाणादेः प्रत्यक्षत्वापत्तिः, रूपावच्छिन्नचैतन्यस्य परिमाणाद्यवच्छिन्नचैतन्यस्य चैकतया रूपावच्छिन्नचैतन्यस्य प्रमातृचैतन्याभेदे परिमाणाद्यवच्छिन्नचैतन्यस्यापि प्रमात्रभिन्नतया परिमाणादिमत्तायाः प्रमातृसत्तातिरिक्तत्वाभावात् इति चेत्, न, तत्तदाकारवृत्त्युपहितत्वस्यापि प्रमातृविशेषणत्वात्। रूपाकारवृत्तिदशायां परिमाणाद्याकारवृत्त्यभावेन परिमाणाद्याकारवृत्त्युपहितप्रमातृचैतन्याभिन्नसत्ताकत्वाभावेन अतिव्याप्त्यभावात्।

Objection: Even then, in the case of the perception, "A coloured jar," the size etc.[1] of the jar would be objects of perception; for since the Consciousness limited by the colour is one with that limited by size etc., and the former is not different from the Consciousness associated with the subject, therefore the Consciousness limited by size etc. is also not different from (that associated with) the subject, and hence the existence of size etc. is not apart from that of (the Consciousness associated with) the subject.

Reply: No, for the fact of having as limiting adjuncts the mental states in the form of those particular objects[2] is also a qualifying attribute of the subject. Thus, when the mental state has the form of colour, there is no mental state in the form of size etc. Hence size etc. not having an existence same as that of the Consciousness associated with the subject, of which the mental state in the form of size etc. is a limiting adjunct, (the definition of perception) does not wrongly extend (to the size etc.).

[[1] That is, all perceptible qualities and actions.
[2] Colour etc., as the case may be.]

नन्वेवं वृत्तावव्याप्तिः, अनवस्थाभिया वृत्तिगोचर-वृत्त्यनङ्गीकारेण तत्र स्वाकारवृत्त्युपहितत्वघटितोक्तलक्षणा-भावात् इति चेत्, न। अनवस्थाभिया वृत्तेर्वृत्त्यन्तरा-विषयत्वेऽपि स्वविषयत्वाभ्युपगमेन स्वविषयवृत्त्युपहित-प्रमातृचैतन्याभिन्नसत्ताकत्वस्य तत्रापि भावात्।

Objection: In that case the definition will not extend to the mental state, for, since for fear of a *regressus in infinitum* you do not admit that a mental state can have for its object another mental state, the definition stated above will not apply there, as one of its factors is that the mental state in the form of the object—here, the mental state itself—is a limiting adjunct (of the Consciousness associated with the subject).[1]

Reply: Not so, for although in order to avoid a *regressus in infinitum* a mental state is not admitted to be the object of another mental state, yet it is assumed to be its own object, and hence, even in the instance cited, there *is* the Consciousness associated with the object, that has an existence not different from that of the Consciousness associated with the subject, of which the mental state, with itself as its own object, is the limiting adjunct.

[[1] For there will be no such thing as a mental state in the form of itself. Hence the definition will be futile in this case.]

एवाञ्चान्तःकरणतद्धर्मादीनां केवलसाक्षिविषयत्वेऽपि तत्तदाकारवृत्त्यभ्युपगमेन उक्तलक्षणस्य तत्रापि सत्तान्नाव्याप्तिः। न चान्तःकरणतद्धर्मादीनां वृत्तिविषयत्वाभ्युपगमे केवलसाक्षिविषयत्वाभ्युपगमविरोध इति वाच्यम्। नहि वृत्तिं विना साक्षिविषयत्वं केबलसाक्षिवेद्यत्वम्, किन्त्विन्द्रियानुमानादिप्रमाणव्यापारमन्तरेण साक्षिविषयत्वम् अत एवाहङ्कारटीकायामाचार्यैरहमाकारान्तःकरणवृत्तिरङ्गीकृता। अत एव च प्रातिभासिकरजतस्थले रजताकाराविद्यावृत्तिः साम्प्रदायिकैरङ्गीकृता। तथाचान्तःकरणतद्धर्मादिषु केवलसाक्षिवेद्येषु वृत्त्युपहितत्वघटितलक्षणस्य सत्त्वान्नाव्याप्तिः। तदयं निर्गलितार्थः— "स्वाकारवृत्त्युपहितप्रमातृचैतन्यसत्तातिरिक्तसत्ताकत्वशून्यत्वे सति योग्यत्वं विषयस्य प्रत्यक्षत्वम्।"

Similarly, although the mind and its attributes,[1] etc.,[2] are objects of the witness (p. 37) alone, yet, as we assume[3] (them to be objects of) mental states in the form of those, the definition mentioned above applies there also, and hence it is not too narrow. It cannot be urged that if the mind and its attributes etc. are assumed to be objects of mental states (in the form of those), it will contradict the assumption that they are cognised by the witness alone; for, being cognised by the witness alone does not mean that they are objects of the witness without the presence of the mental states (corresponding to them), but that they are objects of the witness without the activity of the means of knowledge, such as the organs and inference. Hence the Ācārya,[4] in his gloss, in the passage dealing with egoism,[5] has admitted a mental state in the form of the ego. Hence also, in the case of an illusory[6] piece of silver, a state of *nescience* in the form of the silver has been admitted by the traditional interpreters.[7] So the definition (of perception), of which mental states (in the form of the objects) as limiting adjuncts (of the subject) are a factor, applying to the mind and its attributes, etc., which are cognised by the witness alone, it is not too narrow. Therefore the gist of the matter is this: An object is said to be cognised by perception when it is capable (of being perceived) and is devoid of any existence apart from that of the Consciousness associated with the subject, which (Consciousness) has for its limiting adjunct a mental state in the form of that object.

[[1] Such as pleasure and desire.
[2] Refers to illusions, such as seeing a nacre as silver.

[3] That is, if we admit that the mind and its attributes, as also illusions, are apprehended by mental states in the form of those objects.

[4] Prakāśātma-yati. Note 3 on p. 1.

[5] *Vivaraṇa*, p. 55, l. 21.

[6] *Prātibhāsika*, as opposed to *vyāvahārika* or conventional.

[7] For example, Sarvajñātma-muni (9th century), the author of *Saṁkṣepa-Śārīraka*, a metrical epitome of Śankara's *Śārīraka-Bhāṣya*.]

तत्र संयोग-संयुक्ततादात्म्यादीनां सन्निकर्षाणां चैतन्याभिव्यञ्जकवृत्तिजनने विनियोगः ।

Now the (various) connections of the organs, viz., conjunction,[1] identity with what is conjoined,[2] and so on,[3] are considered to produce mental states that reveal Consciousness.

[[1] *Saṁyoga*, as in the case of substances such as a jar. This is a direct connection.

[2] *Saṁyukta-tādātmya*, as with qualities and other attributes of substances, such as the colour of a jar. Here the organ is connected with the jar, and the colour, according to Vedānta, is identical with that.

[3] Refers to: (i) Identity with what is the same as what is conjoined (*saṁyuktābhinna-tādātmya*), as in the case of the characteristics of a colour, which are identical with it. (ii) Identity, as in the case of sound, which, being a quality of the ether, is identical with it. (iii) Identity with what is the same (*abhinna-tādātmya*), as in the case of the totality of the characteristics of sound (*śabdatva*). This is identical with sound, which again is the same as the ether. Vedānta denies the relation of substantive and qualifying attribute (*viśeṣya-viśeṣaṇa-bhāva*), admitted by Nyāya, as in the sentence, "The ground has no jar." The other connections are practically the same in Nyāya. Only in place of

identity (*tādātmya*) it substitutes inherence (*samavāya*), and in place of the word 'same' (*abhinna*) it uses the word 'inherent' (*samaveta*)].

Four Kinds of Mental States

सा च वृत्तिश्चतुर्विधा—संशयो निश्चयो गर्वः स्मरणमिति। एवंविधवृत्तिभेदेन एममप्यन्तःकरणं मन इति, बुद्धिरिति, अहङ्कार इति, चित्तमिति चाख्यायते। तदुक्तम्—

"मनोबुद्धिरहङ्कारश्चित्तं करणमान्तरम्।
संशयो निश्चयो गर्वः स्मरणं विषया इमे॥"

That (mental) state is of four kinds: doubt, certitude, egoism and recollection. Owing to this diversity of states, the mind, though one, is designated as the *manas*, the intellect, the ego and the *citta*. So it has been said: "The *manas*, the intellect, the ego and the *citta* constitute the internal instrument (mind). Doubt, certitude, egoism and recollection—these are (respectively) their objects."

Determinate and Indeterminate Perception

तच्च प्रत्यक्षं द्विविधम्, सविकल्पकनिर्विकल्पकभेदात्। तत्र सविकल्पकं वैशिष्ट्यावगाहि ज्ञानम्। यथा "घटमहं जानामि" इत्यादिज्ञानम्। निर्विकल्पकन्तु संसर्गानवगाहि ज्ञानम्। यथा "सोऽयं देवदत्तः," "तत्त्वमसि" इत्यादिवाक्यजन्यं ज्ञानम्।

The perception spoken of above is of two kinds: determinate (*savikalpaka*) and indeterminate (*nirvi-*

kalpaka). Of these, the former is that knowledge which apprehends relatedness (of the substantive and the qualifying attribute) (*vaiśiṣṭya*); for example, knowledge such as, "I know the jar."[1] Whereas indeterminate perception is that knowledge which does not apprehend this relatedness; for example, knowledge arising from sentences like, "This is that Devadatta," or "Thou art That" (*Chā*. VI. viii. 7—xvi. 3.)[2]

[[1] Here the object of the knowledge is the jar as related to the subject 'I.' Hence it is determinate knowledge.

[2] In these cases the knowledge arises by ignoring the particular features. For example, 'this' refers to the present and 'that to the past, and these two being contradictory elements, have to be left out of consideration in recognising the person Devadatta. Similarly, in the other example, 'thou' and 'That' referring to something present and absent respectively, these differences have to be ignored before one can grasp the essential unity of the individual self and Brahman. Hence in such cases the knowledge is indeterminate.]

ननु शाब्दमिदं ज्ञानम्, न प्रत्यक्षम्, इन्द्रियाजन्यत्वात्, इति चेत्, न। नहि इन्द्रियजन्यत्वं प्रत्यक्षत्वे तन्त्रम्, दूषितत्वात्, किन्तु योग्यवर्तमानविषयकत्वे सति प्रमाणचैतन्यस्य विषयचैतन्याभिन्नत्वमित्युक्तम। तथाच "सोऽयं देवदत्तः" इति वाक्यजन्यज्ञानस्य सन्निकृष्टविषयतया बहिर्निःसृतान्तःकरणवृत्त्यभ्युपगमेन देवदत्तावच्छिन्नचैतन्यस्य वृत्त्यवच्छिन्नचैतन्याभिन्नतया "सोऽयं देवदत्तः" इति वाक्यजन्यज्ञानस्य प्रस्यक्षत्वम्। एवं "तत्त्वमसि" इत्यादिबाक्य-

जन्यज्ञानस्यापि, तत्र प्रमातुरेव विषयतया तदुभयाभेदस्य सत्त्वात् ।

Objection: But this knowledge is verbal comprehension, not perception, for it is not due to the organs.

Reply: No, for the fact of being due to the organs is not the criterion of perception, since it has already[1] been condemned, but, as has been stated,[2] it is the fact of the Consciousness associated[3] with the means of knowledge not being different from the Consciousness associated with objects, when the latter are present and are capable of being perceived. Thus, as the knowledge due to the sentence, "This is that Devadatta," has for its object something connected with an organ, and as states of the mind that goes out are assumed, the Consciousness limited by Devadatta is not different from that limited by the mental state (in the form of the object), and hence the knowledge due to the sentence, "This is that Devadatta," is a perception. Similarly with the knowledge due to sentences like, "Thou art That," also, for there the subject itself being the object, the condition about the unity of the two is present.

[[1] On p. 13, par. 2.

[2] On p. 26.

[3] That is, limited by the mental state in the form of the objects.]

ननु वाक्यजन्यज्ञानस्य पदार्थसंसर्गावगाहितया कथं निर्विकल्पकत्वम् ? उच्यते । वाक्यजन्यज्ञानविषयत्वे हि

न पदार्थसंसर्गत्वं तन्त्रम्, अनभिमतसंसर्गस्यापि वाक्यजन्यज्ञानविषयत्वापत्तेः, किन्तु तात्पर्यविषयत्वम्। प्रकृते च "सदेव सोम्येदमग्र आसीत्" इत्युपक्रम्य "तत् सत्यम्, स आत्मा, तत्त्वमसि श्वेतकेतो" इत्युपसंहारेण विशुद्धे ब्रह्मणि वेदान्तानां तात्पर्यमवसितम् इति कथं तात्पर्याविषयं संसर्गमवबोधयेत्? इदमेव "तत्त्वमसि" इत्यादिवाक्यानामखण्डार्थत्वं यत् संसर्गानवगाहियथार्थज्ञानजनकत्वमिति। तदुक्तम्।

"संसर्गासङ्गिसम्यग्धीहेतुता या गिरामियम्।
उक्ताखण्डार्थता, यद्वा तत्प्रातिपदिकार्थता ॥"

प्रातिपदिकार्थमात्रपरत्वं वाऽखण्डार्थत्वम् इति चतुर्थपादार्थः।

Objection: Since knowledge due to sentences apprehends the relation subsisting between the meanings of words,[1] how can it be indeterminate?

Reply: The answer is this. For something to be an object of knowledge that is due to sentences, the criterion is not that it should apprehend the relation between the meanings of words—for in that case even something the relation of which is not intended[2] may become an object of such knowledge—but that it should apprehend the intention.[3] And in the passage under discussion, beginning with, "This universe, my dear, was but Existence in the beginning" (*Chā.* VI. ii. 1), and concluding with, "It is the truth, It is the Self, and thou art That, O Śvetaketu" (*Ibid.* VI. xvi.3),[4] the intended purport of Vedāntic texts is held to be the Pure Brahman. So how can it express something that is not the intended meaning? That sentences like, "Thou are That,"[5] convey a simple notion of identity, only means that they produce valid knowledge that does not apprehend the relation (among the meanings of the words in them). So it has been said, "That words[6] produce valid knowledge without reference to the (mutual) relation of their meanings, is what has been spoken of as their conveying a simple notion of indentity. Or it is that which comprises only the meanings[7] of their stems.[8] The meaning of the last foot of the verse (the last sentence) is: Or the conveying of a simple notion of identity (by words) consists in their denoting the meanings of their stems only.[9]

[[1] Any sentence, such as, "Bring the cow," conveys a sense in which the mutual relation of the objects denoted by the different words in that sentence—the nominative, verb and object—is involved. So obviously it is determinate. This is the contention.

[2] For example, when a cricketer ready to play says, "Bring me a bat," nobody thinks of the flying quadruped. But if the sense is to be determined just by the relation of things, denoted by the words, then what is there to prevent that being understood?

[3] In the above example, the cricket accessory.

[4] The passage first occurs in *Chā.* VI. viii. 7, and is repeated nine times to emphasize the central idea of the Upaniṣads, viz., all that exists is Brahman.

[5] Other examples are: "I am Brahman" (*Bṛ.* I. iv. 10), "This self is Brahman" (*Mā,* 2), etc.

[6] Only nouns denoting appositional substances that do not bear a causal relation to one another and are not synonyms, are meant. Otherwise the definition would be too wide.

[7] Direct or implied.

[8] *Tattva-pradipikā* or *Citsukhi,* Ch. I, verse 20. The author Citsukhācārya (13th century), is one of the highest authorities on Advaita Vedānta.

[9] And not the suffixes or case-endings.]

PERCEPTION BY THE WITNESS IN THE SELF AND THE WITNESS IN GOD

तच्च प्रत्यक्षं पुनर्द्विविधम्—जीवसाक्षि ईश्वरसाक्षि चेति। तत्र जीवो नाम अन्तःकरणावच्छिन्नं चैतन्यम्, तत्साक्षी तु अन्तःकरणोपहितं चैतन्यम्। अन्तःकरणस्य विशेषणत्वोपाधित्वाभ्यामनयोर्भेदः। विशेषणञ्च कार्यान्वयि वर्तमानं व्यावर्तकम्, उपाधिश्च कार्यानन्वयी व्यावर्तको वर्तमानश्च। "रूपविशिष्टोघटोऽनित्यः" इत्यत्र रूपं विशेषणम् "कर्णशष्कुल्यवच्छिन्नं नभः श्रोत्रम्" इत्यत्र कर्णशष्कुल्युपाधिः। अयमेवोपाधिर्नैयायिकैः परिचायक इत्युच्यते। प्रकृते चान्तःकरणस्य जड़तया विषयभासकत्वायोगेन विषयभासकचैतन्योपाधित्वम्। अयञ्च जीवसाक्षी प्रत्यात्मं नाना, एकत्वे चैत्रावगते मैत्रस्याप्यनुसन्धानप्रसङ्गः।

That perception is again twofold—that due to the witness in the individual self (*jiva-sākṣin*) and that due to the witness in God (*Iśvarasākṣin*). Now the individual self is Consciousness limited (*avacchinna*) by the mind, and the witness in that is

Consciousness that has the mind as its limiting adjunct (*upādhi*). The difference between them is that in the former the mind is a qualifying attribute (*viśeṣaṇa*) and in the latter a limiting adjunct. A qualifying attribute is that which differentiates,[1] is present,[2] and is connected with (what is predicated in respect of)[3] something[4] related to it[5]; while a limiting adjunct is that which differentiates and is present but is not connected with the predicate in respect of something related to it. In the sentence, "The coloured jar is transitory," the colour is a qualifying attribute,[6] and in the sentence, "The ether enclosed by the auditory passage is the ear."[7] the auditory passage is a limiting adjunct. It is this limiting adjunct that is called an indicator (*paricāyaka*) by the logicians. In the topic under consideration, since the mind is insentient and hence incapable of revealing objects, it is a limiting adjunct of Consciousness, which reveals things. This witness in the individual self is different[8] in each individual. For if it were one, what Caitra has known, Maitra also would recollect.

[[1] Generates the cognition that something is different from another.

[2] This is also a part of the definition. It is omitted in most editions, probably as being obvious.

[3] This portion follows the interpretation of the word *kāryānvayin* by the author's son, Rāmakṛṣṇādhvarin, the writer of the commentary *Vedānta-śikhāmaṇi*. This interpretation certainly makes the definition more comprehensive. But perhaps the author intended to give a simpler definition for practical purposes.

[4] Viz., that which is qualified—the substantive (*viśeṣya*)

[5] The qualifying attribute.

[6] Here the colour differentiates a particular jar that is related to it from other jars. And it is connected (through the jar) with transitoriness, which is predicated only in respect of the jar. Hence colour is a qualifying attribute. In simpler language, the qualifying attribute is a differentiating property and co-exists, in the thing qualified, with what is predicated of it. The *presence* of the colour is presumed from its connection with the jar and transitoriness.

[7] The auditory passage is present, and differentiates the ether enclosed by it from the remaining ether, but it is not connected with the totality of characteristics of an ear as such (*śrotratva*), which is predicated only in respect of the ether related to the auditory passage. Hence the latter is a limiting adjunct. Because, unlike the colour in the other case being transitory, the auditory passage is not an ear, but only the ether enclosed by it is such. In simpler language, a limiting adjunct, while being a differentiating property actually present in the thing of which it is the adjunct, does not co-exist with what is predicated of that.

[8] Although the witness is the same as Brahman, yet since it manifests itself as possessing the limiting adjunct of the mind, it is considered to be different according to different minds.

ईश्वरसाक्षी तु मायोपहितं चैतन्यम्। तच्चैकम्, तदुपाधिभूतमायाया एकत्वात्। "इन्द्रो मायाभिः पुरुरूप ईयते" इत्यादिश्रुतौ 'मायाभि'रिति वहुवचनस्य मायागत-शक्तिविशेषाभिप्रायतया मायागतसत्त्वरजस्तमोरूपगुणाभि-प्रायतया वोपपत्तिः।

"मायान्तु प्रकृतिं विद्यान्मायिनं तु महेश्वरम्।"

"तरत्यविद्यां विततां हृदि यस्मिन्निवेशिते।
योगी मायाममेयाम तस्मै विद्यात्मने नमः ॥"

"अजामेकां लोहितशुक्लकृष्णां
बह्वीः प्रजा सृजमानां सरूपाः।
अजो ह्येको जुषमाणोऽनुशेते
जहात्येनां भुक्तभोगामजोऽन्यः ॥"

इत्यादिश्रुतिस्मृतिषु एकवचनेन लाघवानुगृहीतेन मायाया एकत्वं निश्चीयते।

The witness in God is that Consciousness of which the cosmic illusion (*māyā*) is the limiting adjunct. And it is one, for its limiting adjunct, the cosmic illusion, is one. The plural in Śruti texts such as, "The Supreme Lord is perceived as having manifold forms through His powers of cosmic illusion (*māyābhiḥ*)" (*R.* VI. xlvii. 18), can be explained by a reference to the diversity of powers that are in the cosmic illusion, or to the three ingredients (*guṇas*)—serenity (*sattva*), activity (*rajas*) and inertia (*tamas*)—constituting it. The unity of the cosmic illusion is decided from the use of the singular number, backed by considerations of simplicity (*lāghava*),[1] in such Śruti and Smṛti texts as, "One should know the cosmic illusion to be Nature (*prakṛti*)[2] and the Ruler of that to be Great Lord" (*Śv.* IV. 10); "Salutation to that unknowable Embodiment of Knowledge who being established in the heart, a *yogin* transcends the cosmic illusion—the all-pervading nescience" (*Vis.* V. xvii. 15); "One birthless (masculine) principle (*aja*)[3] attends and follows[4] a birthless (feminine) principle (*ajā*)[5] that is red, white and black,[6] and brings forth a large progeny of similar form[7]; while another birthless principle,[8] having finished its enjoyment of that, gives it up" (*Śv.* IV. 5).[9]

[[1] Explanation of a thing by a minimum number of assumptions: the law of parsimony.

[2] Out of which the whole sentient and insentient universe has proceeded.

[3] The individual self.

[4] And on account of this identification experience happiness and misery and transmigrates.

[5] *Prakṛti* or Nature.

[6] Is composed of the three ingredients (*guṇas*)—activity serenity and inertia, respectively.

[7] That is, also composed of those three ingredients.

[8] One who has acquired discrimination between the self and the cosmic illusion.

[9] The interpretation given above is according to Sāṅkhya. According to Vedānta, the birthless female principle is the primordial state of the universe (*bhūta-prakṛti* or *māyā*). The red, white and black colours stand for the elements—fire, water and earth, respectively (the two invisible elements, air and ether, being understood). If the Sāṅkhyan view of *Prakrti* is modified so as to make it sentient and dependant on God, then Vedānta will have no objection to accepting it as a synonym of *māyā.* The author, who accepts the three *guṇas* as the constituents of *māyā*, may have had some such compromise in his mind.]

ततश्च तदुपहितं चैतन्यम् ईश्वरसाक्षी । तच्चानादि, तदुपाधेर्मायाया अनादित्वात् । मायावच्छिन्नं चैतन्यश्च

परमेश्वरः। मायाया विशेषणत्वे ईश्वरत्वं, उपाधित्वे साक्षित्वम् इतीश्वरत्वसाक्षित्वयोर्भेदः, न तु धर्मिणोरीश्वरतत्साक्षिणोः।

स च परमेश्वर एकोऽपि स्वोपाधिभूतमायानिष्ठसत्त्वरजस्तमोगुणभेदेन ब्रह्माविष्णुमहेश्वरादिशब्दवाच्यतां भजते।

Hence the Consciousness which has that for its limiting adjunct, is the witness in God, and it is without a beginning, because its limiting adjunct, the cosmic illusion, is so. While the Consciousness that is limited by the cosmic illusion is the Supreme Lord. When the cosmic illusion is a qualifying attribute, Consciousness is called God, and when it is a limiting adjunct, it is called the witness (in God). So the distinction is between Godhead and the state of being the witness in God, and not between the two entities possessing those attributes, viz., God and the witness in Him.

That Supreme Lord, although one, is designated by such terms as Brahmā, Viṣṇu and Maheśvara (Śiva),[1] according to (the preponderance of) activity, serenity or inertia, which are the constituents of His limiting adjunct,[2] the cosmic illusion.

[[1] Representing His projecting, maintaining and destroying aspects, respectively.

[2] Qualifying attributes are meant. So also below.]

ननु ईश्वरसाक्षिणोऽनादित्वे "तदैक्षत बहुस्यां प्रजायेय" इत्यादौ सृष्टिपूर्वसमये परमेश्वरस्यागन्तुकमीक्षणमुच्यमानं

कथमुपपद्यते ? उच्यते। यथा विषयेन्द्रियसन्निकर्षादि-कारणवशेन जीवोपाध्यन्तःकरणस्य वृत्तिभेदा जायन्ते, तथा सृज्यमानप्राणिकर्मवशेन परमेश्वरोपाधिभूतमायाया वृत्ति-विशेषाः "इदमिदानीं स्रष्टव्यम्," "इदमिदानीं पालयितव्यम्" "इदमिदानीं संहर्तव्यम्" इत्याद्याकारा जायन्ते। तासाञ्च वृत्तीनां सादित्वात्तत्प्रतिबिम्बितचैतन्यमपि सादीत्युच्यते।

Objection: If the witness in God be without a beginning, how is one to explain the adventitious[1] reflection on the part of the Supreme Lord just before projecting the universe, mentioned in texts like, "It reflected, 'Let Me multiply, let Me be effectively born'" (*Chā.* VI. ii, 3)?

Reply: The answer is this. Just as, owing to the connection of the organs with objects and other such causes, different states arise in the mind, which is the limiting adjunct of the individual self, similarly, owing to the past work of beings that are about to be projected, particular states in the form of, "Now this is to be projected," "Now this is to be maintained," "Now this is to be destroyed," etc., arise in the cosmic illusion, which is the limiting adjunct of the Supreme Lord; and since these states have a beginning, the Consciousness reflected in them is also described as having a beginning.

[[1] Not being present all the time.]

PERCEPTUALITY OF COGNITION DEFINED: THE NATURE OF ERROR

एवं साक्षिद्वैविध्येन प्रत्यक्षज्ञानद्वैविध्यम्। प्रत्यक्षत्वञ्च ज्ञेयगतं ज्ञप्तिगतञ्च निरूपितम्। तत्र ज्ञप्तिगतप्रत्यक्षत्वस्य सामान्यलक्षणं चित्त्वमेव, "पर्वतो वह्निमान्" इत्यादावपि वह्न्याद्याकारवृत्त्युपहितचैतन्यस्य स्वात्मांशे स्वप्रकाशतया प्रत्यक्षत्वात्। तत्तद्विषयांशप्रत्यक्षत्वन्तु पूर्वोक्तमेव। तस्य च भ्रान्तिरूपप्रत्यक्षे नातिव्याप्तिः, भ्रमप्रमासाधारणप्रत्यक्षत्वसामान्यनिर्वचनेन तस्यापि लक्ष्यत्वात्। यदा तु प्रत्यक्षप्रमाया एव लक्षणं वक्तव्यं तदा पूर्वोक्तलक्षणेऽबाधितत्वं विषयविशेषणं देयम्। शुक्तिरूप्यादिभ्रमस्य संसारकालीनबाधविषयप्रातिभासिकरजतादिविषयकत्वेनोक्तलक्षणाभावात् नातिव्याप्तिः।

Thus on account of the twofoldness of the witness, perceptual knowledge is twofold. The character of perception both as regards objects and as regards cognition has been ascertained. Of these, the general definition of perceptuality of cognition is that it is just Consciousness, for even in instances like, "The hill has fire," the Consciousness that has mental states in the form of the fire etc. as limiting adjuncts, being self-revealing in respect of itself, is a perception. As for its perceptuality in respect of its objects, however, it has already[1] been dealt with.[2] It cannot be said that this definition extends unduly to the perception that is of the nature of an illusion; for that too is intended to be covered by the above general definition of perception, which includes both valid knowledge and illusion. When, however, a definition of valid perception alone is to be stated, then in the definition previously mentioned (p. 13) the object has to be qualified by an attribute signifying that it is uncontradicted.[3] Since illusions like that of silver in a nacre have for their objects the illusory silver etc., which are contradicted during the transmigratory state of existence,[4] the above definition does not apply to them, and hence there is no unwarranted extension of it.

[[1] On p. 25 *et seq.*

[2] In the inference, "The hill has fire, because it has smoke," both the hill and the smoke, being visible, are objects of perception, but not the fire, which is being inferred. Hence, if the perception be considered only with regard to the objects, then the fire would be excluded from its scope. But if it be considered in respect of the cognition, then all knowledge being perceptual in respect of itself in Vedānta, the cognition of the fire is a case of perception. So here is the distinction between the perceptuality of cognition with regard to itself and that with regard to its objects.

[3] That is, the last word of the definition on p. 13 should be amplified into, "Object, which must not be contradicted."

[4] That is, even prior to the realisation of one's identity with Brahman. See note 2 on p. 7.]

ननु विसंवादिप्रवृत्त्या भ्रान्तिज्ञातसिद्धावपि तस्य प्रातिभासिकतत्कालोत्पन्नरजतादिविषयकत्वे न प्रमाणम्,

देशान्तरीयरजतस्य क्लृप्तस्यैव तद्विषयत्वसम्भवादिति चेत्, न, तस्यासन्निकृष्टतया प्रत्यक्षविषयत्वायोगात्। न च ज्ञानं तत्र प्रत्यासत्तिः, ज्ञानस्य प्रत्यासत्तित्वे तत एव वह्न्यादेः प्रत्यक्षत्वापत्तौ अनुमानाद्युच्छेदापत्तेः।

Objection (by the logician): Although false knowledge may be established by one's unsuccessful effort,[1] yet there is no proof that it has for its object illusory silver etc. produced at the moment; for it may have for its object silver that is already existent at some other place.[2]

Reply: No, for that, not being connected with the organ,[3] cannot be an object of perception. Nor is knowledge the (needed) connection there, for if it were so, that alone would make fire etc.[5] objects of perception,[6] and this would obliterate inference etc.[7]

[[1] *Visaṁvādi-pravṛtti*, as when we mistake the reflection of a light for a jewel, but on going to the spot to take it, are baffled. This proves that there is such a thing as false knowledge.

[2] According to the logician, all error is knowing one thing for another (*anyathā-khyāti*), as, in the present instance, seeing the silver, already seen somewhere, in the nacre, owing to some defect such as distance or darkness.

[3] Which, according to the logician, is a necessary condition of perception.

[4] Logicians believe in extraordinary perception, which is brought about by three kinds of extraordinary connection between the organ and object. One of these is the connection based on knowledge (*jñāna-lakṣaṇa-sannikarṣa*). A man who knows that sandalwood is fragrant, perceives immediately on *seeing* a piece of it that it is fragrant, and

says, "A fragrant piece of sandalwood." Here the previous knowledge is the connection that enables him to do so. But since the eye is not connected with the fragrance, he perceives it only by the connection based on knowledge. This is also the case with all illusions. For instance, when we mistake a nacre for silver, it is our previous knowledge of silverhood that connects the eye with the silverhood that is perceiced extraordinarily.

[5] Inferred in a hill from smoke.

[6] The Vedāntin argues that if previous knowledge serves as the connection, then the sight of the smoke might as well lead to a perception of the fire, since here also previous knowledge of it would supply the needed connection. So why admit inference etc. as separate means of knowledge? Perception alone would do.

[7] That is, all the means of knowledge except perception.]

ननु रजतोत्पादकानां रजतावयवादीनामभावे शुक्तौ कथं तत्रापि रजतमुत्पद्यते इति चेत्, उच्यते। नहि लोकसिद्धसामग्री प्रातिभासिकरजतोत्पादिका, किन्तु विलक्षणैव। तथाहि—काचादिदोषदूषितलोचनस्य पुरोवर्तिद्रव्यसंयोगादिदमाकारा चाकचिक्याकारा च काचिदन्तःकरणवृत्तिरुदेति। तस्याञ्च वृत्तौ इदमवच्छिन्नचैतन्यं प्रतिबिम्बते। तत्र पूर्वोक्तरीत्या वृत्तेर्निर्गमनेन इदमवच्छिन्नचैतन्यवृत्त्यवच्छिन्नचैतन्यं प्रमातृचैतन्यं चाभिन्नं भवति। ततश्च प्रमातृचैतन्याभिन्नविषयचैतन्यनिष्ठा शुक्तित्व प्रकारिकाऽविद्या चाकचिक्यादिसादृश्यसन्दर्शनसमुद्बोधितरजतसंस्कारसध्रीचीना काचादिदोषसमवहिता रजतरूपार्थाकारेण रजतज्ञानाभासाकारेण च परिणमते।

Objection: In the absence of the parts of silver, etc., which produce the silver, how according to your view also is the silver produced in the nacre?

Reply: The answer is this. It is not the totality of causes as generally accepted that produces the illusory silver, but quite a distinct one. To explain: To a man whose eyes are afflicted with defects such as *kāca*,[1] when the eyes are in contact with a substance in front, there arises a state of the mind in the form of 'this' coupled with 'brightness,'[2] and in that mental state the Consciousness limited by 'this' is reflected. Then, by the issuing of the mind so as to form a state in the manner already[3] mentioned, the Consciousness limited by 'this,' that limited by the mental state, and the Consciousness associated with the subject become one. Thereafter the nescience that[4] is in the form of the nacre and abides in the Consciousness associated with the object, which again is not different from the Consciousness associated with the subject,[5] is joined to the latent impressions of silver roused by seeing points of similarity such as brightness, and in combination with ocular defects such as *kāca*, transforms itself into the object called silver as also the apparent knowledge[6] in the form of that.

[[1] An eye disease in which shining things only are seen.

[2] That is, in the form of "something bright" which has not been truly discerned.

[3] On p. 15.

[4] The adjectival clause refers to the primal nescience (*mūlāvidyā*), which is the material cause of the universe

consisting of the ether etc. It abides in Pure Consciousness, has that for its object, and is destroyed by the indeterminate knowledge of Pure Consciousness. For the distinction between determinate and indeterminate knowledge see p. 32.

[5] That is, Consciousness limited by the mind.

[6] Because it is not a mental state, but a modification of nescience.]

परिणामो नाम उपादानसमसत्ताककार्यापत्तिः। विवर्तो नाम उपादानविषमसत्ताककार्यापत्तिः। प्रातिभासिक-रजतश्चाविद्यापेक्षया परिणाम इति, चैतन्यापेक्षया विवर्त इति चोच्यते। अविद्यापरिणामरूपश्च तद्रजतमविद्या-धिष्ठाने इदमवच्छिन्नचैतन्ये वर्तते, अस्मन्मते सर्वस्यापि कार्यस्य स्वोपादानाविद्याधिष्ठानाश्रितत्वनियमात्।

Transformation (actual change: *pariṇāma*) means the production of an effect that has the same[1] kind of existence as that of its material cause. Apparent change (*vivarta*) means the production of an effect that has a different kind of existence from that of its material cause.[2] The illusory silver is called a transformation in respect of nescience,[3] and an apparent change in respect of Consciousness.[4] And that silver which is a transformation of nescience abides in the substratum of the latter, viz., the Consciousness limited by 'this'[5]; for according to our view, all effects whatsoever abide invariably in the substratum[6] of their material cause, nescience.

[[1] Regarded as either real (*pāramārthika*) or unreal (*apāramārthika*). As in the case of milk and curd, or threads and cloth. Here both cause and effect have an unreal existence.

[2] As when we mistake Brahman as the universe. Here Brahman has a real existence, while the universe has only an unreal existence.

[3] Because both nescience and the illusory silver have an unreal existence, the one being but a modification of the other.

[4] Since Pure Consciousness or Brahman, on which the whole universe is superimposed, has a real existence, and the illusory silver only an unreal existence.

[5] See p. 48.

[6] Pure Consciousness.]

ननु चैतन्यनिष्ठरजतस्य कथमिदं रजतमितिपुरवर्तिना तादात्म्यम् ? उच्यते। यथा न्यायमते आत्मनिष्ठस्य सुखादेः शरीरनिष्ठत्वेनोपलम्भः, शरीरस्य सुखाद्यधिकरणतावच्छेदकत्वात्, तथा चैतन्यमात्रस्य रजतं प्रत्यनधिष्ठानतया, इदमवच्छिन्नचैतन्यस्य तदधिष्ठानत्वेन इदमोऽवच्छेदकतया रजतस्य पुरोवर्तिसंसर्गप्रत्यय उपपद्यते। तस्य च विषयचैतन्यस्य तदन्तःकरणोपहित चैतन्याभिन्नतया विषयचैतन्येऽध्यस्तमपि रजतं साक्षिण्यध्यस्तं केवलसाक्षिवेद्यं सुखादिवदनन्यवेद्यमिति चोच्यते।

Objection: How can the silver that abides in Consciousness be identified with something that is in front,[1] as expressed in the statement, "This is silver"?

Reply: The answer is this. As, in the system of Nyāya, happiness etc., which abide in the soul, are experienced as abiding in the body, since the latter is what determines the fact of the soul's being the substratum of happiness etc.,[2] similarly, since unqualified Pure Consciousness is not the substratum of the silver, but only the Consciousness limited by the meaning of the word 'this' is such, the meaning of the word 'this' being the determining factor of Consciousness being the substratum of the illusory silver—the cognition that the silver is connected[3] with something that is in front, is explicable. And since that Consciousness associated with the object is one with the Consciousness[4] that has the mind as its limiting adjunct, the silver, although it is superimposed on the Consciousness associated with the object, is (virtually) superimposed on the witness, and is (therefore) spoken of as being cognisable by the witness alone[5] and not cognisable through any other agency—like happiness etc.

[[1] While Consciousness is all-pervading.

[2] Acccording to Nyāya, happiness etc., although they are qualities of the soul, are said to be produced in the body, because they are invariably produced within the limits of the body.

[3] By the relation of identity.

[4] That is, the witness.

[5] For the explanation of this term as also the following phrase, see p. 30.]

ननु साक्षिण्यध्यस्तत्वे "अहं रजतम्" इति ; "तद्वान्" इति वा प्रत्ययः स्यात् "अहं सुखी" इतिवत् , इति चेत् , उच्यते। नहि सुखादीनामन्तःकरणावच्छिन्नचैतन्यनिष्ठाविद्याकार्यत्वप्रयुक्तम् "अहं सुखी" इति ज्ञानम् , सुखादीनां घटादिवच्छुद्धचैतन्य एवाध्यासात्। किन्तु यस्य यदा-

कारानुभवाहितसंस्कारसहकृताविद्याकार्यत्वं तस्य तदाकारानुभवविषयत्वम्, इत्येवानुगतं नियामकम्। तथा च इदमाकारानुभवाहितसंस्कारसहिताविद्याकार्यत्वाद् घटादेरिदमाकारानुभवविषयत्वम्, अहमाकारानुभवाहितसंस्कारसहकृताविद्याकार्यत्वादन्तःकरणादेरहमाकारानुभवविषयत्वम्, शरीरेन्द्रियादेरुभयविधानुभवसंस्कारसहिताविद्याकार्यत्वादुभयविधानुभवविषयत्वम्। तथाचोभयविधानुभवः— इदं शरीरम्, अहं देहः, अहं मनुष्यः, अहं ब्राह्मणः; इदं चक्षुः, अहं काणः; इदं श्रोत्रम्, अहं वधिर इति। प्रकृते प्रातिभासिकरजतस्य प्रमातृचैतन्याभिन्नेदमवच्छिन्नचैतन्यनिष्ठाविद्याकार्यत्वेऽपि इदं रजतमिति सत्यस्थलीयेदमाकारानुभवाहितसंस्कारजन्यत्वादिदमाकारानुभवविषयता, न तु "अहं रजतम्" इत्यहमाकारानुभवविषयता इत्यनुसन्धेयम्।

Objection: If (the silver) be superimposed on the witness, the cognition would be, "I am silver," or "I have silver," like, "I am happy."

Reply: The answer is this. The cognition, "I am happy," is not due to happiness etc. being the effects of the nescience that abides in the Consciousness limited by the mind, for happiness etc. are, like a jar and so on, superimposed only on Pure Consciousness; but the universal rule is that a thing is the object of experience in a particular form according as it is the effect of nescience attended with the latent impressions left by an experience of that particular form. So a jar etc. are objects of an experience in the form of 'this', because they are the effects of nescience attended with the latent impressions left by an experience in the form of 'this'; the mind etc. are objects of an experience in the form of 'I', because they are the effects of nescience attended with the latent impressions left by an experience in the form of 'I'; and the body, organs, etc., are objects of an experience in the form of both 'this' and 'I', because they are the effects of nescience attended with the latent impressions of an experience in the form of both. Thus there are two types of experience: "This is the body,"[1] and "I am the body," "I am a man," or "I am a Brāhmana"; "This is the eye," and "I am blind"[2]; "This is the ear," and "I am deaf." In the example cited, although the illusory silver is an effect of nescience abiding in the Consciousness that is limited by 'this', which again is not different from the Consciousness associated with the subject, yet it is the object of an experience in the form of 'this', and not that of an experience in the form of 'I,' expressed in the statement, "I am silver," because it is due to the latent impression left by an experience in the form of 'this' in a genuine case of silver, as expressed in the statement, "This is silver."[3] This should be borne in mind.

[[1] Here the identification is with the body.

[2] Here there is identification with the organs.
[3] The form of the original experience the latent impression of which acts as an auxiliary cause in subsequent superimposed products, is the determining factor regarding the forms of the cognition of the latter.]

नन्वेवमपि मिथ्यारजतस्य साक्षात् साक्षिसम्बन्धितया भानसम्भवे रजतगोचरज्ञानाभासरूपाया अविद्यावृत्तेरभ्युपगमः किमर्थमिति चेत्, उच्यते। स्वगोचरवृत्त्युपहितप्रमातृचैतन्यभिन्नसत्ताकत्वाभावस्य विषयापरोक्षत्वरूपतया रजतस्यापरोक्षत्वसिद्धये तदभ्युपगमात्। नन्विदंवृत्ते रजताकारवृत्तेश्च प्रत्येकमेकैकविषयत्वे गुरुमतवद्विशिष्टज्ञानानभ्युपगमे कुतो भ्रमज्ञानासिद्धिरिति चेत्, न, वृत्तिद्वयप्रतिबिम्बितचैतन्यस्यैकस्य सत्यमिथ्यावस्तुतादात्म्यावगाहित्वेन भ्रमत्वस्वीकारात्। अत एव साक्षिज्ञानस्य सत्यासत्यविषयतया प्रामाण्यानियमादप्रामाण्योक्तिः साम्प्रदायिकानाम्।

Objection: Even then, since the illusory silver can be cognised as being directly connected with the witness, why assume a state of nescience that[1] is an apparent knowledge having the silver for its object?

Reply: The answer is this. It is assumed in order to establish the perceptual character of the cognition of the silver, because the perception of an object consists in its not having an existence apart from that of the Consciousness associated with the subject, of which the state (here, of nescience) cognising the object is a limiting adjunct.[2]

Objection: Since the (mental) state in the form of 'this' and the state (of nescience) in the form of the (illusory) silver have each a separate object, and since, as in the view of the Teacher,[3] a qualified knowledge is not admitted,[4] how can you account for erroneous knowledge?

Reply: Not so, for as one and the same Consciousness reflected in the two states comprehends the identity of a real and an unreal thing, it is admitted to be an error. Therefore the cognition on the part of the witness, having for its object both a real and an unreal thing, and hence lacking[5] uniform validity, is declared as invalid by the traditional interpreters of Vedānta.

[[1] Refers to the 'state.'

[2] See p. 26.

[3] The nickname of Prabhākara, a student of Kumārila Bhaṭṭa (8th century), from whom he differed and founded a new school of the Mīmāṁsā philosophy.

[4] According to his school, the knowledge of 'this" (something in front) is perception, and that of the silver is recollection of a previous genuine experience. The two mental states are distinct, but this is lost sight of in all cases of what is ordinarily called illusion. According to this school, there is no such thing as error, all cognition being valid knowledge.

[5] It is valid in respect of 'this' and invalid in respect of the silver.]

ननु सिद्धान्ते देशान्तरीयरजतमप्यविद्याकार्यमध्यस्तञ्चेति कथं शुक्तिरूप्यस्य ततो वैलक्षण्यम इति चेत्, न।

त्वन्मते सत्यत्वाविशेषेऽपि केषाञ्चित् क्षणिकत्वं केषाञ्चित् स्थायित्वम्, इत्यत्र यदेव नियामकं तदेव स्वभावविशेषादिकं ममापि। यद्वा घटाद्यध्यासे अविद्यैव दोषत्वेन हेतुः, शुक्तिरूप्याद्यध्यासे तु काचादयोऽपि दोषाः। तथा-चागन्तुकदोषजन्यत्वं प्रातिभासिकत्वे प्रयोजकम्। अत एव स्वप्नोपलब्धरथादीनामागन्तुकनिद्रादोषजन्यत्वात् प्राति-भासिकत्वम्।

Objection: According to the tenets of Vedānta, the silver that is elsewhere is also an effect of nescience and superimposed. So how does the silver appearing in the nacre differ from that?

Reply: Not so; for although according to you all things are equally real, some of them are fleeting[1] and others stationary[2]; and whatever may be the determining factor in this, such as peculiar nature, applies to my case also.[3] Or (we may say) in the superimposition[4] of a jar etc., nescience alone, being a defect, is the cause, while in the case of the superimposition of silver on the nacre, and so on, the eye-disease *kāca* etc. also are defects. So the criterion of something being illusory is its being produced by some adventitious defect. Hence a chariot etc. experienced in a dream are illusory, since they are produced by an adventitious defect, viz., sleep.

[[1] Lasting for two moments only. Example of these are sound, knowledge, desire, etc.

[2] As, for instance, a jar.

[3] That is, it is on account of their natural peculiarity etc. that the silver in the one case is conventionally real, and in the other case illusory.

[4] On Pure Consciousness]

Dream Perception

ननु स्वप्नस्थले पूर्वानुभूतरथादेः स्मरणमात्रेणैव व्यवहारोपपत्तौ न रथादिसृष्टिकल्पनम्, गौरवात्, इति चेत्, न, रथादेः स्मृतिमात्राभ्युपगमे "रथं पश्यामि," "स्वप्ने रथमद्राक्षम्" इत्याद्यनुभवविरोधापत्तेः। "अथ रथान् रथयोगान् पथः सृजते" इति रथादिसृष्टिप्रतिपादकश्रुतिविरोधापत्तेश्च। तस्मात् शुक्तिरूप्यवत् स्वप्नोपलब्धरथादयोऽपि प्रातिभासिका यावत्प्रतिभासमवतिष्ठन्ते।

Objection: In the case of dreams, only the recollection of a chariot etc. seen before serves to account for the use of such words; so the creation of a chariot etc. need not be assumed, because it is cumbrous.

Reply: Not so, for if only the recollection of the chariot etc. be assumed, it would contradict such experiences as, "I see a chariot," or "I saw a chariot in a dream." Besides, it would clash with scriptural texts establishing the creation of chariots etc., such as, "But he creates the chariot, the animals to be yoked to them, and the roads" *Bṛ.* IV. iii. 10). Therefore, like the silver appearing in the nacre, the chariot etc. experienced in a dream are also illusory, and stay as long as the illusion lasts.

ननु स्वप्ने रथाद्यधिष्ठानतयोपलभ्यमानदेशविशेषस्यापि तदाऽसन्निकृष्टतया अनिर्वचनीयप्रातिभासिकदेशोऽभ्युपगन्तव्यः, तथा च रथाद्यध्यासः कुत्र इति चेत्, न, चैतन्यस्य स्वयंप्रकाशस्य रथाद्यधिष्ठानत्वात्। प्रतीयमानं रथाद्यस्तीत्येव प्रतीयते इति सद्रूपेन प्रकाशमानं चैतन्यमेवाधिष्ठानम्; देशविशेषोऽपि चिदध्यस्तः प्रातिभासिकः, रथादाविन्द्रियग्राह्यत्वमपि प्रातिभासिकम्, तदा सर्वेन्द्रियाणामुपरमात्। "अहं रथः" इत्यादिप्रतीत्यापादनन्तु पूर्ववन्निरसनीयम्।

स्वप्नरथादयः साक्षान्मायापरिणामा इति केचित्। अन्तकरणद्वारा तत्परिणामा इत्यन्ये।

Objection: In a dream, the particular spot which is experienced as the support of the chariot etc. not being also connected with the eyes at the time, an indescribable illusory spot has to be assumed. So where does the superimposition of the chariot etc. take place?[1]

Reply: The objection is not valid, for Consciousness, which is self-effulgent, is the substratum of the chariot etc. Because the chariot etc. that are experienced (in the dream), are experienced as but existent; hence it is Consciousness manifesting itself as Existence that is the substratum. The particular spot also is superimposed on the Consciousness and is illusory. The fact of the chariot etc. being cognised by the (corresponding) organ is also illusory, for then all organs are at rest. As for the possibility of the experience being in the form of, "I am a chariot,"[2] etc., it should be refuted in the manner already stated.[3]

Some hold that the chariot etc. seen in a dream are direct transformations of the cosmic illusion (*māyā*); others, that they are its transformations through the medium of the mind.

[[1] The implication is that in the absence of the substratum, the superimposition is impossible.

[2] Here and in the following pages the word 'elephant' is substituted for 'chariot' in most of the editions. 'Chariot' is obviously the better reading.

[3] On p. 53.]

Twofold Destruction of Effects: Its Bearing on Error

ननु रथादेः शुद्धचैतन्याध्यस्तत्वे इदानीं तत्साक्षात्काराभावेन जागरणेऽपि स्वप्नोपलब्धरथादयोऽनुवर्तेरन्। उच्यते। कार्यविनाशो हि द्विविधः कश्चिदुपादानेन सह, कश्चित्तु विद्यमान एवोपादाने। आद्यो बाधः, द्वितीयस्तु निवृत्तिः। आद्यस्य कारणमधिष्ठानतत्त्वसाक्षात्कारः, तेन विनोपादानभूताया अविद्याया अनिवृत्तेः। द्वितीयस्य कारणं विरोधिवृत्त्युत्पत्तिर्दोषनिवृत्तिर्वा। तदिह ब्रह्मसाक्षात्काराभावात् स्वप्नप्रपञ्चो मा बाधिष्ट, मुसलप्रहारेण घटादेरिव विरोधिप्रत्ययान्तरोदयेन स्वजनकीभूतनिद्रादिदोषनाशेन वा रथादिनिवृत्तौ को विरोधः?

Objection: If the chariot etc. be superimposed on Pure Consciousness, since this is not realised in the present state,[1] the chariot etc. experienced in a dream would persist even in the awakened state.

Reply: The answer is this. The destruction of an effect is of two kinds. In one the destruction is together with that of the material cause, and in the other the material cause is left untouched. The first is nullification (*bādha*), the second is cessation (*nivṛtti*). The cause of the first is realisation of the truth of the substratum,[2] for without that, nescience,[3] which is the material cause, is not removed. The cause of the second is the rise of a contrary mental state, or the removal of defects. Hence, although in the awakened state the world conjured up in dreams may not be *nullified*[4] in the absence of a realisation of Brahman,[5] yet, like the cessation of a jar etc. by the blow of a club, what is there to prevent the *cessation* of the chariot etc. (seen in a dream), through the rise of a contrary cognition, or through the removal of defects such as sleep that caused them?

[[1] The transmigratory state of existence.

[2] Brahman or Pure Consciousness.

[3] Though earth is commonly spoken of as the material cause of a jar, yet it is but nescience in another form. So that is the true material cause.

[4] That is, destroyed with its material cause, nescience.

[5] That is, of the identity of the individual self with Brahman.]

एवञ्च शुक्तिरूप्यस्य शुक्त्यवच्छिन्नचैतन्यनिष्ठतूलाविद्या-कार्यत्वपक्षे शुक्तिरिति ज्ञानेन तदज्ञानेन सह रजतस्य बाधः। मूलाविद्याकार्यत्वपक्षे तु मूलाविद्याया ब्रह्मसाक्षात्कारमात्र-निवर्त्यतया रजतस्य तत्र शुक्तिज्ञानान्निवृत्तिमात्रम्, मुसल-प्रहारेण घटस्येव।

Thus, according to the view that the silver seen in a nacre is an effect of the subsidiary nescience abiding in the Consciousness limited by the nacre, there is nullification of the silver together with the nescience regarding the nacre by the knowledge that the (supposed) silver is a nacre. While according to the view that it is an effect of the primal nescience, since the latter is destroyed only by the realisation of Brahman, there is just a cessation of the silver through the knowledge that it is a nacre—as in the case of a jar through the blow of a club.

ननु शुक्तौ रजतस्य प्रतिभाससमये प्रातिभासिकसत्ता-भ्युपगमे "नेदं रजतम्" इति त्रैकालिकनिषेधज्ञानं न स्यात्, किन्तु "इदानीमिदं न रजतम्" इति स्यात्, "इदानीं घटः श्यामो न" इतिवत्, इति चेत्, न, नहि तत्र रजतत्वा-वच्छिन्नप्रतियोगिताकाभावो निषेधधीविषयः, किन्तु लौकि-कपारमार्थिकत्वावच्छिन्न-प्रातिभासिकरजतप्रतियोगिताकः, व्यधिकरणधर्मावच्छिन्नप्रतियोगिताकाभावाभ्युपगमात्।

Objection: If we admit an illusory existence for the silver during the time that a nacre appears as that, there would be no (subsequent) knowledge of its negation for all time—past, present and future—in the form, "It is not silver," but it should be of the form, "Now it is not silver," like, "Now the jar is not black."[1]

Reply: No, for the object of the negating knowledge there is not a non-existence[2] the counterpositiveness relating to which is characterised by silverhood, but one[3] the counterpositiveness relating to which, abiding in the illusory silver, is characterised by conventional reality; for we admit that kind of non-existence the counterpositiveness relating to which is characterised by an attribute abiding in a different substratum from its[4] own (*vyadhikaraṇa*).[5]

[[1] That is, the negation should be felt as temporary—just confined to the period of disillusion.

[2] *Non-existence etc.*—That is, an absence of identity, or a non-existence of the form, "It is not silver." The counterpositive (*pratiyogin*) of a non-existence is that whose existence is denied; here, the silver. Counterpositiveness (*pratiyogitā*) is an attribute of that. The distinguishing characteristic (*avacchedaka*) of that counterpositiveness here is silverhood (*rajatatva*: all that makes silver what it is). The plain meaning of the passage is that the denial here is not of all silver as such (but only of illusory silver as possessed of conventional reality).

[3] *One etc.*—That is, a non-existence which may be expressed as: "It is not illusory silver that has conventional reality." The counterpositive of this non-existence is the conventionally real illusory silver, which is a nonentity, for illusory silver never possesses conventional reality like a jar or cloth, being ascertained to be false even during one's relative state of existence. A jar or cloth lacks the absolute reality of Brahman, but it possesses reality in

the popular acceptance of the term, inasmuch as it persists till realisation. Dreams, illusions, etc., are of a much flimsier character, for they are dispelled as soon as a person gets out of those states.

[4] Of the counterpositiveness.

[5] When we say, "A cloth does not exist as a jar," that whose existence is denied is the cloth, which is therefore the counterpositive of this negation. A jar is a different substratum from the cloth. The property of that, viz., jarhood, is the distinguishing characteristic of the counterpositiveness of this negation (*pratiyogitāvacchedaka*). So the non-existence here is *vyadhikarana-dharmāvacchinna-pratiyogitāka-abhāva*, and it is always to be found in a cloth. Similarly, when after mistaking a nacre as silver we have the knowledge, "It is not silver," the absence of illusory silver possessed of conventional reality is always to be met with in the nacre, because, though the latter may sometimes appear as silver, it is never the conventionally real silver.]

ननु प्रातिभासिके रजते पारमार्थिकत्वमवगतं न वा ? अनवगमे प्रतियोगितावच्छेदकावच्छिन्नरजतसत्त्वज्ञानाभावादभावप्रत्यक्षानुपपत्तिः। अवगमेऽपरोक्षावभासस्य तत्कालीनविषयसत्तानियतत्वाद् रजते पारमार्थिकत्वमप्यनिर्वचनीयं रजतवदेवोत्पन्नमिति तदवच्छिन्नरजतसत्त्वे तदवच्छिन्नाभावस्तत्र कथं वर्तत इति चेत्, न, पारमार्थिकत्त्वस्याधिष्ठाननिष्ठस्य रजते प्रतिभाससम्भवेन रजतनिष्ठपारमार्थिकत्वोत्पत्त्यनभ्युपगमात्। यत्रारोप्यमसन्निकृष्टं तत्रैव प्रातिभासिकवस्तूत्पत्तेरङ्गीकारात्। अत एव इन्द्रियसन्निकृष्टतया जवाकुसुमगतलौहित्यस्य स्फटिके भानसम्भवात्,

न स्फटिकेऽनिर्वचनीयलौहित्योत्पत्तिः। नन्वेवं यत्र जपाकुसुमं द्रव्यान्तरव्यवधानादसन्निकृष्टं तत्र लौहित्यप्रतीत्या प्रातिभासिकं लौहित्यं स्वीक्रियतामिति चेत्, न, इष्टत्वात्।

एवं प्रत्यक्षभ्रमान्तरेष्वपि प्रत्यक्षसामान्यलक्षणानुगमो यथार्थप्रत्यक्षलक्षणासद्भावश्च दर्शनीयः।

Objection: In the illusory silver, is the (conventional) reality known or not? If it is unknown, there being an absence of knowledge of the existence (in the illusory silver) of silver that is possessed of the distinguishing characteristic[1] of the counterpositiveness (relating to the absence), there cannot be a perception of the absence.[2] And if the reality is known, since perceptual knowledge depends on the existence of its object at the time, a (conventional) reality that is indescribable is also produced in the silver, just as the latter is (in the nacre); therefore how can there be absence of silver characterised by (conventional) reality in the nacre while there is the presence of silver so characterised?

Reply: Not so; for since it is possible for the (conventional) reality belonging to the substratum[3] (of the illusory silver) to appear in the silver, we do not admit that (conventional) reality is produced in the silver. It is only where the thing superimposed is not connected with the organ, that the origination of an illusory thing is admitted. Hence, there being the possibility of cognition of the redness belonging to a hibiscus in a crystal, since the flower is connected with the organ, there is no origination of an indescribable redness in the crystal.

Objection: In that case, where the hibiscus is not connected with the organ on account of the intervention of some other substance, and yet redness is cognised, you must admit an illusory redness.

Reply: No harm, for we accept this.

Similarly, in other cases of erroneous perception also it may be shown that the general definition of perception is applicable, and that of a valid perception[4] is inapplicable.

[[1] Viz., conventional reality, the counterpositive being the illusory silver.

[2] Of illusory silver possessed of conventional reality. The perception of non-existence depends upon the knowledge of its counterpositive as possessed of its distinguishing characteristic. For instance, the absence of a jar as possessed of jarhood cannot be perceived unless such a jar has already been known. Now, since no illusory silver is ever known to possess conventional reality, the absence of it as possessed of that reality can never be perceived.

[3] The nacre.

[4] Viz., that it must be uncontradicted.]

Perception Through or Without an Organ

उक्तं प्रत्यक्षं प्रकारान्तरेण द्विविधम्—इन्द्रियजन्यं तदजन्यञ्चेति। तत्रेन्द्रियाजन्यं सुखादिप्रत्यक्षम्, मनस इन्द्रियत्वनिराकरणात्। इन्द्रियाणि पञ्च, घ्राणरसनचक्षुः-श्रोत्रत्वगात्मकानि। सर्वाणि चेन्द्रियाणि स्वस्वविषय-

संयुक्तान्येव प्रत्यक्षज्ञानं जनयन्ति। तत्र घ्राणरसनत्वगिन्द्रियाणि स्वस्थानस्थितान्येव गन्धरसस्पर्शोपलम्भान् जनयन्ति, चक्षुःश्रोत्रे तु स्वत एव विषयदेशं गत्वा स्वस्वविषयं गृह्णीतः, श्रोत्रस्यापि चक्षुरादिवत् परिच्छिन्नतया-भेर्यादिदेशगमनसम्भवात्। अत एवानुभवो "भेरीशब्दो मया श्रुतः" इति। वीचीतरङ्गादिन्यायेन कर्णशष्कुली-प्रदेशेऽनन्तशब्दोत्पत्तिकल्पनायां गौरवम्, "भेरीशब्दो मया श्रुतः" इति प्रत्यक्षस्य भ्रमत्वकल्पनायां गौरवञ्च स्यात्।

तदेवं व्याख्यातं प्रत्यक्षम्।

इति वेदान्तपरिभाषायां प्रत्यक्षपरिच्छेदः।

In another way the above-mentioned perception is twofold—that due to the organs, and that not due to them. Of these, that not due to the organs is the perception of happiness etc., for the view that the mind is an organ has already been refuted.[1] The organs are five, consisting of the nose, tongue, eye, ear and skin. And all the organs lead to perceptual knowledge only when they are connected with their respective objects. Among them, the nose, tongue and skin generate congnitions of smell, taste and touch, just remaining at their seats, while the eye and ear apprehend their respective objects by themselves reaching the spot occupied by those objects; because it is possible for the ear, too, to reach the spot occupied by a kettle-drum etc., since it is limited like the eye and so on. Hence we have the experience, "I have heard the sound of the kettle-drum." The assumption[2] that an endless series of sounds is produced in the region of the auditory passage, like a series of waves, or otherwise,[3] is cumbrous, and such also is the assumption that the perception, "I have heard the sound of the kettle-drum," is an illusion.[4]

Thus perception has been explained.

[[1] On p. 12.

[2] Of the Nyāya philosophy.

[3] Refers to the manner of *kadamba* buds, all the filaments of which appear simultaneously.

[4] Because, according to this view, what one hears is a sound of the same *class* as the sound of the kettle-drum.]

CHAPTER II

INFERENCE

INFERENCE IS THE KNOWLEDGE OF INVARIABLE CONCOMITANCE

अथानुमानं निरूप्यते। अनुमितिकरणमनुमानम्। अनुमितिश्च व्याप्तिज्ञानत्वेन व्याप्तिज्ञानजन्या। व्याप्तिज्ञानानुव्यवसायादेस्तत्त्वेन तज्जन्यत्वाभावान्नानुमितित्वम्।

Now inference (*anumāna*) is being described. It is the instrument of inferential knowledge (*anumiti*). And the latter is produced by the knowledge of invariable concomitance (*vyāpti*)[1] purely in its character as the knowledge of invariable concomitance.[2] The apperception[3] etc.[4] of the knowledge of invariable concomitance are not inferential knowledge, because they are not produced by the knowledge of invariable concomitance as such.

[[1] Between the thing to be inferred (*sādhya*) and the reason or ground from which we infer (*hetu*), the latter being the subordinate concomitant (*vyāpya*). In the sentence, "The hill has fire, because it has smoke," fire is the thing to be inferred, the hill is the subject or thing in which it is inferred (*pakṣa*), and smoke is the reason. We know from experience that wherever there is smoke, there is fire. In other words, smoke never exists where fire does not. This is invariable concomitance. According to the Nyāya philosophy, the sight of smoke in the hill, followed by the recollection of this invariable concomitance and the consideration (*parāmarśa*) that the hill has smoke, which is the subordinate concomitant of (i.e. never exists without) fire, leads to the inferential knowledge that the hill has fire. The Vedāntic conception of the origin of inferential knowledge differs from this in certain respects, which will presently be dealt with.

[2] And not as an object etc. See note 4.

[3] See note 6 on p. 21.

[4] Refers to recollection etc. For instance, in the apperception of the knowledge of invariable concomitance (that is, when we know that we have this knowledge), the latter is a cause as an object in the recollection of that, it is a cause as the experience of an identical object (with that of the recollection).]

अनुमितिकरणञ्च व्याप्तिज्ञानम्। तत्संस्कारोऽवान्तर-व्यापारः। न तु तृतीयलिङ्गपरामर्शोऽनुमितौ करणम्, तस्यानुमितिहेतुत्वासिद्ध्या तत्करणत्वस्य दूरनिरस्तत्वात्। न च संस्कारजन्यत्वेनानुमितेः स्मृतित्वापत्तिः, स्मृतिप्रागभाव-जन्यत्वस्य संस्कारमात्रजन्यत्वस्य वा स्मृतित्वप्रयोजकतया संस्कारध्वंससाधारणसंस्कारजन्यत्वस्य तदप्रयोजकत्वात्।

The instrument of inferential knowledge is the knowledge of invariable concomitance. The latent impression of that knowledge is the intermediate operation (*vyāpāra*).[1] But the consideration (*parāmarśa*)—which is the third cognition[2]—of the sign[3] or reason as being present in the thing where something is inferred (*pakṣa*), is not an instrument of inferential knowledge; for since it cannot be proved that it is (even) a cause of inferential knowledge, the question of its being an instrument[4] of that is easily set aside.

It cannot be urged that since inferential knowledge is produced by latent impressions,[5] it comes under recollection; for since the criterion of recollection is the fact that it is produced by the previous non-existence[6] of recollection or by latent impressions alone, the fact of its being produced by latent impressions, which is applicable to their destruction[7] as well (as to recollection), is not a criterion of recollection.

[[1] *Vyāpāra* in *Nyāya* is defined as that which is caused by something else and yet helps to produce the result of that something; the intermediate cause. Here is another point of difference with Nyāya, according to which the operation is *parāmarśa*.

[2] According to the logicians, first we see the presence of smoke in a kitchen etc.; then we recollect that smoke is never without fire; next we consider that the smoke is in the hill where the fire is to be inferred. So consideration is cognition of the reason for the third time, and is an instrument of inferential knowledge. This view of the logicians is rebutted.

[3] *Liṅga*: that from which something is inferred; the reason.

[4] Which is an extraordinary cause.

[5] Which constitute the operation of it.

[6] According to Nyāya, prior to the moment that a positive entity comes into being, there is the previous non-existence of it, which is without a beginning. And when that ceases, the thing is produced.

[7] The destruction of latent impressions would be impossible, were they non-existent. Hence the latter are a cause of that.]

न च यत्र व्याप्तिस्मरणादनुमितिस्तत्र कथं संस्कारो हेतुरिति वाच्यम्, व्याप्तिस्मृतिस्थलेऽपि तत्संस्कारस्यैवानु-

मितिहेतुत्वात्। नहि स्मृतेः संस्कारनाशकत्वनियमः, स्मृतिधारादर्शनात्। न चानुद्बुद्धसंस्कारादप्यनुमित्यापत्तिः, तदुद्बोधस्यापि सहकारित्वात्। ।एवञ्च "अयं धूमवान्" इति पक्षधर्मताज्ञाने "धूमो वह्निव्याप्यः" इत्यनुभवाहित-संस्कारोद्बोधे च सति "वह्निमान्" इत्यनुमितिर्भवति। न तु मध्ये व्याप्तिस्मरणम्, तज्जन्यं "वह्निव्याप्यधूमवानयम्" इत्यादि विशिष्टज्ञानं वा, हेतुत्वेन कल्पनीयम्, गौरवान्माना-भावाच्च। तच्च व्याप्तिज्ञानं वह्निविषयकज्ञानांश एव करणम्, न तु पर्वतविषयकज्ञानांश इति "पर्वतो वह्निमान्" इति ज्ञानस्य वह्न्यंश एव अनुमितित्वम्, न पर्वतांशे, तदंशे प्रत्यक्षत्वस्योपपादितत्वात्।

Nor can it be questioned how, in a case where inferential knowledge arises from recollection, latent impressions can be the cause; for even in the case of a recollection of invariable concomitance, it is the latent impressions of that which are the cause. There is no hard and fast rule that recollection must destroy latent impressions, for we come across a series of recollections. Nor would inferential knowledge arise even from unawakened latent impressions, for the awakening of them is also an auxiliary (to it). Thus the inferential knowledge, "(The hill) has fire," arises when one has knowledge of the reason (smoke) being present in the thing (the hill) where something (fire) is to be inferred, in the form,

"This has smoke," and there is awakening of the latent impression left by the (previous) experience, "Smoke is a subordinate concomitant of fire." But neither the recollection of invariable concomitance nor a qualified knowledge[1] resulting from it, such as, "This has smoke, which is a subordinate concomitant of fire,"[2] should be assumed in between[3] as the cause, for it is cumbrous and unwarranted. That knowledge of invariable concomitance is an instrument[4] only in respect of the knowledge of the fire, and not in respect of that of the hill. Hence the knowledge, "The hill has fire," is inferential only in respect of the fire, and not in respect of the hill, for we have already[5] proved that in respect of the latter the knowledge is a perception.

[[1] A knowledge combining invariable concomitance and the presence of the reason in the subject.

[2] This is consideration (*parāmarśa*)—the knowledge that a thing (e.g. smoke) possessed of the invariable concomitance of some other thing, fire), that is, invariably dependent on it, is present in the subject or the thing where the latter is to be inferred (*pakṣa*).

[3] Between the awakening of the recollection and the inferential knowledge.

[4] Of inferential knowledge.

[5] On pp. 20-21.]

व्याप्तिश्चाशेषसाधनाश्रयाश्रितसाध्यसामानाधिकरण्यरूपा। सा च व्यभिचारादर्शने सति सहचारदर्शनेन गृह्यते। तच्च सहचारदर्शनं भूयोदर्शनं सकृद्दर्शनं वेति विशेषो नादरणीयः सहचारदर्शनस्यैव प्रयोजकत्वात्।

Invariable concomitance is co-existence with the thing to be inferred that must abide in all substratums of the reason. It is apprehended by the observation of concomitance when no violation of the latter has been noticed. As to whether this observation of concomitance should be repeated experience or a first experience, no importance need be attached to this distinction, for the deciding factor is simply the observation of concomitance.

Inference is only Affirmative

तच्चानुमानमन्वयिरूपमेकमेव। न तु केवलान्वयि, सर्वस्यापि धर्मस्यास्मन्मते ब्रह्मनिष्ठात्यन्ताभावप्रतियोगित्वेन अत्यंताभावाप्रतियोगिसाध्यकत्वरूपकेवलान्वयित्वस्यासिद्धेः। नाप्यनुमानस्य व्यतिरेकिरूपत्वम , साध्याभावे साधनाभाव-निरूपितव्याप्तिज्ञानस्य साधनेन साध्यानुमितावनुपयोगात्। कथं तर्हि धूमादावन्वयव्याप्तिमविदुषोऽपि व्यतिरेकव्याप्ति-ज्ञानादनुमितिः? अर्थापत्तिप्रमाणादिति वक्ष्यामः। अत एवानुमानस्य नान्वयव्यतिरेकिरूपत्वम्, व्यतिरेकव्याप्ति-ज्ञानस्य अनुमित्यहेतुत्वात्।

That inference is only of one form,[1] viz., affirmative (*anvayin*),[2] but not purely affirmative (*kevalānvayin*)[3]; for according to our view, every attribute is the counterpositive of the absolute non-existence[4] abiding in Brahman,[5] and hence there is no scope for the purely affirmative inference, in which the thing to be inferred must not be the counterpositive of non-existence. Nor has inference a negative (*vyatirekin*) form[6]; for the knowledge of invariable concomitance subsisting between the *absence* of the thing to be inferred and that of the reason—the former leading to the latter—is of no use[7] for deducing the thing to be inferred from the reason. How then can even a person who is unaware of the affirmative invariable concomitance[8] of smoke etc. (with fire etc.) have inferential knowledge[9] through his knowledge of negative invariable concomitance?[10] From the means of knowledge called presumption (*arthāpatti*), as we shall explain.[11] For this very reason[12] inference has no such form as both affirmative and negative (*anvaya-vyatirekin*),[13] for the knowledge of negative invariable concomitance is not a cause of inferential knowledge.

[[1] Not three, as in Nyāya, viz., purely affirmative (*kevalānvayin*), purely negative (*kevala-vyatirekin*) and both affirmative and negative (*anvaya-vyatirekin*).

[2] In which from the presence of something in a particular place or thing some other thing is inferred. For example, "The hill has fire, because it has smoke."

[3] For example, "A jar is namable, because it is knowable." Here no negative invariable concomitance nor any contrary instance is possible, since, according to the logicians, everything is namable.

[4] As in the proposition, "There is no jar."

[5] Since Brahman is absolutely devoid of attributes, there is always the absence of all attributes in It; and

every attribute is a counterpositive of that non-existence.

[6] Where by the knowledge of negative invariable concomitance between two things we infer the presence of one thing from that of the other. For example, when we infer fire from smoke by the knowledge, "Where there is no fire, there cannot be any smoke," as in a lake. This includes the second form of inference admitted by the logicians, viz., the purely negative, illustrated by the proposition, "Earth is different from other things, because it has smell."

[7] Being too round about a process for the purpose.

[8] For example, "Wherever there is smoke, there is fire."

[9] Such as, "The hill has fire."

[10] For example, "Where there is no fire, there is no smoke."

[11] In Chapter V.

[12] This is explained by the last part of the sentence.

[13] Since negative inference is repudiated by Vedānta, this third form of inference admitted by the logicians, which involves negative inference, is also inadmissible.]

INFERENCE FOR ONESELF AND FOR OTHERS: SYLLOGISM

तच्चानुमानं स्वार्थपरार्थभेदेन द्विविधम्। तत्र स्वार्थन्तूक्तमेव, परार्थन्तु न्यायसाध्यम्। न्यायो नामावयवसमुदायः। अवयवश्च त्रय एव—प्रतिज्ञाहेतूदाहरणरूपाः, उदाहरणोपनयनिगमनरूपा वा। न तु पञ्च, अवयवत्रयेणैव व्याप्तिपक्षधर्मतयोरुपदर्शनसम्भवेनाधिकावयवद्वयस्य व्यर्थत्वात्।

That inference is again twofold according to its division into that meant for oneself and that meant for others. Of these, the former has already[1] been described; the latter, however, requires the help of syllogisms. A syllogism is a group of component parts. These are but three in number, viz., the proposition to be proved, reason and example, or example, application[2] and conclusion, and not five[3]; for, since it is possible to exhibit the invariable concomitance and the presence of the reason in the subject (*pakṣa*) by three component parts only, two additional component parts are useless.

[[1] On p. 71, in the sentence beginning with, "Thus the inferential knowledge," etc.

[2] A statement that the reason (e.g. smoke), which never exists where the thing to be inferred (e.g. fire) does not, is present in the subject of the inference (e.g. a hill).

[3] As the logicians hold. According to them the component parts are: The proposition to be proved (*pratijñā*), reason (*hetu*), example (*udāharaṇa*), application (*upanaya*) and conclusion (*nigamana*). The following are illustrations of these in order:

(1) The hill has fire.
(2) Because it has smoke.
(3) Whatever has smoke has fire, as a kitchen.
(4) This is also like that.
(5) The hill has fire, which is always present where there is smoke.]

Inference Proves the Unreality of the Universe: Definition of Unreality

एवमनुमाने निरूपिते तस्माद् ब्रह्मभिन्ननिखिलप्रपञ्चस्य मिथ्यात्वसिद्धिः। तथाहि—ब्रह्मभिन्नं सर्वं मिथ्या, ब्रह्म-

भिन्नत्वात्, यदेवं तदेवम्, यथा शुक्तिरूप्यम्। न च दृष्टान्त-सिद्धिः, तस्य साधितत्वात्। न चाप्रयोजकत्वम्, शुक्ति-रूप्यरज्जुसर्पादीनां मिथ्यात्वे ब्रह्मभिन्नत्वस्यै लाघवेन प्रयोजकत्वात्। मिथ्यात्वञ्च स्वाश्रयत्वेनाभिमत-यावन्निष्टा-त्यन्ताभावप्रतियोगित्वम्। 'अभिमत'-पदं वस्तुतः स्वाश्रया-प्रसिद्ध्याऽसम्भववारणाय, 'यावत्'-पदमर्थान्तरवारणाय। तदुक्तम्—

"सर्वेषामपि भावानां स्वाश्रयत्वेन सम्मते।
प्रतियोगित्वमत्यन्ताभावं प्रति मृषात्मता ॥" इति।

After inference has thus been set forth, it will prove the unreality of the entire universe, which is other than Brahman. For instance: All that other than Brahman; whatever is such (other than Brahman) is like this (unreal), as silver in a nacre. It cannot be urged that the example cited is unfounded, because it has already been proved.[1] Nor is the reason proffered without any corroborative argument, for in order to prove the unreality of silver in a nacre, of a snake in a rope, etc., it is the fact of their being other than Brahman that is the corroborative argument, because this is simpler.[2] Unreality consists in something[3] being the counterpositive of the absolute non-existence[4] that abides in whatever[5] is supposed[6] to be its substratum. The term 'supposed to be' is used to guard[7] against the futility of the definition on account of the absence of any true substratum of the thing that is unreal, and the word 'whatever' is for precluding a different thing[8] from the one in question. So it has been said,[9] "The unreality of all things whatsoever consists in their being counterpositives of the absolute non-existence that abides in what is supposed to be their substratum."

[[1] On p. 61, in the first paragraph.

[2] Than stating, as one may, that thing is unreal if it is produced by a defect other than nescience.

[3] E.g. silver in the nacre.

[4] As expressed in the sentence, "There is no silver here."

[5] E.g. a nacre.

[6] Not simply actually so. In the case of illusory objects, an actual substratum is not to be found.

[7] Thus, the nacre being the supposed substratum, the definition will apply to it.

[8] Viz., real co-existence, as in the case of the conjunction of a monkey with a tree. Since the conjunction is at the top, but not at the root, there is the non-existence of the conjunction as well as its counterpositive, conjunction, in the same substratum, the tree. And yet the conjunction is not unreal. The word 'whatever,' which connotes the entirety of the supposed substratum, excludes such a case from the purview of the definition.

[9] By Citsukhācārya in the *Citsukhī*, Ch. I, verse 7, p. 39, N. S. Ed.]

यद्वा अयं पट एतत्तन्तुनिष्ठात्यन्ताभावप्रतियोगी, पटत्वात्, पटान्तरवत्—इत्याद्यनुमानं मिथ्यात्वे प्रमाणम्। तदुक्तम्—

"अंशिनः स्वांशगात्यन्ताभावस्य प्रतियोगिनः।
अंशित्वादितरांशीव, दिगेषैव गुणदिषु॥" इति।

Or the proof of a thing's unreality is an inference like the following: "The cloth is a counterpositive of the absolute non-existence[1] abiding in these threads, because it is a cloth; as is the case with any other cloth." So it has been said,[2] "Things[3] that have parts are counter-positives of the non-existence abiding in those parts,[4] because they have parts; as in the case with other things that have parts. With regard to quality etc.[5] (also), the same kind of inference holds good."[6]

[[1] That is, a non-existence of the form, "There is no cloth here."

[2] *Op cit.*, Ch. I, verse 8, p. 40.

[3] E.g. a cloth.

[4] Viz., threads.

[5] Refers to action, generic attribute (*jāti*), etc.

[6] For example, "This colour of the cloth is a counterpositive of the absolute non-existence abiding in the cloth, because it is a colour; as is the case with other colours." Similarly, other qualities as also generic attributes etc. are to be taken as counterpositives of the absolute non-existence abiding in those threads.]

न च घटादेर्मिथ्यात्वे "सन् घटः" इति प्रत्यक्षेण बाधः, अधिष्ठानब्रह्मसत्तायास्तत्र विषयतया घटादेः सत्यत्वासिद्धेः।

It cannot be urged that if a jar etc. are unreal, it would contradict the perception, "The jar is existent"; for since the existence of the substratum of the jar, viz., Brahman, is the object of this perception, the reality of a jar etc. is unfounded.

न च नीरूपस्य ब्रह्मणः कथं चाक्षुषादिज्ञानविषयतेति वाच्यम्, नीरूपस्यापि रूपादेः प्रत्यक्षविषयत्वात्। न च नीरूपस्य द्रव्यस्य चक्षुराद्ययोग्यत्वमिति नियमः, मन्मते ब्रह्मणो द्रव्यत्यासिद्धेः। गुणाश्रयत्वं समवायिकारणत्वं वा द्रव्यत्वम् इति तेऽभिमतम्। न हि निर्गुणस्य ब्रह्मणो गुणाश्रयता, नापि समवायिकारणता, समवायासिद्धेः। अस्तु वा द्रव्यत्वं ब्रह्मणः, तथापि नीरूपस्य कालस्येव चाक्षुषादिज्ञानविषयत्वे न बिरोधः।

It cannot be urged: How can Brahman, which is colourless, be an object of ocular[1] cognition? For colour etc., which are without colour,[2] are objects of perception. Nor does the accepted principle that a colourless *substance* is incapable of being perceived by the eye etc. (go against us), for according to our view, the fact of Brahman's being a substance is unfounded. You hold that a substance is that which is the substratum of qualities, or which is an inherent cause. But Brahman, which is devoid of qualities, cannot be the substratum of qualities; nor is It an inherent cause, for inherence is unfounded.[3] Or, even if Brahman be admitted to be a substance, still there is no contradiction in Its being an object of ocular cognition, like time, which is colourless.[4]

[[1] The printed editions read *cākṣuṣādi* (ocular *or any other*). The word *ādi* (etc.) is obviously out of place here, as also in the last sentence of this paragraph.

[2] Because, according to Nyāya, a quality or action does not possess any other quality or action.
[3] See p. 23, l. 5, and note 2 on p. 24.
[4] According to the Mīmāṁsakas, in every perception the particular time also is perceived. See p. 5, l. 14, and note 5 on p. 6.]

EXISTENCE IS THREEFOLD

यद्वा त्रिविधं सत्त्वम्—पारमार्थिकं व्यावहारिकं प्रातिभासिकञ्चेति। पारमार्थिकं सत्त्वं ब्रह्मणः, व्यावहारिकं सत्त्वमाकाशादेः, प्रातिभासिकं सत्त्वं शुक्तिरजतादेः। तथा च "घटः सन्" इति प्रत्यक्षस्य व्यावहारिकसत्त्वविषयत्वेन प्रामाण्यम्। अस्मिन् पक्षे घटादेर्ब्रह्मणि निषेधो न स्वरूपेण, किन्तु पारमार्थिकत्वेनैवेति न विरोधः। अस्मिन् पक्षे च मिथ्यात्वलक्षणे पारमार्थिकत्वावच्छिन्नप्रतियोगिताकत्वमत्यन्ताभावविशेषणं द्रष्टव्यम्। तस्मादुपपन्नं मिथ्यात्वानुमानमिति।

इति वेदान्तपरिभाषायामनुमानपरिच्छेदः।

Or (we may say) there are three kinds of existence: absolute,[1] conventional[2] and illusory.[3] Absolute existence belongs to Brahman, conventional existence to the ether etc., and illusory existence to silver in a nacre, etc. Thus the perception, "The jar is existent," is valid, as it treats of conventional existence. In this alternative, the negation of a jar etc. in Brahman is not a negation of those things as they actually are,[4] but only as absolute reality.[5] Again, in this alternative, we should understand that in the definition[6] of unreality the absolute non-existence is to be so qualified as to convey the additional idea, "And the counterpositiveness relating to which is characterised by absoluteness."[7] Therefore the inference about the unreality (of the universe) is valid.

[[1] Which remains uncontradicted for all time.

[2] Which abides till the realisation of one's identity with Brahman—that is, what is popularly known as real.

[3] Which is destroyed as soon as the obstacles to proper vision, such as distance, defects of the eye and sleep, are removed ; e.g. a mirage.

[4] That is, as phenomenal entities.

[5] Which Brahman alone is.

[6] Given on p. 77, ll. 22-25.

[7] The above words should be added at the end of the sentence setting forth the definition.]

CHAPTER III

COMPARISON

अथोपमानं निरूप्यते। तत्र सादृश्यप्रमाकरणमुपमानम्। तथा हि—नगरेषु दृष्टगोपिण्डस्य पुरुषस्य वनं गतस्य गवयेन्द्रियसन्निकर्षे सति भवति प्रतीतिः "अयं पिण्डो गोसदृशः" इति। तदनन्तरञ्च भवति निश्चयः "अनेन सदृशी मदीया गौः" इति। तत्रान्वयव्यतिरेकाभ्यां गवयनिष्ठगोसादृश्यज्ञानं करणम्, गोनिष्ठगवयसादृश्यज्ञानं फलम्।

Now comparison is being described. The instrument of the valid knowledge of similarity is comparison. For instance, a man who has seen a cow's form in cities and has gone to a forest, where his eyes have come in contact with a gayal (*gavaya*), has the cognition,[1] "This thing is like a cow." Then he has the conviction, "My cow is like this." Here, by a process of agreement and difference,[2] the knowledge of that likeness of a cow which exists in a gayal is the instrument, and the knowledge of that likeness of a gayal which exists in a cow is the result.[3]

[[1] Which is a perception.

[2] When there is the preceding knowledge, there is the succeeding conviction; otherwise not.

[3] That is, comparison.]

न चेदं प्रत्यक्षेण सम्भवति, गोपिण्डस्य तदेन्द्रियासन्निकर्षात्। नाप्यनुमानेन, गवयनिष्ठगोसादृश्यस्य अतल्लिङ्गत्वात्। नापि

मदीया गौरेतद्गवयसदृशी,
एतन्निष्ठसादृश्यप्रतियोगित्वात्,
यो यद्गतसादृश्यप्रतियोगी स तत्सदृशः,
यथा मैत्रनिष्ठसादृश्यप्रतियोगी चैत्रो मैत्रसदृशः—

इत्यनुमानात् तत्सम्भव इति वाच्यम्। एवंविधानुमानानवतारेऽपि "अनेन सदृशी मदीया गौः" इति प्रतीतेरनुभवसिद्धत्वात्, "उपमिनोमि" इत्यनुव्यवसायाच्च। तस्मादुपमानं मानान्तरम्।

इति वेदान्तपरिभाषायामुपमानपरिच्छेदः।

This is not possible through perception, for then the cow's form is not in contact with the eyes. Nor is it possible through inference,[1] for that likeness of a cow which exists in a gayal cannot be the sign (reason) for inferring the likeness of a gayal in a cow. Nor can it be urged that this is possible through the following inference:

My cow is like this gayal.

Because it corresponds to its likeness existing in a gayal.

That which corresponds to its likeness existing in a thing is like the latter.

As Caitra, who corresponds to his likeness existing in Maitra, is like him.

For even without this sort of inference, the cognition, "My cow is like this," is a matter of common experience, and one has also the apperception,[2] "I am comparing[3] (the two," Hence comparison is a distinct means of knowledge.

[[1] As it is held by Sāṅkhya and Vaiśeṣika.

[2] See note 6 on p. 21.

[3] *Not inferring.*]

CHAPTER IV

VERBAL TESTIMONY

अथागमो निरूप्यते। यस्य वाक्यस्य तात्पर्यविषयीभूत-संसर्गो मानान्तरेण न बाध्यते तद्वाक्यं प्रमाणम्। वाक्य-जन्यज्ञाने च आकांक्षायोग्यताऽऽसत्तयस्तात्पर्यज्ञानश्चेति चत्वारि कारणानि।

Now verbal testimony is being discussed. That sentence is a means of valid knowledge in which the relation (among the meanings of words) that is the object of its intention[1] is not contradicted by any other means[2] of valid knowledge. The knowledge arising from a sentence has four causes, viz., expectancy, consistency, contiguity and the knowledge of the intention.[3]

[[1] That is, the relation intended by the sentence.

[2] Than verbal testimony. That is, perception etc.

[3] In Nyāya, it is the *knowledge* of all the four that is the cause.]

Expectancy

तत्र पदार्थानां परस्परजिज्ञासाविषयत्वयोग्यत्वमाकांक्षा। क्रियाश्रवणे कारकस्य, कारकश्रवणे क्रियायाः, करणश्रवणे इतिकर्तव्यतायाश्च जिज्ञासाविषत्वात्। अजिज्ञासोरपि वाक्यार्थबोधात् 'योग्यत्व'मुपात्तम्। तदवच्छेदकश्च क्रियात्व-कारकत्वादिकमिति नातिव्याप्तिः गौरश्व इत्यादौ।

अभेदान्वये च समानविभक्तिकपदप्रतिपाद्यत्वं तदवच्छेदकमिति "तत्त्वमस्या"दिवाक्येषु नाव्याप्तिः ।

Of these, expectancy is the capacity of the meanings of words to become objects of inquiry regarding each other. For when we hear a word signifying an action, something connected with the latter becomes an object of our inquiry; when we hear a word meaning something connected with an action, that action becomes such an object; and when we hear a word conveying the instrument of an action, its *modus operandi* becomes an object of our inquiry.[1] The word 'capacity' is inserted (in the definition), because even one who is not inclined to inquire comprehends the meaning of a sentence. Since the determining characteristic (*avacchedaka*)[2] of that capacity is the fact of being an action, that of being something connected with an action (*kārakatva*), and so on, the definition is not too wide so as to include words (in the nominative case) like, 'A cow,' 'A horse,' etc.[3] While in cases where words in apposition bring out an identity of meaning, that determining characteristic is the fact of being signified by words having the same case-ending; hence the definition is not too narrow to include sentences like, "Thou art That" (*Cha.* VI viii. 7 ff).[4]

[[1] For example, when somebody says, 'Bring,' we are inclined to ask: 'What?' or 'Whom?' Similarly, when we hear the word 'him,' we expect a verb like 'bring." And when we hear the sentence, "One who desires heaven should perform the new- and full-moon sacrifices," the concluding phrase (which in Sanskrit is in the instrumental case) leads us to inquire into its steps—how exactly the sacrifice should be done.

[2] By which instances of that kind of capacity can be spotted out and grouped together.

[3] Which do not, according to the rules of Sanskrit grammar, normally suggest any corresponding terms, as do words in the accusative and other cases.

[4] Here the words 'Thou' and 'That', being ppositional, might be excluded from the purview of the definition, if the determining characteristic of the capacity for rousing inquiry were the same as before. Hence a different one is given.]

एतादृशाकांक्षाभिप्रायेणैव बलाबलाधिकरणे "सा वैश्वदेव्यामिक्षा, वाजिभ्यो वाजिनम्" इत्यत्र वैश्वदेवयागस्यामिक्षान्वितत्वेन न वाजिनाकांक्षा इत्यादिव्यवहारः। ननु तत्रापि वाजिनस्य जिज्ञासाऽविषयत्वेऽपि तद्योग्यत्वमस्त्येव, प्रदेयद्रव्यत्वस्य यागनिरूपितजिज्ञासाविषयतावच्छेदकत्वादिति चेत्, न, स्वसमानजातीयपदार्थान्वयबोधविरहसहकृतप्रदेयद्रव्यत्वस्यैव तदवच्छेदकत्वेन वाजिनद्रव्यस्य स्वसमानजातीयामिक्षाद्रव्यान्वयबोधसहकृतत्वेन तादृशावच्छेदकत्वाभावात्। आमिक्षायान्तु नैवम्, वाजिनान्वयस्य सदानुपस्थितत्वात्। उदाहरणान्तरेष्वपि दुर्बलत्वप्रयोजक आकांक्षाविरह एव द्रष्टव्यः।

It is in view of such expectancy that under the topic of "Relative Strength,"[1] in the passage,

"Those curds belong to the Viśvadevas, and the whey is for the Vājins,"[2] the procedure is laid down to the effect that there is no expectancy of the whey,[3] since the sacrifice pertaining to the Viśvadevas has connection with curds only.[4]

Objection: Even there,[5] although the whey is not actually an object of inquiry, yet it certainly has the capacity for being such, because the determining characteristic of something being an object of inquiry in connection with sacrifices is the fact of its being an article of offering.

Reply: Not so; for the determining characteristic in question is the fact of something[6] being an article of offering *in the absence of* an apprehension of the connection[7] of something else[8] of the same class[9] as itself; and as with regard to the article whey there *is* an apprehension of the connection of another thing of the same class as itself, viz., curds, the whey[10] has not such a determining characteristic. But in the case of the curds, it is not so; for then[11] there is no apprehension of the connection of the whey. In other instances[12] also, it is the absence of expectancy that should be understood to be the criterion of weakness.

[[1] Topic 7 of Jaimini's *Pūrva-Mīmāṁsā-Sūtras* III. iii., aphorism 14 of which reads as follows: "Where direct enunciation (case-endings, affixes, etc.—*śruti*), indication (*liṅga*), supplementary statement (*vākya*), context (*prakaraṇa*), order (*sthāna*) and derivation (*samākhyā*) relate to the same thing, each succeeding item is weaker, because it conveys its meaning in a more distant way" —that is, through the medium of the preceding ones.

[2] The passage is actually discussed in Śabara's commentary, not in chapter III, but under II. ii. 23. The discussion on it, however, is based on the relative strength of the first and third of the above tests for determining "the parts of a sacrifice," which is the subject-matter of the second chapter, the issue being whether the offering of the whey is a part of the sacrifice relating to the Viśvadevas. This is decided negatively on the ground that direct enunciation is stronger than supplementary statement. The words immediately preceding those quoted in the text are: "In hot milk one should put curd."

[3] Which belongs to another sacrifice, viz., that relating to the Vājins.

[4] Because of direct enunciation, viz., the adjectival suffix.

[5] In the sacrifice relating in the Viśvadevas.

[6] E.g. curds.

[7] With the *Vaiśvadeva* sacrifice. So also three lines later.

[8] Viz., whey.

[9] As being an article of offering.

[10] Which is not an article of offering of the kind specified above.

[11] At the time of the verbal comprehension of the meaning of the word first heard, viz., 'curds.'

[12] Where the relative strength of the other items in the series, such as direct enunciation and indication, is the issue. For examples of these see *op cit.*]

Consistency and Contiguity

योग्यता तात्पर्यविषयसंसर्गाबाधः । "वह्निना सिञ्चति" इत्यादौ तादृशसंसर्गबाधान्न योग्यता । "स प्रजापतिरात्मनो वपामुदखिदत्" इत्यादावपि तात्पर्यविषयीभूतपशुप्राशस्त्याबाधात् योग्यता । "तत्त्वमस्या"-दिवाक्येष्वपि वाच्याभेदबाधेऽपि लक्ष्यस्वरूपाभेदे बाधाभावात् योग्यता ।

Consistency is non-contradiction of the relation[1] that is intended. Since in sentences like, "He is sprinkling (plants) with fire," there is contradiction of such a relation, they have no consistency. Even sentences like, "That Prajāpati took out his own omentum" (*Tai.* S. II. 1. i. 4, adapted), have consistency, because there is non-contradiction of the object of the intention, viz., an eulogy on animals.[2] Sentences like, "Thou art That" (*Chā.* VI. viii. 7 ff), also have consistency, because, although there is contradiction of the identity of their direct meanings,[3] still there is non-contradiction of the identity of their implied meaning, viz., their real essence.[4]

[[1] Between one thing and another signified by two words.

[2] As a result of the offering of his omentum by Prajāpati, a large number of kids were born. And kids are prescribed as offerings for the attainment of children and animals. Hence the sentence quoted is meant simply to extol animals, and from that standpoint it is consistent.

[3] Viz., the individual self and God, respectively, that are as the poles asunder as regards power, knowledge, etc.

[4] Viz., the Brahman without attributes, which is the underlying essence of both.]

आसत्तिश्चाव्यवधानेन पदजन्यपदार्थोपस्थितिः। मानान्तरोपस्थापितपदार्थस्यान्वयबोधाभावात् 'पदजन्या' इति। अत एवाश्रुतस्थले तत्तत्पदाध्याहारः। 'द्वारम्' इत्यादौ 'पिधेहि' इति। अत एव 'इषे त्वा' इत्यादिमन्त्रे 'छिनद्मि'

इति पदाध्याहारः। अत एव विकृतिषु "सूर्याय जुष्टं निर्वपामि" इति पदप्रयोगः।

Contiguity is the apprehension,[1] without an interval, of the meanings[2] of words that is produced by those words. The clause, "That is produced by those words," is inserted, since the meanings of words apprehended by other means[3] of knowledge do not lead to any (verbal) comprehension of their mutual connection. Hence in cases where particular words are not uttered, they are to be supplied; as, for instance, in the case of the word *dvāram* (the door), the word *pidhehi* (shut) is to be supplied. Hence (also) in the *mantra* beginning with, "For the sake of rain[4] thee,[5]" (*Vāj. S.* I, i. 22, *Taj. S.* I. i. 1, etc.), the words "I cut" are to be supplied. Hence (again) in the variant sacrifices the words should run as follows: "To (the god) Sun[6] I offer thee so as to please him."[7]

[[1] Recollection by association.

[2] The things signified by them.

[3] Such as perception and inference.

[4] As the producer of crops.

[5] The branch of a *palāśa* tree (*Butea Frondosa*) is being addressed.

[6] Or any other deity, according to the sacrifice.

[7] Addressed to an oblation of rice-cake. In the typical sacrifice (*prakṛti*), the deity of which is Fire, the words of the *mantra* are: "To (the god) Fire I offer thee so as to please him" (*Tai. S.* I. 1. iv. 2). In the variant sacrifice (*vikrti*), the word 'Fire' is changed into 'Sun' to suit the deity. In a typical sacrifice all the details are given; in a variant sacrifice the points of difference only are noted.]

SIGNIFICANCE OF WORDS

पदार्थश्च द्विविधः—शक्यो लक्ष्यश्चेति। तत्र शक्ति-र्नाम पदानामर्थेषु मुख्या वृत्तिः। यथा 'घट'-पदस्य पृथु-बुध्नोदराद्याकृतिविशिष्टे वस्तुविशेषे वृत्तिः। सा च शक्तिः पदार्थान्तरम्, सिद्धान्ते कारणेषु कार्यानुकूलशक्तिमात्रस्य पदार्थान्तरत्वात्। सा च तत्तत्पदजन्यपदार्थज्ञानरूपकार्या-नुमेया। तादृशशक्तिविषयत्वं शक्यत्वम्।

The meanings of words are of two kinds—primary and implied. Now significance (*śakti*) is the direct reference of words to their meanings. As, the word 'jar' refers to a particular thing of a form having a large bottom and body etc. That significance is a distinct category,[1] for, according to Vedānta, any power in a cause tending to produce an effect comes under a distinct category. And it is to be inferred from its effect, viz., the comprehension of the meanings of particular words produced by those words. To be signified (*śakyatva*) is to be an object of (the comprehension produced by) such significance.[2]

[[1] According to the logicians, significance (*śakti*) is the relation of a word to its meaning. It is of the form of a divine will that such and such a word should mean such and such a thing. And they do not admit its being a distinct category. The Mīmāṁsakas, however, side with the Vedāntists.

[2] That is, something is said to be directly meant by a word when it is known through the significance of that word.]

तच्च जातेरेव, न व्यक्तेः, व्यक्तीनामानन्त्येन गुरुत्वात्। कथं तर्हि गवादिपदाद्व्यक्तिभानमिति चेत्, जातेर्व्यक्तिसमानसंवित्संवेद्यत्वादिति ब्रूमः। यद्वा गवादिपदानां व्यक्तौ शक्तिः स्वरूपसती, न तु ज्ञाता, हेतुः; जातौ तु सा ज्ञाता हेतुः। न च व्यक्त्यंशे शक्तिज्ञानमपि कारणम्, गौरवात्। जातिशक्तिमत्त्वज्ञाने सति व्यक्तिशक्तिमत्त्वज्ञानं विना व्यक्तिधीविलम्बाभावाच्च। अत एव न्यायमतेऽप्यन्वये शक्तिः स्वरूपसतीति सिद्धान्तः।

That capacity of being signified belongs to a generic attribute (*jāti*),[1] not to individuals,[2] for individuals being infinite in number, it would be cumbrous (to assume otherwise). It may be urged: How, then, are individuals known through words like 'cow'? The answer is: Because the same cognition that comprehends a generic attribute also comprehends the individuals. Or (we may put it this way): With regard to individuals, the significance of words like 'cow' is (a cause of verbal comprehension) *per se*,[3] not as being known; while with regard to a generic attribute, it is a cause as being known. It cannot be urged that the knowledge of significance in respect of individuals also is a cause, for it would be a cumbrous assumption. And, besides, (even) in the absence of a knowledge that significance refers to individuals, there is no delay[4] in knowing those individuals, simply when one is aware that significance refers to the (corresponding) generic attribute. Therefore, even in the Nyāya philosophy, the conclusion is that significance (of words) regarding the logical connection is (a cause of verbal comprehension) *per se.*[5]

[[1] Meaning the common property of a class, which characterises all the individuals comprised in that class; for example, jarhood, which is found in all jars. This kind of generic attribute is admitted in Vedānta. What was refuted on p. 22 was the technical interpretation of the term as a distinct category upheld by the logicians.

[2] According to the logicians, however, it belongs to the individual possessed of a particular generic attribute and form.

[3] That is, by its mere existence.

[4] Which would be inevitable if the knowledge of significance as referring to individuals were a cause of verbal comprehension.

[5] Not as being known.]

ज्ञायमानशक्तिविषयत्वमेव वाच्यत्वमिति जातिरेव वाच्या। अथवा व्यक्तेर्लक्षणयाऽवगमः। यथा "नीलो घटः" इत्यत्र 'नील'-शब्दस्य नीलगुणविशिष्टे लक्षणा, तथा जातिवाचकस्य तद्विशिष्टे लक्षणा। तदुक्तम् "अनन्यलभ्यः शब्दार्थः" इति। एवं शक्यो निरूपितः।

A direct meaning (*vācya*) is that which is an object of significance as being known. Hence a generic attribute alone is directly meant. Or (we may say) individuals are comprehended by implication (*lakṣaṇā*). As in the phrase, "A blue jar," the word 'blue' implies something possessed of the blue colour as a quality, similarly a work meaning a generic attribute may convey by implication an individual possessing it. So it has been said[1]:

"The meaning of a word is to be obtained from no other source[2] (than the word itself)." Thus the primary meaning of a word has been ascertained.

[[1] By the Mīmāṁsakas.
[2] Than significance and implication.]

Implication: Its Varieties

अथ 'लक्ष्य'-पदार्थो निरूप्यते। तत्र लक्षणाविषयो लक्ष्यः। लक्षणा च द्विविधा—केवललक्षणा लक्षितलक्षणा चेति। तत्र शक्यसाक्षात्सम्बन्धः केवललक्षणा। यथा "गङ्गायां घोषः" इत्यत्र प्रवाहसाक्षात्सम्बन्धिनि तीरे 'गङ्गा'-पदस्य केवललक्षणा। यत्र शक्यपरम्परासम्बन्धेनार्थान्तरप्रतीतिस्तत्र लक्षितलक्षणा, यथा 'द्विरेफ'-पदस्य रेफद्वये शक्तस्य 'भ्रमर'-पदघटित-परम्परासम्बन्धेन मधुकरे वृत्तिः। गौण्यपि लक्षितलक्षणैव। यथा "सिंहो मानवकः" इत्यत्र 'सिंह'-शब्दवाच्यसम्बन्धिक्रौर्यादिसम्बन्धेन मानवकस्य प्रतीतिः।

Now the meaning implied by a word is being described. An implied meaning is the object implied by a word. Implication is of two kinds—pure and double. Of these, pure implication is the direct relation to the primary meaning of a word. As, in the sentence, "The cowherd colony is on (lit., in) the Ganges," the word 'Ganges' refers by pure implication[1] to the bank (of the river), which is directly related to the stream. Double implication occurs where, by an indirect relation to the primary meaning of a word, some other meaning is known. As, the word *dvirepha*, which signifies two r's, refers to a bee by an indirect relation arrived at through the intermediary word *bhramara*.[2] What is called figurative use is also nothing but double implication. As, in the sentence, "The boy is a lion," the boy is known through his relation to ferocity etc., which are associated with what is primarily meant by the word 'lion.'

[[1] Because the colony cannot be *in* the river.

[2] '*Dvirepha*' literally means two r's. From this we are led by pure implication to something containing two r's, viz., the word *bhramara*. Then by a second implication of the word *dvirepha*, we get its meaning, viz., a bee. Hence this is an instance of double implication.]

प्रकारान्तरेण लक्षणा त्रिविधा—जहल्लक्षणा, अजहल्लक्षणा, जहदजहल्लक्षणा चेति। तत्र शक्यमनन्तर्भाव्य यत्रार्थान्तरप्रतीतिस्तत्र जहल्लक्षणा। यथा "विषँ भुंक्ष्व" इत्यत्र स्वार्थं विहाय शत्रुगृहे भोजननिवृत्तिर्लक्ष्यते। यत्र शक्यार्थमन्तर्भाव्यैवार्थान्तरप्रतीतिः, तत्राजहल्लक्षणा, यथा "शुक्लो घटः" इति। अत्र हि 'शुक्ल'-शब्दः स्वार्थं शुक्लगुणमन्तर्भाव्यैव तद्वति द्रव्ये लक्षणया वतते। यत्र हि विशिष्टवाचकः शब्द एकदेशं विहाय एकदेशे वर्तते तत्र जहदजहल्लक्षणा, यथा "सोऽयं देवदत्तः" इति। अत्र हि पदद्वयवाच्ययोर्विशिष्टयोरैक्यानुपपत्त्या पदद्वयस्य विशेष्यमात्र-

परत्वम्। यथा वा "तत्त्वमसि" इत्यादौ 'तत्'-पदवाच्यस्य सर्वज्ञत्वादिविशिष्टस्य 'त्वं'-पदवाच्येनान्तःकरणविशिष्टेनैक्यायोगात् ऐक्यसिद्ध्यर्थं स्वरूपे लक्षणेति साम्प्रदायिकाः।

In another way, implication is of three kinds—exclusive (*jahat*), inclusive (*ajahat*) and quasi-inclusive (*jahad-ajahat*). Of these, exclusive implication occurs where, excluding the primary meaning, some other meaning is comprehended. As, in the sentence, "Take poison,"[1] discarding the original meaning of the words, abstention from eating in an enemy's house is implied. Inclusive implication occurs where, along with the primary meaning, some other meaning is comprehended: as, "A white jar." Here the word 'white' includes its original meaning, viz., the quality white colour, and yet refers by implication to a substance possessing it. Quasi-inclusive implication occurs where a word signifying some qualified entity discards one part of its meaning and refers to another part; as, "This is that Devadatta." Here, since the qualified entities primarily meant by the two words[2] cannot be identical,[3] the latter refer only to the substantive (*viśeṣya*).[4] Or[5] as, according to the traditional interpreters of Vedānta, in a sentence like, "Thou art That" (*Chā.* VI viii. 7 ff.), since the entity meant by the word 'That', viz., God as possessed of omniscience etc., cannot be identical with what is meant by the word 'Thou,' viz., the individual self endowed with a mind, therefore in order to make their identity possible, the words refer by implication to their essential nature.[6]

[1 Addressed to a person going to eat in an enemy's house.
2 'This' and 'that.'
3 Because 'this' refers to Devadatta as associated with the present time and 'that' to Devadatta as associated with the past.
4 Just the person Devadatta, unrelated to time past or present.
5 This is a Vedic example; the other is a popular one.
6 Viz., the Brahman without attributes.]

वयन्तु ब्रूमः—"सोऽयं देवदत्तः," "तत्त्वमसि" इत्यादौ विशिष्टवाचकपदानामेकदेशपरत्वेऽपि न लक्षणा, शक्त्युपस्थितविशिष्टयोः अभेदान्वयानुपपत्तौ विशेष्ययोः शक्त्युपस्थितयोरेव अभेदान्वयाविरोधात्। यथा "घटोऽनित्यः" इत्यत्र 'घट'-पदवाच्यैकदेशघटत्वस्यायोग्यत्वेऽपि योग्यघटव्यक्तया सहानित्यत्वान्वयः। यत्र पदार्थैकदेशस्य विशेषणतयोपस्थितिः, तत्रैव स्वातन्त्र्येण उपस्थितये लक्षणाभ्युपगमः। यथा "नित्यो घटः" इत्यत्र 'घट'-पदात् घटत्वस्य शक्त्या स्वातन्त्र्येणानुपस्थितया तादृशोपस्थित्यर्थं 'घट-पदस्य घटत्वे लक्षणा। एवमेव "तत्त्वमसि" इत्यादिवाक्येऽपि न लक्षणा, शक्त्या स्वातन्त्र्येणोपस्थितयोः 'तत्त्वं'-पदार्थयोरभेदान्वये बाधकाभावात्। अन्यथा "गेहे घटः," "घटे रूपम्," "घटमानय" इत्यादौ घटत्वगेहत्वादेरभिमतान्वयबोधायोग्यतया तत्रापि 'घटा'-दिपदानां विशेष्यमात्रपरत्वं लक्षणयैव स्यात्। तस्मात् "तत्त्वमसि" इत्यादिवाक्येषु आचार्याणां लक्षणोक्तिरभ्युपगमवादेन बोध्या।

We, however, maintain that in sentences like, "This is that Devadatta," and "Thou art That," although words signifying qualified entities refer only to one portion of their meaning, yet there is no implication; for, notwithstanding the fact that two qualified entities presented (to the mind) by significance[1] cannot be (logically) connected with each other to convey an identical meaning, there is no contradiction in connecting two substantives, also presented by significance, so as to yield an identity of meaning. As, in the sentence, "The jar is transitory," although it is inconsistent[2] to connect with transitoriness only one part[3] of what is meant by the word 'jar', viz., jarhood, yet it is all right with regard to an individual jar, which is capable of being so connected.[4] Only where one part of the meaning of a word is presented as a qualifying attribute (*viśeṣaṇa*), implication is admitted in order that the meaning may be presented independently.[5] As, in the sentence, "The jar is eternal," since jarhood is not independently presented[6] by the significance of the word 'jar,' the latter refers by implication to jarhood, in order to effect such cognition. Similarly, in sentences like, "Thou art That," there is also no implication, because the meanings of the words 'Thou' and 'That' are presented independently by significance (of those two words), and there is no obstacle to their being logically connected so as to mean an identical thing. Otherwise,[7] in sentences like, "There is a jar in the house," "There is colour in the jar," and "Bring the jar," since jarhood, householdhood, etc.,[8] are incapable of leading to the desired comprehension of the logical connection,[9] therefore even in these cases words such as 'jar' would convey mere substantives just by implication. Therefore the statement about implication by the (traditional) teachers in sentences like, "Thou art That," should be understood as mere tentative admission.

[[1] Of the two words 'this' and 'that' in the first example, and 'thou' and 'That' in the second.

[2] From the logician's standpoint, because jarhood, being a generic attribute, is according to him eternal.

[3] In Nyāya, the significance of a word is with regard to individuals comprised in a genus. See note 2 on p. 95.

[4] Because individual jars are perishable.

[5] As a substantive.

[6] According to Nyāya.

[7] If implication be admitted even with regard to words signifying independent substantives.

[8] Which are presented as qualifying attributes.

[9] Of the meanings of words comprising those sentences.]

जहदजहल्लक्षणोदाहरणन्तु "काकेभ्यो दधि रक्ष्यताम्" इत्याद्येव, तत्र शक्यकाकत्वपरित्यागेन अशक्यदध्युपघातकत्वपुरस्कारेणाकाकेऽपि 'काक'-शब्दप्रवृत्तेः ।

Examples of quasi-inclusive implication, however, are only sentences like these: "Protect the curd from the crows"; for here the word 'crows' gives up its characteristic yielding the primary meaning, viz., crowhood,[1] and refers, through the attribute[2] of being a spoiler of the curd, which is not the characteristic yielding the primary meaning, to creatures other than crows as well.

[[1] The word *'śakya'* in the text stands for *śakyatāvacchedaka.*
[2] Possessed by crows.]

लक्षणाबीजन्तु तात्पर्यानुपपत्तिरेव, न तु अन्वयानुपपत्तिः ; "काकेभ्यो दधि रक्ष्यताम्" इत्यत्र अन्वयानुपपत्त्यभावात्, "गङ्गायां घोषः" इत्यादौ तात्पर्यानुपपत्तेरपि सम्भवात्।

The root of implication, however, is the frustration of intention alone, and not that of the logical connection (of words); for in the sentence, "Protect the curd from the crows," there is no frustration of the logical connection, and in sentences like, "The cowherd colony is in (on) the Ganges," there is the possibility of a frustration of intention as well.

[[1] But there is a frustration of the speaker's intention, the word 'crows' being intended by the speaker to mean all pests.]

लक्षणा च न पदमात्रवृत्तिः, किन्तु वाक्यवृत्तिरपि। यथा "गम्भीरायां नद्यां घोषः" इत्यत्र "गम्भीरायां नद्याम्" इति पदद्वयसमुदायस्य तीरे लक्षणा। ननु वाक्यस्याशक्ततया कथं शक्यसम्बन्धरूपा लक्षणा? उच्यते। शक्त्या यत् पदसम्बन्धेन ज्ञाप्यते तत्सम्बन्धो लक्षणा। शक्तिज्ञाप्यश्च यथा पदार्थस्तथा वाक्यार्थोऽपीति न काचिदनुपपत्तिः।

Implication belongs not to words alone,[1] but also to a group of words. As, in the sentence, "There is a cowherd colony in (on) the deep river," the group consisting of the two words 'deep river' refers by implication to its bank. It may be urged: Since a group of words does not possess significance (*śakti*), how can it have implication, which is a relation to what is conveyed by significance? The answer is this: Implication is a relation to what is conveyed by significance, which is a relation of words[2] (to their meanings). And just as the meaning of a word is conveyed by significance, so is also that of a group of words. Hence there is no anomaly.

[[1] As Nyāya holds.
[2] Not a group of words.]

एवमर्थवादवाक्यानां प्रशंसारूपाणां प्राशस्त्ये लक्षणा, "सोऽरोदीत्" इत्यादिनिन्दार्थवादवाक्यानां निन्दितत्वे लक्षणा। अर्थवादगतपदानां प्राशस्त्यादिलक्षणाभ्युपगमे एकेन पदेन लक्षणाया तदुपस्थितिसम्भवे पदान्तरवैयर्थ्य स्यात्। एवञ्च विध्यपेक्षितप्राशस्त्यरूपपदार्थप्रत्यायकतया अथवादपदसमुदायस्य पदस्थानीयतया विधिवाक्येनैक-वाक्यत्वं भवति, इत्यर्थवादवाक्यानां पदैकवाक्यता। क्व तर्हि वाक्यैकवाक्यता? यत्र प्रत्येकं भिन्नभिन्नसंसर्गप्रतिपादकयो-र्वाक्ययोराकांक्षावशेन महावाक्यार्थबोधकत्वम्। यथा "दर्शयूर्णमासाभ्यां स्वर्गकामो यजेत" इत्यादिवाक्यानां "समिधो यजति" इत्यादिवाक्यानाञ्च परस्परापेक्षिताङ्गाङ्गि-

भावबोधकतया एकवाक्यता। तदुक्तं भट्टपादैः—
"स्वार्थबोधे समाप्तानामङ्गाङ्गित्वाद्यपेक्षया।
वाक्यानामेकवाक्यत्वं पुनः संहत्य जायते॥" इति।

Thus (Vedic) corroborative statements (*artha-vāda*) that are of the nature of eulogies refer by implication to praiseworthiness,[1] while depreciatory statements like, "He cried" (*Tai.* S. I. v. i. 1),[2] refer by implication to blameworthiness.[3] If the *words* comprising a corroborative statement be admitted to refer by implication to praiseworthiness etc., then, it being possible for one of those words to convey that through implication, the other words would be redundant. So the group of words comprising a corroborative statement virtually serves as one word, inasmuch as it leads to the apprehension of that meaning of the words, viz., praiseworthiness, which is required by the injunction, and thus it constitutes a unitary passage[4] with the sentence setting forth the injunction. Hence corroborative statements constitute (what is called) a unitary passage in respect of a word. Where, then, does a unitary passage in respect of a sentence occur?—Where two sentences, each of which conveys distinct relations (between its words and their meanings), express, by virtue of their expectancy, the meaning of a longer passage. As, a sentence like, "One who desires heaven should perform the new- and full-moon sacrifices,[5] and one like, "One should perform the Samidh sacrifice" (*Ait.* Br. VI 4), form a unitary passage, inasmuch as they express the mutually expected relation of whole and part. So it has been stated by the illustrious Kumārila Bhaṭṭa: "Sentences that are complete in themselves as regards the expression of their meanings, again combine in view of their relation of whole and part etc. and become a unitary passage" (*Tantra-Vārtika*, verse 4, under *Pū. Mī. Sū.* I. iv. 24).

[[1] Of actions prescribed by the Vedic injunctions.

[2] The story is this: Once the deity Fire ran away with some precious booty the gods had deposited with him. When they chased him, he cried, and his tears became silver. Hence silver should not be given as remuneration to the priests in the Barhis sacrifice; for it is sure to cause weeping in the sacrificer's family within a year.

[3] Of actions prohibited by the Vedas.

[4] Amplifying the purport of the injunction.

[5] These are the main sacrifices, of which the Samidh sacrifice, named after its deity and forming the first of the five Prayāja sacrifices, is a part. Hence the two sentences, although complete in themselves, form one whole—a unitary passage.]

एवं द्विविधोऽपि पदार्थो निरूपितः। तदुपस्थितिश्चासत्तिः। सा च शाब्दबोधे हेतुः, तथैवान्वयव्यतिरेकदर्शनात्। एवं महावाक्यार्थबोधेऽवान्तरवाक्यार्थबोधो हेतुः, तथैवान्वयाद्यवधारणात्।

Thus both the varieties of the meanings of words have been determined. Contiguity is the knowledge[1] of those. It is also a cause of verbal comprehension, for we observe just that kind of agreement and difference (between them).[2] Similarly, the comprehension of the meanings of subsidiary sentences is a cause of the comprehension of a composite passage, for we have a certitude about such agreement etc.[3] between them.[4]

[[1] Recollection produced by the utterance of words.

[2] If there is that recollection, there is verbal comprehension; otherwise not.

[3] Refers to difference.

[4] If the meanings of the component sentences are grasped, then the meaning of the paragraph also is grasped; otherwise not.]

INTENTION

क्रमप्राप्तं तात्पर्यं निरूप्यते। तत्र तत्प्रतीतीच्छयोच्चरितत्वं न तात्पर्यम्; अर्थज्ञानशून्येन पुरुषेणोच्चरिताद्वेदादर्थप्रत्ययाभावप्रसङ्गात्, "अयमध्यापकोऽव्युत्पन्नः" इति विशेषदर्शनेन तात्पर्यभ्रमस्याप्यभावात्। न चेश्वरीयतात्पर्यज्ञानात् तत्र शाब्दबोध इति वाच्यम्, ईश्वरानङ्गीकर्तुरपि तद्वाक्यार्थप्रतिपत्तिदर्शनात्। उच्यते। तत्प्रतीतिजननयोग्यत्वं तात्पर्यम्। "गेहे घटः" इति वाक्य गेहे घटसंसर्गप्रतीतिजननयोग्यम्, न तु पटसंसर्गप्रतीतिजननयोग्यमिति तद्वाक्यं घटसंसर्गपरम्, न तु पटसंसर्गपरमित्युच्यते।

Now intention, which comes next in order, is being described. Regarding this (we must know that) intention is not the utterance (of words) with the object of producing the cognition of a particular thing, for then Vedic texts uttered by a person who does not know their meaning would not be intelligible, and there can be no error[1] also about (the speaker's) intention,[2] since the listener has a specific comprehension,[3] as (expressed in his words), "This teacher does not understand (what he utters)." It cannot be urged that in the case cited above,[4] verbal comprehension takes place from a knowledge of God's intention,[5] for we find that even a person who does not believe in God[6] understands the meaning of the Vedic passages.[7] (What, then, *is* intention?) This is being stated: Intention is the capacity to produce cognition of a particular thing. The sentence, "There is a jar in the house," is capable of producing a cognition of the relation of a jar, and not that of a cloth, to the house. Hence that sentence is said to mean the relation of a jar, and not that of a cloth (to the house).

[[1] In the mind of the listener.
[2] Viz., his desire to convey a particular meaning.
[3] Which settles the question of error.
[4] Where one listens to Vedic or other words uttered by a person who does not understand them.
[5] Because He produced the Vedas.
[6] As the author of the Vedas.
[7] Uttered by one who does not know their meaning.]

ननु "सैन्धवमानय" इत्यादिवाक्यं यदा लवणानयनप्रतीतीच्छया प्रयुक्तं तदापि अश्वसंसर्गप्रतीतिजनने स्वरूपयोग्यतासत्त्वात् लवणपरत्वज्ञानदशायामप्यश्वादिसंसर्गज्ञानापत्तिरिति चेत्, न, तदितरप्रतीतीच्छयानुच्चरितत्वस्यापि तात्पर्यं प्रति विशेषणत्वात्। तथा च यद्वाक्यं यत्प्रतीति-

जननस्वरूपयोग्यत्वे सति यदन्यप्रतीतीच्छया नोच्चरितम्, तद्वाक्यं तत्संसर्गपरमित्युच्यते। शुकादिवाक्ये अव्युत्पन्नोच्चरितवेदवाक्यादौ च प्रतीतीच्छाया एवाभावेन तदन्यप्रतीतीच्छयोच्चरितत्वाभावेन लक्षणसत्त्वान्नाव्याप्तिः। न चोभयप्रतीतीच्छयोच्चरितेऽव्याप्तिः, तदन्यमात्रप्रतीतीच्छयाऽनुच्चरितत्वस्य विवक्षितत्वात्।

Objection: A sentence like, "Bring the *saindhava*,"[1] even when it is uttered with the object of producing the cognition that salt should be brought, has the potentiality of producing the cognition that it relates to a horse; hence, even when one has the knowledge that it means salt, one may have the idea that it relates to a horse or the like.

Reply: Not so; for (the definition of) intention has the additional qualifying attribute that the sentence must not be uttered with the object of producing the cognition of anything else but that (which is intended by the words). So a sentence that has the potentiality of producing the cognition of a particular thing, and at the same time is not uttered with the object of producing the cognition of anything else, is said to relate to that particular thing.[2] In the case of words uttered by a parrot etc., and of Vedic or other sentences uttered by a person ignorant of their meaning, since there is no desire at all to produce any cognition, and consequently there is the absence of an utterance with the object of producing the cognition of anything else but that (which is in view), the definition is applicable, and hence it is not too narrow. Nor is it too narrow to include a sentence uttered to mean both salt and horse (for instance); for the idea (behind the definition) is that the sentence must not be uttered with the object of producing the cognition of that only which is other than the thing in view.

[[1] Lit., a product of *sindhu*, which (among other things) means a sea, as also the territory called Sind. Hence the word means both salt and a species of horse.

[2] So, although '*saindhava*' may mean a horse, it will not be taken in that sense if somebody who is eating utters the sentence, because it has not been uttered to mean a horse.]

उक्तप्रतीतिमात्रजननयोग्यतायाश्चावच्छेदिका शक्तिः। अस्माकं मते सर्वत्र कारणतायाः शक्तेरेवावच्छेदकत्वान्न कोऽपि दोषः।

The determining characteristic of the capacity (of words) to produce just the above-mentioned cognition is inherent power (*śakti*). Since, according to us, inherent power alone is everything the determining characteristic of casuality,[1] there is no anomaly here.

[[1] As in the case of fire, for instance, the reason why it can burn things is that it possesses that inherent power, so in the case of words, the reason for their conveying particular meanings is to be sought in their inherent power, viz., significance.]

एवं तात्पर्यस्य तत्प्रतीतिजनकत्वरूपस्य शाब्दज्ञानजनकत्वे सिद्धे चतुर्थवर्णके तात्पर्यस्य शाब्दज्ञानहेतुत्वनिराकरणवाक्यं तत्प्रतीतीच्छयोच्चरितत्वरूपतात्पर्यनिराकरणपरम्, अन्यथा तात्पर्यनिश्चयफलकवेदान्तविचारवैयर्थ्यप्रसङ्गात्। केचित्तु—शाब्दज्ञानत्वावच्छेदेन न तात्पर्यज्ञानं हेतुरित्येवंपरं चतुर्थवर्णकवाक्यम्; तात्पर्यसंशयविपर्ययोत्तरशाब्दज्ञानविशेषे च तात्पर्यज्ञानं हेतुरेव; इदं वाक्यमेतत्परमुतान्यपरमिति संशये तद्विपर्यये च तदुत्तरवाक्यार्थविशेषनिश्चयस्य तात्पर्यनिश्चयं विनाऽनुपपत्तेरित्याहुः।

It thus being proved that intention, which is the (capacity for) generation of the cognition of a particular thing, is the cause of verbal comprehension, the passage[1] in the fourth chapter (*varṇaka*) *of the Vivaraṇ*[2] refuting the causality of intention in producing verbal comprehension, is meant to refute the contention[3] that intention is the utterance (of words) with the object of producing the cognition of a particular thing. Otherwise discussions on Vedānta, which result in a certitude about the intention, would be futile. Some,[4] however, maintain: The passage in the fourth chapter of the *Vivaraṇa* means that knowledge of the intention is not a cause of all verbal comprehension; but that with regard to the particular verbal comprehension that takes place after a doubt or error regarding the intention, it certainly is a cause; for in case of a doubt as to whether a particular sentence means this or something else, as also of an error regarding it, the ascertainment of its particular meaning thereafter can not take place without the ascertainment of the intention.

[[1] Pp. 181-182, V. S. S.
[2] See footnote 3 on p. 1.
[3] Of the logicians.
[4] The reference is to the author of the *Abheda-ratnākara.*]

तच्च तात्पर्यं वेदे मीमांसापरिशोधितन्यायादेवावधार्यते, लोके तु प्ररकणादिना। तत्र लौकिकवाक्यानां मानान्तरावगतार्थतयाऽनुवादकत्वम्, वेदे तु वाक्यार्थस्यापूर्वतया नानुवादकत्वम्। तत्र लोके वेदे च कार्यपराणामिव सिद्धार्थानामपि प्रामाण्यम्, "पुत्रस्ते जातः" इत्यादिषु सिद्धार्थेऽपि पदानां सामर्थ्यावधारणात्। अत एव वेदान्तवाक्यानां ब्रह्मणि प्रामाण्यम्। यथा चैतत् तथा विषयपरिच्छेदे वक्ष्यते।

That intention is determined with regard to the Vedas only by reasoning rectified by the principles of interpretation, while with regard to secular sentences, by means of the context etc.[1] Of these, secular sentences are of the nature of restatements, since their meanings are primarily apprehended through other means of knowledge; but with regard to the Vedas, since the meanings of Vedic sentences are known at first hand, they are not of the nature of restatements. Now, both in secular and Vedic sentences, even statements of fact are, like those conveying something to be done, means of valid knowledge; for in utterances like, "A son has been born to you," words are definitely known to have the power of conveying meanings that are statements of fact. Hence Vedāntic sentences are means of valid knowledge with regard to Brahman.[2] How this is so, will be dealt with in the chapter relating to the subject-matter of Vedānta.[3]

[[1] Refers to the words of a trustworthy person, and so on.

[2] Which is an eternal Reality.

[3] Chapter VII.]

The Authority of the Vedas Explained

तत्र वेदानां नित्यसर्वज्ञपरमेश्वरप्रणीतत्वेन प्रामाण्यमिति-नैयायिकाः। वेदानां नित्यत्वेन निरस्तसमस्तपुंदूषणतया प्रामाण्यमित्यध्वरमीमांसकाः। अस्माकं तु मते वेदो न नित्यः, उत्पत्तिमत्त्वात्। उत्पत्तिमत्त्वञ्च "अस्य महतो भूतस्य निःश्वसितमेतद्यदृग्वेदो यजुर्वेदः सामवेदोऽथर्ववेदः" इत्यादिश्रुतेः।

Now, according to the logicians, the Vedas are means of valid knowledge because they are produced by God, who is eternal and omniscient. According to the Mīmāṁsakas who deal with sacrifices, the Vedas are means of valid knowledge because they are eternal and as such free from all human defects.

In our view, however, the Vedas are not eternal, for they have an origin, which is proved by such Śruti texts as, "The *Ṛg-Veda*, *Yajur-Veda*, *Sāma-Veda*, *Atharva-Veda* are (like) the breath of this infinite Reality" (*By.* II. iv. 10, adapted).

नापि वेदानां त्रिक्षणावस्थायित्वम्, "य एव वेदो देवदत्तेनाधीतः सः एव मयामि" इत्यादिप्रत्यभिज्ञाविरोधात्। अत एव गकारादिवर्णानामपि न क्षणिकत्वम्, "सोऽयं गकारः" इत्यादिप्रत्यभिज्ञाविरोधात्। तथा च वर्णपदवाक्य-समुदायस्य वेदस्य वियदादिवत् सृष्टिकालीनोत्पत्तिकत्वं प्रलयकालीनध्वंसप्रतियोगित्वञ्च, न तु मध्ये वर्णाना-मुत्पत्तिविनाशौ, अनन्तगकारादिकल्पनायां गौरवात्। अनुच्चारणदशायां वर्णानामनभिव्यक्तिस्तदुच्चारणरूपव्यञ्जका-भावात् न विरुध्यते, अन्धकारस्थघटानुपलम्भवत्। "उत्पन्नो गकारः" इत्यादिप्रत्ययस्तु "सोऽयं गकारः" इत्यादिप्रत्य-भिज्ञाविरोधादप्रमाणम्। वर्णाभिव्यञ्जकध्वनिगतोत्पत्ति-निरूपितपरम्परासम्बन्धविषयत्वेन प्रमाणं वा। तस्मान्न वेदानां क्षणिकत्वम्।

And the Vedas have not a duration of three moments only,[1] for it clashes with such recognition as, "The same Veda that was studied by Devadatta was also studied by me." Hence also the syllables such as *ga* are not momentary, for it contradicts such recognition as, "This is that syllable *ga*." So the Vedas, which are a collection of syllables, words and sentences, originate like the ether etc. at the time of cosmic projection, and are counterpositives of the destruction that takes place[2] at the time of cosmic dissolution. It is not that the syllables are subject to origin and destruction in the interim, for it is cumbrous to assume an endless series of the syllable *ga*, for instance. The non-manifestation of the syllables during the time they are not uttered, is nothing contradictory, because then there is an absence of the revealing medium, viz., utterance—as with the non-apprehension of a jar in darkness.[3] As for the cognition, "The syllable *ga* has been produced," and so on, it is invalid, since it contradicts such recognition as, "This is that syllable *ga*." Or it may be valid as being indirectly related to the origin abiding in the inarticulate sound that manifests the syllable.[4] Therefore the Vedas are not momentary.

[[1] The view of some logician of the old school.

[2] That is, they are destroyed at that time.

[3] When a light is brought, the jar is visible. Similarly, utterance reveals the already existing syllable *ga*.

[4] The origin of the sound revealing the syllable is transferred to the latter.]

ननु क्षणिकत्वाभावेऽपि वियदादिप्रपञ्चवदुत्पत्तिमत्त्वेन परमेश्वरकर्तृकतया पौरुषेयत्वादपौरुषेयत्वं वेदनामिति तव सिद्धान्तो भज्येत इति चेत्, न। न हि तावत् पुरुषेण उच्चार्यमाणत्वं पौरुषेयत्वम्, गुरुमतेऽप्यध्यापकपरम्परया पौरुषेयत्वापत्तेः। नापि पुरुषाधीनोत्पत्तिकत्वं पौरुषेयत्वम्, नैयायिकाभिमतपौरुषेयत्वानुमानेऽस्मदादिना सिद्धसाधना-

पत्तेः। किन्तु सजातीयोच्चारणानपेक्षोच्चारणविषयत्वम्। तथा च सर्गाद्यकाले परमेश्वरः पूर्वसर्गसिद्धवेदानुपूर्वीसमानानुपूर्वीकं वेदं विरचितवान्, न तु तद्विजातीयं वेदमिति न सजातीयोच्चारणानपेक्षोच्चारणविषयत्वं पौरुषेयत्वं वेदस्य। भारतादीनान्तु सजातीयोच्चारणमनपेक्ष्यैवोच्चारणमिति तेषां पौरुषेयत्वम्। एवं पोरुषेयापौरुषेयभेदेन द्विविध आगमो निरूपितः।

इति वेदान्तपरिभाषायामागमपरिच्छेदः।

Objection: Although the Vedas are not momentary, yet, on account of their having an origin like the ether and other phenomenal things, and being connected with a person in that they are the handiwork of God, your tenet that they are not connected with a person would be shattered.

Reply: No. In the first place, connection with a person does not mean being uttered by a person, for even according to the school of the Teacher,[1] the Vedas would be connected with persons, being handed down from one teacher to another. Nor does connection with a person mean having an origin due to a person, for that inference[2] about the personal origin of the Vedas which is approved by the logicians is condemned by our school as proving what is already established.[3] But it is being the object of utterance that is independent of any utterance of the same kind. For instance, in the beginning of cosmic projection, the Lord produced Vedas having a sequence of words similar to that which had already existed in the Vedas in the previous cosmic projection, and not Vedas of a different type. Hence the Vedas, not being the object of utterance that is independent of any utterance of the same kind, are not connected with a person. The utterance of the *Mahābhārata* etc., however, is not at all dependent on any utterance of the same kind. Hence they are connected with a person. Thus two kinds of verbal testimony have been determined, viz., that which is connected with a person, and that which is not.

[[1] See note 3 on p. 55.

[2] Viz., that the Vedas are connected with a person, because they consist of sentences, as is the case with the *Mahābhārata* etc.

[3] By the Vedas, e.g. *Bṛ.* II. iv. 10.]

CHAPTER V

PRESUMPTION

CONDITIONS OF PRESUMPTION

इदानीमर्थापत्तिर्निरूप्यते। तत्रोपपाद्यज्ञानेनोपपादक-कल्पनमर्थापत्तिः। तत्रोपपाद्यज्ञानं करणम्, उपपादकज्ञानं फलम्। येन विना यदनुपपन्नं तत् तत्रोपपाद्यम। यस्या-भावे यस्यानुपपत्तिः तत् तत्रोपपादकम्। यथा रात्रिभोजनेन विना दिवाऽभुञ्जानस्य पीनत्वमनुपपन्नम्, इति तादृशं पीनत्वमुपपाद्यम्; यथा वा रात्रिभोजनस्याभावे तादृश-पीनत्वस्यानुपपत्तिः, इति रात्रिभोजनमुपपादकम्।

Now presumption (*arthāpatti*) is being described. It is the assumption of an explanatory fact (*upapādaka*) from a knowledge of the thing to be explained (*upapādya*). Here the knowledge of the thing to be explained is the instrument, and the knowledge of the explantory fact is the result. That which is inexplicable without (the assumption of) something, is the thing to be explained with reference to the latter, and that in the absence of which something is inexplicable, is the explanatory fact with reference to the latter. As, the stoutness of a man who does not eat at day-time is inexplicable unless we assume his eating at night; hence such stoutness is the thing to be explained. Again, in the absence of eating at night such stoutness is inexplicable; hence eating at night is the explanatory fact.

रात्रिभोजनकल्पनारूपायां प्रमितौ "अर्थस्य आपत्तिः" कल्पना इति षष्ठीसमासेन 'अर्थापत्ति'-शब्दो वर्तते; कल्पनाकरणे पीनत्वादिज्ञाने तु "अर्थस्य आपत्तिः कल्पना यस्मात्" इति बहुव्रीहिसमासेन वर्तते, इति फलकरणयोरुभयोस्तत्पदप्रयोगः।

With regard to the (resulting) valid knowledge, viz., the assumption of eating at night, the word *arthāpatti* is a compound of the class known as *Ṣaṣṭhī-tatpuruṣa,* meaning 'the assumption (*āpatti*) of a thing (*artha*).' But with regard to the instrument of the assumption, viz., the knowledge of stoutness etc., the word is a compound of the class known as *Bahuvrīhi,* meaning 'that from which a thing is assumed.' Hence the word *arthāpatti* applies both to the result and to the instrument.

Two Varieties of Presumptive Knowledge

सा चार्थापत्तिर्द्विविधा—दृष्टार्थापत्तिः श्रुतार्थापत्तिश्चेति। तत्र दृष्टार्थापत्तिर्यथा, "इदं रजतम्" इति पुरोवर्तिनि प्रतिपन्नस्य रजतस्य "नेदं रजतम्" इति तत्रैव निषिध्यमानत्वं सत्यत्वेऽनुपपन्नम्, इति रजतस्य सद्भिन्नत्वं सत्यत्वात्यन्ताभाववत्त्वं वा मिथ्यात्वं कल्पयति। श्रुतार्थापत्तिर्यथा, यत्र श्रूयमाणवाक्यस्य स्वार्थानुपपत्तिमुखेन अर्थान्तरकल्पनम्। यथा "तरति शोकमात्मवित्" इत्यत्र श्रुतस्य

शोकशब्दवाच्यबन्धजातस्य ज्ञाननिवर्त्यत्वस्यान्यथानुपपत्त्या बन्धस्य मिथ्यात्वं कल्प्यते। यथा वा "जीवी देवदत्तो गृहे न" इति वाक्यश्रवणानन्तरं जीविनो गृहासत्त्वं बहिःसत्त्वं कल्पयति।

That presumption[1] is of two kinds—presumption from what is seen and presumption from what is heard. Of these, presumption from what is seen is as follows: If silver has been (wrongly) apprehended in something[2] in front as, "This is silver," and (later) it is denied[3] in that very things as, "This is not silver," this denial would be unreasonable if the silver were real. So one assumes that the silver is false, that is, other than real, or possessed of the absolute non-existence of reality. Presumption from what is heard occurs where, on account of the incongruity of the direct meaning of a sentence that is being heard, one assumes a different meaning for it. As, in the sentence, "The knower of the Self transcends grief" (*Chā.* VII. i. 3), since the manifold bonds signified by the word 'grief'—which actually occurs in the Śruti—cannot otherwise[4] be reasonably destroyed by realisation, they are assumed to be false. Or[5] as, after one has heard the sentence, "Devadatta is living, but not at home," the absence from home of a person who is alive makes one assume that he is outside.

[[1] According to the first interpretation of the word; that is, the resulting knowledge, not the instrument.

[2] Other than silver.

[3] As a result of closer inspection.

[4] Unless they are unreal from the absolute standpoint.

[5] This is a familiar example of the Mīmāṁsakas.]

Twofold Presumption from What is Heard

श्रुतार्थापत्तिश्च द्विविधा—अभिधानानुपपत्तिः अभिहितानुपपत्तिश्च। तत्र यत्र वाक्यैकदेशश्रवणेऽन्वयाभिधानानुपपत्त्या अन्वयाभिधानोपयोगि पदान्तरं कल्प्यते तत्राभिधानानुपपत्तिः। यथा 'द्वारम्' इत्यत्र 'पिधेहि' इति पदाध्याहारः, यथा वा "विश्वजिता यजेत" इत्यत्र 'स्वर्गकाम'-पदाध्याहारः।

Presumption from what is heard, again, is of two kinds—(that due to) failure of expression (intention) (*abhidhānānupapatti*) and (that due to) incongruity of meaning (*abhihitānupapatti*). Of these, the former occurs where, on hearing part of a sentence, there is failure of the expression of (i.e. intention regarding) the logical connection (*anvayābhidhāna*), and for that reason some additional word helpful to the latter is assumed. As, after the word *dvāram* (door), the word *pidhehi* (shut) is supplied; or[1] as with the words, "should perform the *Viśvajit* sacrifice," the words, "One who desires heaven," are supplied.[2]

[[1] This is a Vedic example, as the other is a conventional one.

[2] The sentence, to be complete, requires a subject, and a man who is possessed of desires can be the required agent. Now it is an accepted principle with the Mīmāṁsakas that where no result is specifically mentioned for an action enjoined by the Śrutis, heaven is assumed to be that result. See *Pū Mī. Sū.* IV. iii. 15.]

ननु 'द्वारम्' इत्यादावन्वयाभिधानात् पूर्वम्, इदमन्वयाभिधानं पिधानापस्थापकपदं विनाऽनुपपन्नमिति कथं ज्ञानमिति चेत्, न, 'अभिधान'-पदेन करणव्युत्पत्या तात्पर्यस्य विवक्षितत्वात्। तथा च द्वारकर्मकपिधानक्रियासंसर्गपरत्वं पिधानोपस्थापकपदं विनाऽनुपपन्नमिति ज्ञानं तत्रापि सम्भाव्यते।

Objection: In the case of a word like *dvāram*, before the expression (*abhidhāna*) of the logical connection, how can one know that this expression fails without a word meaning shutting?

Reply: Not so; for the word *abhidhāna* (lit., expression), by a derivation signifying instrumentality,[1] means 'intention.'[2] Thus even in this case the knowledge is possible that the sentence cannot convey a relation[3] (of the word *dvāram*) to the act of shutting, having for its object the door, without some word signifying shutting.

[[1] Signifying that *by means of* which the meaning of the sentence is expressed, and not the *act* of expressing.

[2] Of the sentence, a part of which, viz., the word *dvāram*, has been heard.

[3] Which is the 'intention' of the sentence.]

अभिहितानुपपत्तिस्तु यत्र वाक्यावगतोऽर्थोऽनुपपन्नत्वेन ज्ञातः सन्नर्थान्तरं कल्पयति तत्र द्रष्टव्या। तथा "स्वर्गकामो ज्योतिष्टोमेन यजेत" इत्यत्र स्वर्गसाधनत्वस्य क्षणिकयागगततयाऽवगतस्यानुपपत्त्या मध्यवर्त्यपूर्वं कल्प्यते।

(Presumption from what is heard due to) incongruity of meaning, however, is to be looked for where the meaning understood from a sentence is found to be incongruous and leads to the assumption of some other thing. As, in the sentence, "One who desires heaven should perform the Jyotiṣṭoma sacrifice," since the property of leading to heaven, which is cognised as abiding in the transitory sacrifice, is incongruous,[1] an intermediate thing,[2] viz., the unseen result (*apūrva*),[3] is assumed.

[[1] Because the effect, viz., heaven, will be attained at some remote future time, while the sacrifice is short-lived.

[2] Serving as the operation or intermediate cause (*vyāpāra*). See note 1 on p. 70.

[3] Postulated by the Mīmāṁsakas to explain the above incongruity. It lasts till the fruition of the ultimate result, viz., heaven or hell.]

न चेयमर्थापत्तिरनुमानेऽन्तर्भवितुमर्हति, अन्वयव्यप्तिज्ञानेनान्वयिन्यनन्तर्भावात्। व्यतिरेकिणश्चानुमानत्वं प्रागेव निरस्तम्। अत एवार्थापत्तिस्थले 'अनुमिनोमि' इति नानुव्यवसायः, किन्तु "अनेन इदं कल्पयामि" इति।

This presumption cannot be included in inference.[1] For since affirmative invariable concomitance[2] cannot be apprehended here, it cannot be classed under affirmative inference[3]; and we have already[4] refuted the contention that inference through negative invariable concomitance is also an inference. Hence in cases of presumption the appreception[5] is not, "I am inferring it," but, "I am assuming it from this."

[[1] As the logicians hold.
[2] Between the reason and the thing to be inferred, that is, between living and existence outside home, in the instance cited (p. 119). Living proves only existence.
[3] The only kind of inference admitted by Vedānta.
[4] On p. 74.
[5] See note 6 on p. 21.]

ननु अर्थापत्तिस्थले "इदमनेन विनाऽनुपपन्नमिति ज्ञान करणम्" इत्युक्तम्; तत्र किमिदं "तेन विनाऽनुपपन्नत्वम्"? तदभावव्यापकाभावप्रतियोगित्वमिति ब्रूमः।

It may be urged: It has been stated[1] that in cases of presumption[2] the instrument is the knowledge, "This is inexplicable without such and such;" now what is this 'inexplicability without such and such'? We reply: It is the counterpositiveness[3] of a non-existence[4] that includes (necessarily signifies) the non-existence of something else.[5]

[[1] In effect. See p. 117.
[2] See note 1 on p. 119.
[3] See note 2 on p. 62.
[4] Of the thing to be explained, e.g. stoutness.
[5] The explanatory fact, e.g. eating at night, in the case of a man fasting by day. Since stoutness depends on this, where it is wanting, stoutness also is wanting.]

एवमर्थापत्तेर्मानान्तरत्वसिद्धौ व्यतिरेकि नानुमानान्तरम्, "पृथिवीतरेभ्यो भिद्यते" इत्यादौ गन्धवत्त्वमितरभेदं विनाऽनुपपन्नमित्यादिज्ञानस्य करणत्वात्। अत एवानुव्यवसायः "पृथिव्यामितरभेदं कल्पयामि" इति।

इति वेदान्तपरिभाषायामर्थापत्तिपरिच्छेदः।

Thus presumption being proved to be a distinct means of valid knowledge, inference of the negative form is not a variety of inference.[1] For in a sentence like, "Earth is different from other things (for it has smell)," the knowledge that the possession of smell is impossible without difference from other things, is the instrument (of presumption).[2] For this very reason[3] the appreciation is, "I am *assuming*[4] difference from other things in earth."

[[1] It should not be reckoned as a distinct kind of inference, as is done by the logicians, but instances of the kind should be classed under presumption.

[2] So one must not think that owing to the absence of an instrument of presumption, as described on p. 117, this is not a case of presumption, but of inference of the negative form, advocated by the logicians. According to them, this negative form of inference is resorted to only in cases where the thing to be inferred has no similar instance. For instance, in the example cited above, the thing to be inferred is different from other things, and this can exist in earth alone, which, however, is the subject of the inferential knowledge (*pakṣa*), and as such the presence in it of the thing to be inferred is disputed. In negative invariable concomitance, the absence of the reason (e.g. smell) is of wider extension than the absence of the thing to be inferred (e.g. difference from other things), and from the former the latter is inferred. This method of inference is adopted, since otherwise no example is available.

[3] Because the knowledge of incongruity as such is the instrument of presumption.

[4] Not, "I am inferring."]

CHAPTER VI

NON-APPREHENSION

NON-APPREHENSION: MEANING OF ITS CAPACITY

इदानीं षष्ठं प्रमाणं निरूप्यते। ज्ञानकरणाजन्याभावानुभवासाधारणकारणमनुपलब्धिरूपं प्रमाणम्। अनुमानादिजन्यातीन्द्रियाभावानुभवहेतावनुमानादावतिव्याप्तिवारणायाजन्यान्तं पदम्। अदृष्टादौ साधारणकारणेऽतिव्याप्तिवारणायासाधारणेति। अभावस्मृत्यसाधारणहेतुसंस्कारेऽतिव्याप्तिवारणायानुभवेति विशेषणम्। न चातीन्द्रियाभावानुमितिस्थलेऽप्यनुपलब्ध्यैवाभावो गृह्यताम्, विशेषाभावादिति वाच्यम्। धर्माधर्माद्यनुपलब्धिसत्त्वेऽपि तदभावानिश्चयेन योग्यानुपलब्धेरेवाभावग्राहकत्वात्।

Now the sixth means[1] of valid knowledge is being described. The means of valid knowledge known as non-apprehension is the extraordinary cause of that apprehension of non-existence which is not due to knowledge as an instrument.[2] The clause, "Which is not due," etc. is inserted to preclude the definition from unduly extending to an inference or the like which causes that apprehension of the non-existence of imperceptible objects which is due to inference etc.[3] The word 'extraordinary' is used to prevent a too wide extension to such general causes[4] as merit and demerit. And the qualifying term 'apprehension'[5] is for precluding a similar unwarranted extension to latent impressions, which are the extraordinary cause of a recollection of non-existence. It cannot be urged that even in the case of an inferential knowledge about the non-existence of imperceptible objects, the non-existence may as well be grasped through non-apprehension, since there is no difference.[6] For although merit and demerit etc. may not be perceptible, still, there being no certitude of their non-existence, only a non-apprehension that is possessed of capacity (*yogyānupalabdhi*) is (to be regarded as) the instrument of an apprehension of non-existence.

[[1] Viz., non-apprehension.

[2] Inference, comparison, verbal testimony and presumption, dealt with in the four preceding chapters, are all due to knowledge, viz., that of invariable concomitance, similarity, words possessing an intention, and the thing to be explained, respectively. Hence these are excluded from the purview of the definition.

[3] Refers to verbal testimony and presumption.

[4] Other general causes are space, time and God.

[5] Instead of the general term 'knowledge,' which includes recollection.

[6] Between the two cases, both being non-existence.]

ननु केयं योग्यानुपलब्धिः ? किं योग्यस्य प्रतियोगिनोऽनुपलब्धिः ? उत योग्येऽधिकरणे प्रतियोगिनोऽनुपलब्धिः ? नाद्यः, स्तम्भे पिशाचादिभेदस्याप्रत्यक्षत्वापत्तेः ;

नान्त्यः, आत्मनि धर्माद्यभावस्यापि प्रत्यक्षत्वापत्तेरिति चेत्, न, "योग्या चासावनुपलब्धिश्चेति" कर्मधारयाश्रयणात्। अनुपलब्धेर्योग्यता च तर्कितप्रतियोगिसत्त्वप्रसञ्जितप्रतियोगिकत्वम्। यस्याभावो गृह्यते, तस्य यः प्रतियोगी तस्यसत्त्वेनाधिकरणे तर्कितेन प्रसञ्जनयोग्यमापादनयोग्यं प्रतियोग्युपलब्धिस्वरूपं यस्यानुपलम्भस्य तत्त्वं तदनुपलब्धेर्योग्यत्वमित्यर्थः। तथाहि—स्फीतालोकवति भूतले यदि घटः स्यात् तदा घटोपलम्भः स्यादित्यापादनसम्भवात् तादृशभूतले घटाभावोऽनुपलब्धिगम्यः। अन्धकारे तु तादृशापादनासम्भवान्नानुपलब्धिगम्यता। अत एव स्तम्भे तादात्म्येन पिशाचसत्त्वे स्तम्भवत् प्रत्यक्षत्वापत्त्या तदभावोऽनुपलब्धिगम्यः। आत्मनि धर्मादिसत्त्वेऽप्यस्यातीन्द्रियतया निरुक्तोपलम्भापादनासम्भवात् न धर्माद्यभावस्यानुपलब्धिगम्यत्वम्।

Objection: What is the *yogyānupalabdhi*?[1] Is it the non-apprehension of something capable of being perceived that abides in something else? Or is it the non-apprehension of something abiding in a substratum that is capable of being perceived? It cannot be the former, for then the difference[2] a pillar has from a ghoul, for instance, would be imperceptible. Nor can it be the latter, for then even the non-existence of merit etc. in the self would be perceptible.[3]

Reply: Not so, for the compound used in the word is *Karmadhāraya,* meaning 'a non-apprehension that is possessed of capacity.' And the capacity of non-apprehension is the fact of being that whose counterpositive is assumed from the hypothetical existence of (the object of) that counterpositive. That is to say, the capacity of non-apprehension is the fact of its being a non-apprehension whose counterpositive, viz., apprehension, may be assumed[4] from the existence, assumed[5] in the substratum,[6] of the counterpositive[7] of that non-existence[8] of a thing which is apprehended.[9] For instance, if there be a jar on a well-lighted floor, then there would be an apprehension of the jar—on account of the possibility of this supposition, the non-existence of the jar on such a floor is to be known through non-apprehension. But such a supposition being impossible in darkness, the absence of the jar in that case cannot be known through non-apprehension. Again, if there be a ghoul in a pillar by a relation of identity, it would be perceptible like the pillar; hence[10] its absence[11] is to be known through non-apprehension. But although merit etc. exist in the self, since these are imperceptible,[12] there is no possibility of the above-mentioned supposition regarding aprehension, and hence the absence of merit etc. cannot be known through non-apprehension.[13]

[[1] The word can be expounded in three ways, as meaning: a non-apprehension *that* is possessed of capacity; a non-apprehension *of* something that is capable of being perceived; and a non-apprehension in something that is jerceptible. In the first, the compound is *Karmadhāraya* (cf. blackbird); in the second it is *Ṣaṣṭhi-tatpuruṣa* (cf. riverside); and in the third, it is *Saptami-tatpuruṣa* (cf. homespun). The second and third alternatives are being rejected one by one in favour of the first.

[2] A difference of the form, "The pillar is not a ghoul." This difference is perceptible. But if the first interpretation be taken, then the ghoul being by nature imperceptible, non-apprehension would have no capacity here to distinguish the pillar from the ghoul; but as a matter of fact, it does. This is the difficulty.

[3] According to the logicians, merit and demerit are imperceptible, but the self, in which they abide, is perceptible to the mind. Hence, according to the second interpretation, merit etc. would be known to be absent through non-apprehension; but they are not. This is the anomaly.

[4] In the form, "The jar would be perceived (were it here)."

[5] In the form, "If the jar were here."

[6] Of the non-existence mentioned in the last clause of this sentence; e.g. a floor.

[7] E.g. a jar.

[8] E.g. non-existence of a jar.

[9] Through non-apprehension.

[10] Since non-apprehension that is possessed of capacity is the means of valid knowledge regarding non-existence.

[11] That is, a difference of the form, "The pillar is not a ghoul."

[12] If there be merit etc. in the self, they would be perceptible.

[13] Because there is not possessed of capacity.]

Non-apprehension Cannot Be Replaced By Perception

ननूक्तरीत्याऽधिकरणेन्द्रियसन्निकर्षस्थले अभावस्यानुपलब्धिगम्यत्वं त्वदनुमतम्; तत्र क्लृप्तेन्द्रियमेवाभावाकारवृत्तावपि करणम्, इन्द्रियान्वयव्यतिरेकानुविधानादिति चेत्, न। तत्प्रतियोग्यनुपलब्धेरप्यभावग्रहे हेतुत्वेन क्लृप्तत्वेन करणत्वमात्रस्य कल्पनात्; इन्द्रियस्य चाभावेन समं सन्निकर्षाभावेनाभावग्रहाहेतुत्वात्, इन्द्रियान्वयव्यतिरेकयोरधिकरणज्ञानाद्युपक्षीणत्वेनान्यथासिद्धेः।

Objection[1]: In cases where there is a contact[2] between the organ and the substratum of non-existence, you maintain that the non-existence is cognised in the above-mentioned manner[3] through non-apprehension. There, with regard to the mental state[4] in the form of the non-existence also, it is the prescribed[5] organ that should be the instrument, in deference to the association (of the cognition of non-existence) with the organ by the method of agreement and difference.[6]

Reply: Not so, for the non-apprehension of the counterpositive of non-existence being also prescribed as a cause of the apprehension of non-existence, we simply assume that (non-apprehension) to be the instrument.[7] Moreover, since the organ, not being in contact with non-existence,[8] cannot be a cause[9] of the apprehension of non-existence, and since the association with the organ by the method of agreement and difference exhausts[10] itself by generating a knowledge[11] of the substratum of the non-existence and so on,[12] the organ is a superfluity.[13]

[[1] By the logician.

[2] Without which even non-apprehension would be inoperative.

[3] By the argument, "If there were a jar here, it would be perceived."

[4] Which must be assumed in the apprehension of non-existence.

[5] Admitted as the instrument for the perception of objects.

[6] If the eye is in contact with the floor, the non-existence of the jar etc. is apprehended; otherwise not.

[7] According to Nyāya as well as Vedānta the organ and non-apprehension are both causes. What the Vedāntin does is to call the latter an instrument, or an extraordinary cause. That is all.

[8] As maintained by the logician, but with its substratum.

[9] Much less an instrument.

[10] So it cannot in addition lead to an apprehension of non-existence.

[11] Which in its turn causes the apprehension of non-existence.

[12] Refers to the knowledge of positive things that abide in the substratum.

[13] *Anyathā-siddha*—an attendant circumstance not to be confounded with a cause, which must be a necessary invariable antecedent. For example, a potter's father with regard to a jar made by the former. For other instances see the *Bhāṣā-Paricchedа*, verses 19-22.]

ननु "भूतले घटो न" इत्याद्यभावानुभवस्थले भूतलांशे प्रत्यक्षत्वमुभयसिद्धमिति तत्र वृत्तिनिर्गमनस्यावश्यकत्वेन भूतलावच्छिन्नचैतन्यवत् तन्निष्ठघटाभावावच्छिन्नचैतन्यस्यापि प्रमात्रभिन्नतया घटाभावस्य प्रत्यक्षतैव सिद्धान्तेऽपि इति चेत्, सत्यम्, अभावप्रतीतेः प्रत्यक्षत्वेऽपि तत्कारणस्यानुपलब्धेर्मानान्तरत्वात्। नहि फलीभूतज्ञानस्य प्रत्यक्षत्वे तत्करणस्य प्रत्यक्षप्रमाणतानियतत्वमस्ति। "दशमस्त्वमसि" इत्यादिवाक्यजन्यज्ञानस्य प्रत्यक्षत्वेऽपि तत्करणस्य वाक्यस्य प्रत्यक्षप्रमाणभिन्नप्रमाणत्वाभ्युपगमात्।

Objection: In cases of apprehension of non-existence, such as, "There is no jar on the floor," that it is a perception in respect of the floor is accepted by both.[1] Hence, it being necessary that the mental state should reach there,[2] the Consciousness limited by the non-existence of the jar abiding in the floor is, like the Consciousness limited by the floor, not different from the subject,[3] and therefore the non-existence of the jar is but an object of perception[4] even in Vedānta.

Reply: It is true; for although the apprehension of non-existence is perceptual knowledge, its instrument, viz., non-apprehension, is a distinct means of knowledge. There is no fixed rule that if the resulting knowledge be perceptual, its instrument, too, must be the means of knowledge called perception; for although the knowledge generated by a sentence like, "You are the tenth man,"[5] is perceptual, yet its instrument, viz., the sentence, is admitted to be a distinct means[6] of knowledge from that called perception.

[[1] Vedānta and Nyāya.

[2] See p. 15.

[3] Consciousness limited by the mind. See p. 15.

[4] And not of non-apprehension. See p. 16.

[5] See note 1 on p. 19.

[6] Viz., verbal testimony.]

फलवैजात्यं विना कथं प्रमाणभेद इति चेत्, न, वृत्ति-वैजात्यमात्रेण प्रमाणवैजात्योपपत्तेः। तथाच घटाद्यभावाकारवृत्तिर्नेन्द्रियजन्या, इन्द्रियस्य विषयेणासन्निकर्षात्, किन्तु घटाद्यनुपलब्धिरूपमानान्तरजन्येति भवत्यनुपलब्धेर्मानान्तरत्वम्।

Objection: How can there be a different means of knowledge unless the resulting knowledge is of a different class?

Reply: Not so, for simply from the fact of the mental state being of a different class, we understand that the means of knowledge must be different. Thus the mental state in the form of the absence of a jar etc. is not generated by the organ, for the latter is not in contact with the object,[1] but it is generated by a distinct means of knowledge, viz., non-apprehension of the jar etc. Hence non-apprehension is a distinct means of valid knowledge.

[[1] Viz., the absence of a jar etc.]

ननु अनुपलब्धिरूपमानान्तरपक्षेऽभावप्रतीतेः प्रत्यक्षत्वे घटवति घटाभावभ्रमस्यापि प्रत्यक्षत्वापत्तौ तत्राप्यनिर्वचनीय-घटाभावोऽभ्युपगम्येत। न चेष्टापत्तिः, तस्य मायोपादानकत्वेऽभावत्वानुपपत्तेः; मायोपादानकत्वाभावे मायायाः सफलकार्योपादानत्वानुपपत्तिरिति चेत्, न। घटवति घटाभावभ्रमो न तत्कालोत्पन्नघटाभावविषयकः, किन्तु भूतलरूपादौ विद्यमानो लौकिको घटाभावो भूतले आरोप्यते इत्यन्यथाख्यातिरेव, आरोप्यसन्निकर्षस्थले सर्वत्रान्यथाख्यातेरेव व्यवस्थापनात्।

Objection: Admitting that non-apprehension is a distinct means of knowledge, since the apprehension of non-existence is perceptual knowledge, even a mistaken apprehension of the non-existence of a jar in a place containing a jar would be perceptual knowledge, and hence even in such a case one will have to admit an indescribable non-existence of the jar.[1] You cannot say this is a welcome objection, for if that non-existence be a product of the cosmic illusion (*māyā*), it cannot reasonably be a non-existence;[2] and if it be not a product of the cosmic illusion, the latter cannot be held to be the material cause of all effects whatsoever.[3]

Reply: Not so. The mistaken apprehension of the non-existence of a jar in a place containing a jar has not for its object an instantly produced non-existence of the jar, but inasmuch as that normal non-existence of a jar which is already present in the colour etc.[4] of the floor, is superimposed on the floor, it is but a case of mistaking one thing for another;[5] for in a case[6] where there is contact of the thing superimposed with the organ, it is this mistaking of one thing for another[7] that is always held to be the fact.

[[1] As in the case of a rope mistaken for a snake.

[2] Because the cosmic illusion as a positive entity can produce only positive entities.

[3] Which is a postulate of Vedānta.

[4] E.g. touch. A jar never exists in qualities etc.

[5] *Anyathā-khyāti,* advocated by the logicians.

[6] See p. 64.

[7] And not a knowledge of something that is indescribable, that is, neither same as nor different from the actual entity (*anirvacanīya-khayātī*).]

अस्तु वा प्रतियोगिमति तद्भावभ्रमस्थले तद्भावस्यानिर्वचनीयत्वम्, तथापि तदुपादानं मायैव। नह्युपादानोपादेययोरत्यन्तसाजात्यम्, तन्तुपटयोरपि तन्तुत्वपटत्वादिना वैजात्यात्, यत्किञ्चित्साजात्यस्य मायया अनिर्वचनीयघटाभावस्य च मिथ्यात्वधर्मस्य विद्यमानत्वात्। अन्यथा व्यावहारिकं घटाभावं प्रति कथं मायोपादानमिति कुतो नाशङ्केथाः? न च विजातीययोरप्युपादानोपादेयभावे ब्रह्मैव जगदुपादानं स्यादिति वाच्यम्, प्रपञ्चविभ्रमाधिष्ठानत्वरूपस्य तस्येष्टत्वात्, परिणामित्वरूपस्योपादानत्वस्य निरवयवे ब्रह्मण्यनुपपत्तेः। तथाच प्रपञ्चस्य परिणाम्युपादानं माया, न ब्रह्म, इति सिद्धान्त इत्यलमतिप्रसङ्गेन।

Or, in cases where there is a mistaken apprehension of the non-existence of a thing in a substratum containing it, we may concede that the non-existence in question is indescribable; still its material cause is but the cosmic illusion. It is not that the material cause and the effect must be altogether similar, for even threads and a cloth are heterogeneous in respect of their attributes such as threadhood and clothhood; and there is some homogeneity between the cosmic illusion and the indescribable non-existence of a jar, viz., in respect of the attribute of falsity. Otherwise,[1] why don't you raise the objection how the cosmic illusion can be the material cause of the conventional non-existence[2] of a jar? Nor can you urge that even if two heterogeneous things may stand to each other in the relation of material cause and effect, it is Brahman[3] that should be the material cause of the universe. For Brahman is accepted as that, as being the substratum of the phantasm of the universe; but being devoid of parts, It cannot be the transformative material cause of the universe. So the conclusion of Vedānta is that the transformative material cause of the universe is the cosmic illusion, not Brahman. There is no need to dilate on the point.

[[1] That is, if the cosmic illusion be not the material cause of this non-existence.

[2] As opposed to illusory non-existence. That is, where the jar is actually non-existent.

[3] And not the cosmic illusion.]

FOUR KINDS OF NON-EXISTENCE

स चाभावश्चतुर्विधः—प्रागभावः प्रध्वंसाभावोऽत्यन्ताभावोऽन्योन्याभावश्चेति। तत्र मृत्पिण्डादौ कारणे कार्यस्य घटादेरुत्पत्तेः पूर्वं योऽभावः स प्रागभावः। स च भविष्यतीति प्रतीतिविषयः। तत्रैव घटस्य मुद्गरपातानन्तरं योऽभावः स प्रध्वंसाभावः। ध्वंसस्यापि स्वाधिकरणकपालनाशे नाश एव। न च घटोन्मज्जनापत्तिः, घटध्वंसध्वंसस्यापि घटप्रतियोगिकध्वंसत्वात्; अन्यथा प्रागभावध्वंसात्मकघटस्य विनाशे प्रागभावोन्मज्जनापत्तिः। न चैवमपि यत्र ध्वंसाधिकरणं नित्यं तत्र कथं ध्वंसनाश इति वाच्यम्। तादृशमधिकरणं यदि चैतन्यव्यतिरिक्तं तदा तस्य नित्यत्वमसिद्धम्, ब्रह्मव्यतिरिक्तस्य सर्वस्य ब्रह्मज्ञाननिवर्त्यताया वक्ष्यमाणत्वात्। यदि च ध्वंसाधिकरणं चैतन्यं तदाऽसिद्धिः, आरोपितप्रतियोगिकध्वंसस्याधिष्ठाने प्रतीयमानस्याधिष्ठानमात्रत्वात्। तदुक्तम्—"अधिष्ठानावशेषो हि नाशः कल्पितवस्तुनः" इति एवं शुक्तिरूप्यविनाशोऽपीदमवच्छिन्नचैतन्यमेव।

That non-existence is of four kinds—previous non-existence, non-existence as destruction, absolute non-existence and mutual non-existence. Of these, previous non-existence is the absence of an effect such as a jar in its cause, a lump of clay, for example, before the effect has originated.

It is the object of a cognition that the thing will come into being. Non-existence as destruction is the absence of a jar in that very thing,[1] after the jar has been dealt a blow with a club. (This non-existence as) destruction is also certainly destroyed[2] when its substratum, the pieces of a jar, is destroyed. It cannot be urged that this would lead to a reappearance of the jar, for even the destruction of destruction of a jar is a destruction of which the counterpositive is the jar.[3] Otherwise, when a jar, which represents the destruction of its previous non-existence, ceases to be, the previous non-existence would reappear.[4] It cannot be questioned how there can be a cessation of destruction where the substratum of the destruction is eternal.[5] For if such substratum be apart from Consciousness, then its eternity is untenable, because it will be stated later on[6] that everything but Brahman terminates with the realisation of Brahman. And if the substratum of the destruction be Consciousness, this[7] is also untenable, for a destruction the counterpositive of which is fancied, and which merely appears in its substratum, is nothing but that substratum. So it has been said: "The destruction of an imaginary thing is but its being reduced to its substratum." Similarly, the destruction of silver appearing in a nacre is nothing but Consciousness limited by 'this.'[8]

[[1] Viz., the material cause, such as a lump of clay.

[2] This is contrary to the view of the logicians, according to whom it has a beginning, but no end.

[3] And not the preceding destruction alone. That is to say, when a jar is first broken into pieces, it is destroyed, and when these pieces are further broken, the previous destruction ends. But this end of destruction does not mean that the jar re-emerges, on the analogy of two negatives making an affirmative. For we still cognise that the jar has been destroyed.

[4] Which the logicians do not admit.

[5] As, for instance, in the case of an atom, which is the substratum of the destruction of a dyad.

[6] In Chapter VIII.

[7] Your objection that destruction is indestructible.

[8] Something shining connected with the eye, subsequently identified as a nacre. See p. 48.]

यत्राधिकरणे यस्य कालत्रयेऽप्यभावः सोऽत्यन्ताभावः ; यथा वायौरूपात्यन्ताभावः। सोऽपि वियदादिवत् ध्वंसप्रतियोग्येव। "इदमिदं न" इति प्रतीतिविषयोऽन्योन्याभावः। अयमेव विभागो भेदः पृथक्त्वश्चेति व्यवह्रियते, भेदातिरिक्तपृथक्त्वादौ प्रमाणाभावात्। अयं चान्योन्याभावोऽधिकरणस्य सादित्वे सादिः, यथा घटे पटभेदः ; अधिकरणस्यानादित्वेऽनादिरेव, यथा जीवे ब्रह्मभेदः, ब्रह्मणि वा जीवभेदः। द्विविधोऽपि भेदो ध्वंसप्रतियोग्येव, अविद्यानिवृत्तौ तत्परतन्त्राणां निवृत्त्यवश्यम्भावात्।

That whose non-existence in a particular substratum is for all time—past, present and future—has absolute non-existence (there); as, the absolute non-existence of colour in air. It, too, is indeed the counterpositive of destruction,[1] like the ether etc., Mutual non-existence is what[2] is an object of the cognition, "This is not such and such." It is this difference that is designated as disjunction and separateness etc. are something over and above difference (mutual non-existence). This mutual non-existence is possessed of a beginning when its substratum has a beginning;[3] as, the difference a jar has from a cloth.[4] But it is indeed without a beginning when its substratum is such; as, the difference of the individual self from Brahman, or the difference of Brahman from the individual self. Both these kinds of difference are indeed the counterpositives of destruction,[5] for when nescience ceases, all that depend on it necessarily cease.

[[1] That is, is subject to destruction—not eternal, as in Nyāya.

[2] Both of which are distinct qualities according to Nyāya.

[3] According to Nyāya, mutual non-existence is eternal.

[4] A difference of the form, "A jar is not a cloth."

[5] That is, are subject to destruction or transitory.]

Mutual Non-existence is Twofold

पुनरपि भेदो द्विविधः—सोपाधिको निरुपाधिकश्चेति। तत्रोपाधिसत्ताव्याप्यसत्ताकत्वं सोपाधिकत्वम्; तच्छून्यत्वं निरुपाधिकत्वम्। तत्राद्यो तथा एकस्यैवाकाशस्य घटाद्युपाधिभेदेन भेदः; यथा वा एकस्य सूर्यस्य जलभाजनभेदेन

भेदः। तथाच एकस्यैव ब्रह्मणोऽन्तःकरणभेदाद्भेदः। निरुपाधिकभेदो यथा घटे पटभेदः।

Difference is again of two kinds—conditioned and unconditioned. Of these, conditioned difference is that the existence of which is the subordinate concomitant (*vyāpya*)[1] of the existence of its limiting adjunct (*upādhi*), and unconditioned difference is that which has not this kind of existence. An example of the first of these is this: One and the same ether is differentiated by different limiting adjuncts such as a jar.[2] Or as the one sun is manifold according to different water vessels.[3] Thus one and the same Brahman appears as different owing to different minds.[4] Unconditioned difference is—as is the difference a jar has from a cloth.[5]

[1 See note 1 on p. 68.

2 Here the existence of the ether enclosed by the jar is the subordinate concomitant of the existence of the jar; that is, it is never present where the latter is not.

3 In which the sun is reflected. The two examples point respectively to what is known as the doctrine of (apparent) limitation (*avacchinna-vāda*) and the doctrine of reflection (*pratibima-vāda*), with regard to the relation between the individual self and the Supreme Self or Brahman.

4 Serving either as (apparent) limiting adjuncts or as reflecting media.

5 See note 4 on p. 140.]

न च ब्रह्मण्यपि प्रपञ्चभेदाभ्युपगमेऽद्वैतविरोधः, तात्त्विकभेदानभ्युपगमेन वियदादिवदद्वैताव्याघातकत्वात्; प्रपञ्चस्याद्वैते ब्रह्मणि कल्पितत्वाङ्गीकारात्। तदुक्तं सुरेश्वराचार्यैः—

"अच्नमा भवतः केयं साधकत्वप्रकल्पने ।
किं न पश्यसि संसारं तत्रैवाज्ञानकल्पितम् ॥"

इति । अत एव विवरणेऽविद्यानुमाने प्रागभावव्यतिरिक्तत्व-विशेषणम् , तत्त्वप्रदीपिकायामविद्यालक्षणे भावत्व-विशेषणं च सङ्गच्छते ।

It cannot be urged that if a difference in the form of the universe be ammitted even in Brahman, it will contradict Monism. For since real difference is not admitted, the universe does not, like the ether[1] etc., serve as an impediment to Monism; because it is admitted to be superimposed on Brahman, the One without a second. So it has been said by Sureśvarācārya: "Why this intolerance of yours about Brahman being assumed to be an aspirant? Don't you see that the (whole) universe has been superimposed on Brahman Itself through ignorance?" (*Bṛ. Vā.* I. iv. 1279). Hence[2] the qualifying epithet, 'Other than previous non-existence,' in the inference[3] regarding nescience in the *Vivaraṇa*,[4] as also the qualifying clause, 'Which is a positive entity,' in the definition[5] of nescience in the *Tattva-pradīpikā*[6] is appropriate.

[[1] The distinction between the all-pervading ether and that enclosed by a jar is only apparent, there being only one indivisible ether. So with Brahman.

[2] Because Vedānta admits nescience to be the positive entity that projects the universe. Or, because Vedānta admits fourfold negation.

[3] The reference is to the following passage, "One may also infer: Valid cognition, which is in dispute, must be produced by something *other than its previous non-existence* (viz., nescience), which covers the objects (e.g. a jar) of that cognition and is removed by it, and which co-exists with that cognition; for it reveals undiscovered objects; as is the case with the first beam of a lamp in darkness" (V. S. S., p. 13, 11. 4-7).

[4] See note 3 on p. 1.

[5] The definition is like this: "Nescience is that which is a positive entity without a beginning and is terminated by knowledge" (N. S. Ed., p. 57).

[6] Under verse 9 of Chapter I. See note 8 on p. 37.]

एवं चतुर्विधानामभावानां योग्यानुपलब्ध्या प्रतीतिः; तत्रानुपलब्धिर्मानान्तरम् ।

The cognition of the above four kinds of non-existence is through non-apprehension that is possessed of capacity. Hence non-apprehension is a separate means of knowledge.

THE VALIDITY OF KNOWLEDGE IS INTRINSIC AND SELF-EVIDENT

एवमुक्तानां प्रमाणानां प्रामाण्यं स्वत एवोत्पद्यते ज्ञायते च। तथाहि स्मृत्यनुभवसाधारणं संवादिप्रवृत्त्यनुकूलं तद्वति तत्प्रकारकज्ञानत्वं प्रामाण्यम्। तच्च ज्ञानसामान्य-सामग्रीप्रयोज्यं, न त्वधिकं गुणमपेक्षते, प्रमामात्रेऽनुगतगुणा-भावात्। नापि प्रत्यक्षप्रमायां भूयोऽवयवेन्द्रियसन्निकर्षः, रूपादिप्रत्यक्षे आत्मप्रत्यक्षे च तदभावात्, सत्यपि तस्मिन्

"पीतः शङ्खः" इति प्रत्यक्षस्य भ्रमत्वाच्च। अत एव न सल्लिङ्गपरामर्शादिकमप्यनुमित्यादिप्रमायां गुणः, असल्लिङ्ग-परामर्शादिस्थलेऽपि विषयाबाधेनानुमित्यादेः प्रमात्वात्। न चैवमप्रमापि प्रमा स्यात्, ज्ञानसामान्यसामग्र्या अविशेषादिति वाच्यम्। दोषाभावस्यापि हेतुत्वाङ्गीकारात्। न चैवं परतस्त्वम्, आगन्तुकभावकारणापेक्षायामेव परतस्त्वात्।

The validity of knowledge generated by the above-mentioned means of knowledge originates by itself and is self-evident.[1] To explain: Valid knowledge is that knowledge regarding something[2] possessing a particular attribute,[3] which has that attribute as its feature (*prakāra*),[4] which is conducive to successful effort,[5] and which includes recollection as well as fresh experience.[6] That validity is due to the totality[7] of causes producing knowledge in general, and does not depend on extra merit,[8] for there is no merit that abides in all valid knowledge. Nor is the contact of an organ with a large number of parts (of the object) a merit of valid perception, for it is absent in the perception of colour etc.[9] as also of the self,[10] and in spite of the contact, the perception, "The conch is yellow," is an error. Hence a valid consideration[11] of the sign, or the like,[12] is also not a merit of other forms of valid knowledge such as inferential knowledge, for even when there is a fallacious consideration of the sign and so forth, inferential knowledge etc. are valid if their objects are uncontradicted.[13] It cannot be urged that in that case[14] even invalid knowledge would be valid knowledge, since the totality of causes of knowledge in general is the same; for the absence of defects is also admitted to be a cause. Nor does valid knowledge become thereby dependent on other things, for dependence comes only when adventitious *postive* entities act as causes.

[[1] Both the points are denied by logicians.

[2] E.g. a floor containing a jar, or silver possessed of silverhood.

[3] Viz., the jar, or silverhood.

[4] In the phrase 'a floor containing a jar,' the jar is the qualifying attribute (*viśeṣaṇa*). Similarly in the word 'silver,' silverhood is that attribute. The qualifying attribute of a thing that is known is the feature (*prakāra*) in the knowledge of the thing. Hence the gist of this portion of the definition is: Valid knowledge is knowing a thing as it is, and not as something else, which would be error. For instance, the sentence, "The lake has fire," does not give us valid knowledge, for a lake contains water, and not fire.

[5] One that can be fulfilled. When we see a real piece of silver, our effort to take it can materialise. Not so, however, when we mistake a nacre as silver. This latter leads to unsuccessful effort. See p. 46.

[6] On p. 5 two definitions of valid knowledge were given, in the second one of which recollection was included. The present definition is relating to that. According to Nyāya, recollection is not valid knowledge.

[7] Viz., the conjunction of the self and mind, sense-contact with objects etc.

[8] As the logicians say. Particulars of these merits or favourable conditions are enumerated in the *Bhāṣā-Paricceheda*, verses 132-134.

[9] Refers to taste, smell, etc., which also have no parts.

[10] Which has no parts.

[11] See p. 69, bottom. For the consideration to be valid, the sign also must be true.

[12] Refers to consistency etc.

[13] That is, accidentally happen to be true.

[14] If validity is held to depend on the totality of causes of valid knowledge in general.]

ज्ञायते च प्रामाण्यं स्वतः। स्वतो ग्राह्यत्वञ्च दोषाभावे सति यावत्स्वाश्रयग्राहकसामग्रीग्राह्यत्वम्। स्वाश्रयो वृत्ति-ज्ञानम्, तद्ग्राहकं साक्षिज्ञानम्। तेनापि वृत्तिज्ञाने गृह्यमाणे तद्गतं प्रामाण्यमपि गृह्यते। न चैवं प्रामाण्यसंशयानुप-पत्तिः, तत्र संशयानुरोधेन दोषस्यापि सत्त्वेन दोषाभाव-घटितस्वाश्रयग्राहकाभावेन तत्र प्रामाण्यस्यैवाग्रहात्। यद्वा यावत्स्वाश्रयग्राहकग्राह्यत्वयोग्यत्वं स्वतस्त्वम्। संशय-स्थले प्रामाण्यस्योक्तयोग्यतासत्त्वेऽपि दोषवशेनाग्रहात् न संशयानुपपत्तिः।

The validity of knowledge is also spontaneously apprehended.[1] Spontaneous apprehension is the fact of being grasped by the totality[2] of causes that apprehend the substratum[3] of the validity, provided no defect is present. The substratum of the validity is the Consciousness manifested as the mental state,[4] and the cause of its cognition is the Consciousness designated as the witness.[5] That too, when it apprehends the Consciousness manifested as the mental state, apprehends the validity of the latter as well. It cannot be urged that in that case[6] there cannot be any room for doubt about the validity of knowledge. For in order that doubt may arise, there must be some defect also in such a case, and therefore, owing to an absence of the totality of causes of apprehending the substratum[7] of the validity, which (totality) is bound up with an absence of defects, there would be no apprehension at all of the validity of the knowledge. Or spontaneity (self-evidence)[8] is the capacity of being cognised by all that apprehends the substratum of the validity. In a case of doubt, although the validity may possess that capacity, yet it is not apprehended on account of some defect. Hence there is a reasonable chance for doubt.

[[1] That is, is self-evident. Not, as in Nyāya, to be established by inference.

[2] That is, all the causes involved in the act of cognition by the witness.

[3] The knowledge, 'This is a jar.'

[4] A modification of the mind in the form of the object. See p. 15.

[5] Consciousness having the mind as its limiting adjunct. See p. 38. The witness, however, is only one of the causes. See note 2 above.

[6] If the validity of knowledge be self-evident.

[7] See note 3.

[8] Of the validity of knowledge.]

अप्रामाण्यन्तु न ज्ञानसामान्यसामग्रीप्रयोज्यम्, प्रमाया-मप्यप्रामाण्यापत्तेः; किन्तु दोषप्रयोज्यम्। नाप्यप्रामाण्यं यावत्स्वाश्रयग्राहकग्राह्यम्, अप्रामाण्यघटकतदभाववत्त्वादे-र्वृत्तिज्ञानानुपनीतत्वेन साक्षिणा ग्रहीतुमशक्यत्वात्। किन्तु विसंवादिप्रवृत्त्यादिलिङ्गकानुमित्यादिविषय इति परत एवा-प्रामाण्यमुत्पद्यते ज्ञायते च।

इति वेदान्तपरिभाषायामनुपलब्धिपरिच्छेदः।

The invalidity of knowledge, however, is not due to the totality of causes of knowledge in general, for in that case even valid knowledge would be invalid;[1] but it is due to some (adventitious) defect. Nor is the invalidity apprehended by all[2] that apprehends its substratum. For since the circumstances leading to the invalidity, for example, the fact of (the object known) having the *absence* of the qualifying attribute,[3] are not presented[4] by the cognition in the form of the mental state, the witness cannot apprehend them; but it is the object of an inferential knowledge,[5] for instance,[6] that has for its sign unsucessful effort etc.[7]. Thus the invalidity of knowledge arises and is apprehended through some extraneous agency alone.

[[1] Being produced by the same cause.

[2] Same as the totality of causes.

[3] Presented in the erroneous knowledge of the thing.

[4] When a nacre is mistaken for silver, there is no mental state in the form of the nacre or the absence of silver.

[5] For example, "This knowledge of silver is invalid, for it leads to unsuccessful effort."

[6] Refers to verbal comprehension etc.—for example, if somebody says, "This is not silver, but a nacre."

[7] Refers to sleep etc.]

CHAPTER VII

THE SUBJECT-MATTER OF VEDĀNTA

Twofold Validity of the Means of Knowledge

एवं निरूपितानां प्रमाणानां प्रामाण्यं द्विविधम्—व्यावहारिकतत्त्वावेदकत्वं पारमार्थिकतत्त्वावेदकत्वञ्चेति। तत्र ब्रह्मस्वरूपावगाहिप्रमाणव्यतिरिक्तानां सर्वप्रमाणानामाद्यं प्रामाण्यम्, तद्विषयाणां व्यवहारदशायां बाधाभावात्। द्वितीयन्तु जीवब्रह्मैक्यपराणां "सदेव सोम्येदमग्र आसीत्" इत्यादिनां "तत्त्वमसि" इत्यन्तानाम्, तद्विषयस्य जीवपरैक्यस्य कालत्रयांबाध्यत्वात्। तच्चैक्यं 'तत्त्वं'-पदार्थज्ञानाधीनज्ञानमिति प्रथमं 'तत्'-पदार्थो लक्षणप्रमाणाभ्यां निरूप्यते।

The validity of the means of knowledge that have been described in the above manner is of two kinds—as setting forth conventional reality and as setting forth absolute reality. Of these, the validity of all means of knowledge except that[1] which apprehends the true nature of Brahman is of the first variety, since their objects are free from contradiction during the phenomenal state of existence.[2] The second kind of validity belongs to Vedāntic texts that set forth the identity of the individual self with Brahman, for instance, those beginning with, "This universe, my dear, was but Existence in the beginning" (*Chā.* VI. ii. 1), and ending with, "Thou art

That" (*Ibid.* VI. viii. 7—xvi. 3); for the thing they teach viz., the identity of the individual self with the Supreme Self, is uncontradictable for all time—past, present and future. And since the realisation of that identity depends on a knowledge of the meanings of the words 'That' and 'thou,' the meaning of the word 'That' is being first ascertained with the help of characteristics and the means of knowledge.

[[1] That is, verbal (scriptural) testimony.

[2] That is, prior to the realisation of one's identity with Brahman.]

Essential and Secondary Characteristics of Brahman

तत्र लक्षणं द्विविधम्—स्वरूपलक्षणं तटस्थलक्षणञ्चेति। तत्र स्वरूपमेव लक्षणं स्वरूपलक्षणम्। यथा सत्यादिकं ब्रह्मस्वरूपलक्षणम्, "सत्यं ज्ञानामनन्तं ब्रह्म," "आनन्दो ब्रह्मेति व्यजानात्" इत्यादिश्रुतेः। ननु स्वस्य स्ववृत्तित्वाभावे कथं लक्षणत्वमिति चेत्, न, स्वस्यैव स्वापेक्षया धर्मिधर्मभावकल्पनया लक्ष्यलक्षणत्वसम्भवात्। तदुक्तम्—"आनन्दो विषयानुभवो नित्यत्वञ्चेति सन्ति धर्माः, अपृथक्त्वेऽपि चैतन्यात् पृथगिवावभासन्ते" इति।

Now characteristics are of two kinds—essential and secondary. Of these, essential characteristics (*svarūpa-lakṣaṇa*) consist in the very nature (*svarūupa*) of a thing. As, Truth etc. are essential characteristics of Brahman, for this is borne out of such Śruti texts as, "Brahman is Truth, Knowledge and Infinitude" (*Tai.* II. 1) and "He knew that Bliss was Brahman" (*Ibid.* III. 6).

Objection: Since a thing cannot abide in itself, how can it be a characteristic (of itself)?

Reply: Not so, for since the same thing can be conceived of as both a possessor of attributes and an attribute with regard to itself, it can be a thing having a characteristic as also a characteristic.[1] So it has been stated, "Bliss, the experience of objects and eternity are the attributes. Although these are not separate from Consciousness (Brahman), they appear to be so" (*Pañcapādikā*, p. 4, 1. 3).

[[1] That is to say, Truth, Knowledge, etc. *are* Brahman, but they are *assumed* to be Its attributes. Hence these can be regarded as both.]

तटस्थलक्षणं नाम यावल्लक्ष्यकालमनवस्थितत्वे सति यद्व्यावर्तकं तदेव। यथा गन्धवत्त्वं पृथिवीलक्षणम्, महाप्रलये परमाणुषु, उत्पत्तिकाले घटादिषु च गन्धाभावात्। प्रकृते च जगज्जन्मादिकारणत्वम्। अत्र 'जगत्'-पदेन कार्यजातं विवक्षितम्। कारणत्वञ्च कर्तृत्वम्, अतोऽविद्यादौ नातिव्याप्तिः। कर्तृत्वञ्च तत्तदुपादानगोचरापरोक्षज्ञान-चिकिर्षाकृतिमत्त्वम्। ईश्वरस्य तावदुपादानगोचरापरोक्ष-ज्ञानसद्भावे—

"यः सर्वज्ञः सर्ववित्, यस्य ज्ञानमयं तपः।
तस्मादेतद्ब्रह्म नाम रूपमन्नञ्च जायते॥"

इत्यादिश्रुतिर्मानम्; तादृशचिकीर्षासद्भावे च "सोऽकामयत बहु स्यां प्रजायेय" इत्यादिश्रुतिर्मानम्; तादृशकृतौ च "तन्मनोऽकुरुत" इत्यादिवाक्यम्।

A secondary characteristic is that which, though not lasting as long as the thing possessing it, yet differentiates it from other things. As, the possession of smell is a (secondary) characteristic of earth, for there is no smell in atoms (of earth) at the dissolution of the universe, nor in jars etc. at the time of their origin. With regard to the subject under discussion (Brahman), Its being the cause of the birth etc.[1] of the universe is such a characteristic. Here the word 'universe' means the sum total of effects. And casuality is agency. Hence the characteristic does not unwarrantedly extend to nescience etc.[2] Agency is the possession of immediate knowledge, the desire to do and volition regarding particular material causes.[3] About God's possessing immediate knowledge of all material causes, Śruti texts like the following are evidence: "From Him who knows all things generally and particularly, and whose meditation is a (natural) result of His knowledge, are produced this Hiranyagarbha,[4] and names, colours and foods" (*Mu.* I. i. 9). About His possessing the above kind of desire to do, Śruti texts like, "It desired:

Let Me multiply, let Me effectively born" (*Tai.* II. 6), are evidence. And about that kind of volition of His, passages like, "He produced the mind"[5] (*Bṛ.* I. ll. 1), (are proofs).

[[1] Refers to maintenance and dissolution.

[2] Refers to Nature and atoms, for example, which, being insentient, are not agents.

[3] Of things to be done.

[4] The 'effect-Brahman,' that is, Brahman as the sum total of the manifested universe in its subtle form.

[5] That is, concerning all material causes of things to be done.]

ज्ञानेच्छाद्यन्यतमगर्भं लक्षणत्रितयं विवक्षितम्, अन्यथा व्यर्थविशेषणापत्तेः। अत एव जन्मस्थितिध्वंसानामन्यतमस्यैव लक्षणे प्रवेशः। एवञ्च लक्षणानि नव सम्पद्यन्ते। ब्रह्मणो जगज्जन्मादिकारणत्वे च "यतो वा इमानि भूतानि जायन्ते, येन जातानि जीवन्ति, यत् प्रयन्त्यभिसंविशन्ति" इत्यादिश्रुतिर्मानम्।

Here three characteristics, each embodying only one of the items—knowledge, desire, etc.,[1] are meant; for otherwise it would involve the fallacy of 'redundant qualifying attributes.'[2] For the same reason only one of the items—origin, maintenance and dissolution, should at a time enter into the characteristic. Thus we get altogether nine[3] characteristics (of Brahman). As regards Brahman's being the cause of the origin etc. of the universe, Śruti texts like the following are proofs: "From which these beings[4] are born, through which they live after birth and to which they (finally) return and become merged" (*Tai.* III. i).

[[1] Refers to volition.

[2] As in the sentence, "The hill has fire, because it has *blue* smoke." Here the word 'blue' is redundant, smoke alone being sufficient for inferring the presence of fire.

[3] By combining knowledge, desire and volition severally with cosmic origin, maintenance and dissolution.

[4] From Hiraṇyagarbha down to a clump of grass.]

यद्वा निखिलजगदुपादानत्वं ब्रह्मणो लक्षणम् । उपादानत्वञ्च जगदध्यासाधिष्ठानत्वम्, जगदाकारेण परिणममानमायाधिष्ठानत्वं वा । एतादृशमेवोपादानत्वमभिप्रेत्य "इदं सर्वं यदयमात्मा," "सच्च त्यच्चाभवत्," "बहु स्यां प्रजायेय" इत्यादिश्रुतिषु ब्रह्मप्रपञ्चयोस्तादात्म्यव्यपदेशः । "घटः सन्," "घटो भाति," "घट इष्टः" इत्यादिलौकिकव्यपदेशोऽपि सच्चिदानन्दरूपब्रह्मैक्याध्यासात् ।

Or the characteristic of Brahman is Its being the material cause of the entire universe. By 'material cause' is meant the substratum of the superimposition of the universe, or the substratum of the cosmic illusion (*māyā*) that transforms itself in the shape of the universe. It is in view of such material causality that Brahman and the universe have been described as identical in Śruti texts like the following: "This all is the Self" (*Bṛ.* II. iv. 6), "It became the gross and the subtle" (*Tai.* II. 6), and "Let Me multiply, let Me be effectively born" (*Ibid.* II. 6; *Chā.* VI. ii. 3). Conventional statements like, "The jar exists," "The jar is manifest," and "The jar is desirable," are also on account of the superimposition of its identity with Brahman, the Existence-Knowledge-Bliss Absolute.[1]

[[1] In superimposition there is an exchange of characteristic between the substratum and the thing superimposed.]

नन्वानन्दात्मकचिदध्यासात् घटादेरिष्टत्वव्यवहारे दुःखस्यापि तत्राध्यासात् तस्यापीष्टत्वव्यवहारापत्तिरिति चेत्, न; "आरोपे सति निमित्तानुसरणम्, न तु निमित्तमस्तीत्यारोपः," इत्यभ्युपगमेन दुःखादौ सच्चिदंशाध्यासेऽपि आनन्दांशाध्यासाभावात्। जगति नामरूपांशद्वयव्यवहारस्तु अविद्यापरिणामात्मकनामरूपसम्बन्धात्। तदुक्तम्—

"अस्ति भातिप्रियं रूपं नाम चेत्यंशपञ्चकम्।
आद्यं त्रयं ब्रह्मरूपं जगद्रूपं ततो द्वयम्॥" इति॥

Objection: If a jar etc. are treated as desirable on account of their superimposition on the Consciousness that is Bliss, then, since pain also is superimposed on That, it too would be treated as desirable.

Reply: No; for accepting the principle, "If there is superimposition, its cause may be traced; but it does not follow that just because there is a cause, there must be superimposition," although there may be a superimposition on pain of the Existence and Knowledge aspects (of Brahman), there is no superimposition of the Bliss aspect. The application of the two aspects, viz., name and form, with regard to the universe is due to its relation to name and form, which are the modifications of nescience. So it has been said: "Existence, manifestation, agreeableness, form and name—these are the five aspects (of phenomena). The first three are characteristics of Brahman, and the next two of the universe."[1]

[[1] Śaṅkarācārya's *Vākya-sudhā*, 20. So the relation of Brahman to name and form and that of the universe to existence etc. are but cases of a transference of attributes.]

Cosmogony: its Order

अथ जगतो जन्मक्रमो निरूपते। तत्र सर्गाद्यकाले परमेश्वरः सृज्यमानप्रपञ्चवैचित्र्यहेतुप्राणिकर्मसहकृतोऽपरिमितानिरूपितशक्तिविशेषविशिष्टमायासहितः सन् नामरूपात्मकनिखिलप्रपञ्चं प्रथमं बुद्धावाकलय्य "इदं करिष्यामि" इति सङ्कल्पयति, "तदैक्षत बहु स्यां प्रजायेय," "सोऽकामयत बहु स्यां प्रजायेय" इत्यादिश्रुतेः। तत आकाशादीनि पञ्चभूतान्यपञ्चीकृतानि तन्मात्रपदप्रतिपाद्यान्युत्पद्यन्ते। तत्राकाशस्य शब्दो गुणः, वायोस्तु शब्दस्पर्शौ, तेजसस्तु शब्दस्पर्शरूपाणि, अपां तु शब्दस्पर्शरूपरसाः, पृथिव्यास्तु

शब्दस्पर्शरूपरसगन्धाः। न तु शब्दस्याकाशमात्रगुणत्वं, वाय्वादावपि तदुपलम्भात्। न चासौ भ्रमः, बाधकाभावात्।

Now the order of the manifestation of the universe is being described. At the beginning of creation, the Supreme Lord, aided by the (past) actions[1] of beings, which are the causes of the variety of the universe that is about to be created, as also by the cosmic illusion,[2] which is endowed with an unlimited and inscrutable power, first conceives in His mind the entire universe[3] consisting of names and forms, and resolves, "I shall do this"; for the Śruti says, "It reflected: Let Me multiply, let Me be effectively born" (*Chā.* VI. ii. 3), "It desired: (Let Me multiply, let Me be effectively born" (*Tai.* II. 6), etc.. From that the five[4] simple[5] elements beginning with the ether, which are signified by the word *tanmātra*[6] (subtle element), are produced. Of these, the property of the ether is sound; those of air are sound and touch; those of fire are sound, touch and colour; those of water are sound, touch, colour and taste; and those of earth are sound, touch, colour, taste and smell. Sound is not the property of the ether alone, for it is found in air etc. also. Nor is this an error, for there is nothing to contradict it.

[[1] This explains the difference that we find in the universe. For these not God, but the beings themselves, are responsible.

[2] *Māyā*, which is the material cause.

[3] As it was in the previous cycle (*kalpa*). So the present manifested universe is a replica of the previous one.

[4] Ether, air, fire (or light), water and earth.

[5] Not combined with the other four; hence subtle. For the process of combination see p. 162.

[6] Lit. 'only that,' that is, not combined with the other elements.]

इमानि भूतानि त्रिगुणमायाकार्याणि त्रिगुणानि। गुणाः सत्त्वरजस्तमांसि। एतैश्च सत्त्वगुणोपेतैः पञ्चभूतैर्व्यस्तैर्यथाक्रमं श्रोत्रत्वक्चक्षूरसनघ्राणानि पञ्चज्ञानेन्द्रियाणि जायन्ते। एतैरेव सत्त्वगुणोपेतैः पञ्चभूतैर्मिलितैर्मनोबुद्ध्यहङ्कारचित्तानि जायन्ते। श्रोत्रादीनां पञ्चानां क्रमेण दिग्वातार्कवरुणाश्विनोधिष्ठातृदेवताः। मन आदीनां चतुर्णां क्रमेण चन्द्रचतुर्मुखशङ्कराच्युता अधिष्ठातृदेवताः।

These elements, being effects of the cosmic illusion, which is made up of the three ingredients (*guṇas*), are (also) composed of the three ingredients. The ingredients are serenity (*sattva*), activity (*rajas*) and inertia (*tamas*). From these five elements as particularly possessed of the ingredient of serenity, taken singly, are produced in order[1] the five sense-organs known as the ear, skin, eye, tongue and nose. From these same five elements as particularly possessed of the ingredient of serenity, taken in combination,[2] are produced the *manas*,[3] the intellect, the ego and the *citta*.[4] The presiding deities of the five organs beginning with the ear are the Quarters,

Air, the Sun, Varuṇa (the god of water) and the two Aśvins, respectively.[5] The presiding deities of the four beginning with the *manas* are the Moon, Brahmā, Śiva and Viṣṇu respectively.

[[1] The ear from the ether, the skin from air, the eye from light, and so on.

[2] The text of this line has a different reading: **एतेभ्यः पुनराकाशादिगतसात्त्विकांशेभ्यो मिलितेभ्यः,** meaning, "From these portions of the ether etc., again, that are characterised by serenity, taken in combination."

[3] The mind as doing the function of deliberation. See p. 32.

[4] The mind as doing the function of recollection.

[5] The Quarters control the ear, Air the skin, the Sun the eye, and so on.]

एतैरेव रजोगुणोपेतैः पञ्चभूतैर्यथाक्रमं वाक्पाणिपाद-पायूपस्थाख्यानि कर्मेन्द्रियाणि जायन्ते। तेषाञ्च क्रमेण वह्नीन्द्रोपेन्द्रमृत्युप्रजापतयोऽधिष्ठातृदेवताः। रजोगुणोपेतैः पञ्चभूतैरेव मिलितैः पञ्च वायवः प्राणापानव्यानोदान-समानाख्या जायन्ते। तत्र प्राग्गमनवान् वायुः प्राणो नासादिस्थानवर्ती। अर्वाग्गमनवानपानः पाय्वादिस्थानवर्ती। विष्वग्गमनवान् व्यानः अखिलशरीरवर्ती। ऊर्ध्वगमनवानुत्क्रमणवायुरुदानः कण्ठस्थानवर्ती। अशितपीतान्नादिसमीकरणकरः समानः नाभिस्थानवर्ती।

From these same five elements (taken singly) as particularly possessed of the ingredient of activity, are produced in order the organs of action we call the tongue, the hand, the feet, the anus and the organ of generation. Their presiding deities are Agni (Fire), Indra, Viṣṇu, Yama (Death) and Prajāpati, respectively. The same five elements as particularly possessd of the ingredient of activity, taken in combination, produce the five vital forces named *prāṇa, apāna, vyāna, udāna* and *samāna*. Of these, *prāṇa* is the vital force that moves forward and has its seat in the region of the nose etc.[1] *Apāna* is what moves downwards and has its seat in the region of the anus etc. *Vyāna* is what moves in all directions and pervades the whole body. *Udāna* is the vital force that moves upwards and helps (the soul's) departure from the body; it has its seat in the region of the throat. *Samāna* is what metabolises the food etc., that we eat and drink and has its seat in the region of the navel.

[[1] Refers to the mouth, heart, etc. Authorities differ slightly as to the seats and functions of the five vital forces.]

तैरेव तमोगुणोपेतैरपञ्चीकृतभूतैः पञ्चीकृतभूतानि जायन्ते। "तासां त्रिवृतं त्रिवृतमेकैकां करवाणि" इति श्रुतेः पञ्चीकरणोपलक्षणार्थत्वात्।

Out of the same simple elements as particularly possessed of the ingredient of inertia, are produced the compound elements that are combined with the other four. For the Śruti text, "Let Me make each one of these[1] a triple[2] entity" (*Chā.* VI. iii. 3), is indicative of combination of each element with the other four[3] (*pañcī-karaṇa*).

[[1] Fire, water and food or earth.

[2] With a preponderance in each one of that particular element in the ratio of four to one.

[3] Not with the other two only; for the creation of fire was presumably preceded by that of the ether and air. Thus the mention of only three elements in *Chā.* V. ii. 3-4 will harmonise with that of five elements in *Tai.* III. 1.]

Combination of the Elements

पञ्चीकरणप्रकारश्चेत्थम्—आकाशमादौ द्विधा विभज्य त्तयोरेकं भागं पुनश्चतुर्धा विभज्य तेषां चतुर्णामंशानां वाय्वादिषु चतुर्षु भूतेषु संयोजनम। एवं वायुं द्विधा विभज्य तयोरेकं भागं पुनश्चतुर्धा विभज्य तेषां चतुर्णा-मंशानामाकाशादिषु संयोजनम्। एवं तेज आदीनामपि। तदेवमेकैकभूतस्यार्धं स्वांशात्मकम्, अर्धान्तरं चतुर्विध-भूतमयमिति पृथिव्यादिषु स्वांशाधिक्यात् पृथिव्यादि-व्यवहारः। तदुक्तम्—"वैशेष्यात्तु तद्वादस्तद्वादः" इति।

The process of combination with the other four elements is as follows: First dividing the ether into two, and again dividing one of these halves into four, each one of these four parts is to be added to (halves of) the (other) four elements—air and the rest.[1] Similiarly, dividing air into two, and again dividing one of these halves into four, each one of these parts is to be added to (halves of) the (other) four elements—ether and so forth. Similarly with fire etc. also. Thus half of each (compound) element consists, in the above manner, of itself, and the other half, of the remaining four elements. So the use of the terms 'earth' and so on with regard to earth and the other elements is on account of the preponderance of their own parts in them. Hence it has been said, "But the use of particular names is on account of the preponderance (of that element)."[2]

[[1] That is, each compound element will consist of half of itself and one-eigth of each of the other four.

[2] *Br.* S. II. iv. 22. The repetition of the last word in the original, omitted in the translation, marks the close of the chapter.]

Superior and Inferior Subtle Bodies

पूर्वोक्तैरपञ्चीकृतभूतैर्लिङ्गशरीरं परलोकयात्रानिर्वाहकं मोक्षपर्यन्तस्थायि मनोबुद्धिभ्यामुपेतं ज्ञानेन्द्रियपञ्चक-कर्मेन्द्रियपञ्चक-प्राणादिपञ्चकसंयुक्तं जायते। तदुक्तम्—

"पञ्चप्राणमनोबुद्धिदशेन्द्रियसमन्वितम्।
अपञ्चीकृतभूतोत्थं सूक्ष्माङ्गं भोगसाधनम्॥" इति।

तच्च द्विविधम्—परमपरञ्च। परं हिरण्यगर्भलिङ्गशरीरम्, अपरमस्मदादिलिङ्गशरीरम्। तत्र हिरण्यगर्भलिङ्गशरीरं महत्तत्त्वम्, अस्मदादिलिङ्गशरीरञ्चाहङ्कार इत्याख्यायते।

Out of the above-mentioned simple elements is made the subtle body (*liṅga-śarīra*), consisting of the *manas* and intellect as well as the five sense-organs, the five organs of action and the five vital forces. It helps (the soul's) passage to other worlds and lasts till liberation.[1] So it has been said. "The subtle body, consisting of the five vital forces, the *manas,* the intellect and the ten organs, is produced from the simple elements, and is the means of (the soul's) experiencing the results of (its) actions" (Śaṅkarācārya's *Ātma-bodha,* 13). It is of two kinds—superior and inferior. The superior one is the subtle body of Hiraṇyagarbha;[2] the inferior one is the subtle body of beings like us. Of these, the subtle body of Hiranyagarbha is called *mahat-tattva* (the cosmic intellect), while that of people like us is called the ego.

[[1] The fall of the body after the realisation of one's identity with Brahman.

[2] The being identified with the sum total of all minds. See also note 4 on p. 154.]

Origin of the Various Worlds and Bodies

एवं तमोगुणयुक्तेभ्यः पञ्चीकृतभूतेभ्यो भूम्यन्तरिक्ष-स्वर्महर्जनतपःसत्यात्मकस्योर्ध्वलोकसप्तकस्य अतल-वितल-सुतल-तलातल-रसातल-महातल-पातालाख्यस्य अधोलोक-सप्तकस्य ब्रह्माण्डस्य जरायुजाण्डजस्वेदजोद्भिज्जाख्यचतु-र्विधस्थूलशरीराणाञ्चोत्पत्तिः। तत्र जरायुजानि जरायुभ्यो जातानि मनुष्यपश्वादिशरीराणी। अण्डजान्यण्डेभ्यो

जातानि पक्षिपन्नगादिशरीराणी। स्वेदजानि स्वेदाज्जातानि यूकमशकादिशरीराणि। उद्भिज्जानि भूमिमुद्भिद्य जातानि वृक्षादीनि। वृक्षादीनामपि पापफलभोगायतनत्वेन शरीरत्वम्।

Similarly, from the compounded elements as particularly possessed of the ingredient of inertia is produced the universe consisting of the seven upper worlds, viz., earth, sky, heaven, *mahar*, *jana*, *tapas* and *satya*, and the seven nether worlds, viz., *atala*, *vitala*, *sutala*, *talātala*, *rasātala*, *mahātala* and *pātāla*, as also the four kinds of gross bodies, viz., those born of the mother's womb, those born of eggs, those born of moisture and those that shoot from the earth. Of these, those born of the mother's womb are the bodies of men, cattle, etc.; those born of eggs are the bodies of birds, snakes, etc.; those born of moisture are the bodies of lice, mosquitoes, etc.; and those that shoot from the earth are plants etc. Plants are also bodies, since they are the seats in which the results of (past) sins are experienced.[1]

[[1] As we know from the scriptures. Cf. *Manu Saṁhitā* XII. 9.]

तत्र परमेश्वरस्य पञ्चतन्मात्राद्युत्पत्तौ सप्तदशावयवोपेत-लिङ्गशरीरोत्पत्तौ हिरण्यगर्भस्थूलशरीरोत्पत्तौ च साक्षात् कर्तृत्वम्, इतरनिखिलप्रपञ्चोत्पत्तौ च हिरण्यगर्भादिद्वारा, "हन्ताहमिमास्तिस्रो देवता अनेन जीवेनात्मनानुप्रविश्य नामरूपे व्याकरवाणि" इति श्रुतेः।

Now, in the origination of the five subtle elements etc.,[1] the subtle body[2] consisting of seventeen[3] components, and the gross body[4] of Hiraṇyagarbha, God is a direct agent; while in the origination of all the rest of the universe He is such through the medium of Hiraṇyagarbha and others.[5] For the Śruti says, "Well, let Me enter these three deities[6] as this individual self and manifest name and form" (*Chā.* VI. iii. 2).

[[1] Refers to the five gross elements.
[2] Superior and inferior.
[3] See p. 164, top.
[4] That is, the gross universe. Here Hiraṇyagarbha is identified with Virāj, who represents the sum total of all gross bodies.
[5] Refers to the Prajāpatis, the progenitors of different beings.
[6] Fire, water and earth.]

हिरण्यगर्भो नाम मूर्तित्रयादन्यः प्रथमो जीवः ।
"स वै शरीरी प्रथमः स वै पुरुष उच्यते ।
आदिकर्ता स भूतानां ब्रह्माग्रे समवर्तत ॥"
"हिरण्यगर्भः समवर्तताग्रे," इत्यादिश्रुतेः ।
एवं भूतभौतिकसृष्टिर्निरूपिता ।

Hiraṇyagarbha is the first individual to be born, and is different from the Trinity (Brahmā, Viṣṇu and Śiva). (Witness the Smṛti text), "He indeed is the first embodied being. He indeed is called a person (*puruṣa*). He is the first progenitor of beings. (That) Brahmā appeared first of all (*Śiv.* V. I. viii, 22; *Mār.* XIV. 64; etc.).

As also the Śruti text, "Hiraṇyagarbha appeared first of all," etc. (*Ṛ*. X. cxxi. 1; *Vāj*. S. XIII. 4; etc.).

Thus the projection of the elements and of things made up of the elements has been described.

Four Kinds of Cosmic Dissolution

इदानीं प्रलयो निरूप्यते। प्रलयो नाम त्रैलोक्यविनाशः। स च चतुर्विधः—नित्यः प्राकृतो नैमित्तिक आत्यन्तिकश्चेति। तत्र नित्यः प्रलयः सुषुप्तिः, तस्याः सकलकार्यप्रलयरूपत्वात्। धर्माधर्मपूर्वसंस्काराणाञ्च तदा कारणात्मनाऽवस्थानम्। तेन सुप्तोत्थितस्य न सुखदुःखाद्यनुपपत्तिः, न वा स्मरणानुपपत्तिः। न च सुषुप्तौ अन्तःकरणस्य विनाशे तदधीनप्राणादिक्रियानुपपत्तिः, वस्तुतः श्वासाद्यभावेऽपि तदुपलब्धेः पुरुषान्तरविभ्रममात्रत्वात्, सुप्तशरीरोपलम्भवत्। न च एवं सुप्तस्य परेतादविशेषः, सुप्तस्य हि लिङ्गशरीरं संस्कारात्मनाऽत्रैव वर्तते, परेतस्य तु लोकान्तरे इति वैलक्षण्यात्।

Now cosmic dissolution is being described. It is the destruction of the world in general. It is of four kinds—diurnal, basic, occasional and absolute. Of these, diurnal (*nitya*) dissolution is the condition of profound sleep, for it represents the dissolution of all effects. Merit, demerit and past latent impressions then remain in their causal form. Hence, for a person awaking from sleep, pleasure, pain, etc. are not incongruous; nor is recollection inexplicable. In profound sleep, though the mind is destroyed, yet the function of respiration etc., which depend on that, are not incongruous, because, though really there are no respiration etc.,[1] yet their cognition is just a phantasy of another person,[2] like the cognition of the body of a sleeping man..[3] It cannot be urged that in that case a sleeping man would be indistinguishable from a dead man; for there is this distinction that the subtle body of a sleeping man remains here itself in the form of latent impressions, while that of a dead man remains in another world.

[[1] To the sleeping man.
[2] Viz., the on-looker.
[3] Who does not feel it himself, and therefore for him it does not exist.]

यद्वा अन्तःकरणस्य द्वे शक्ति—ज्ञानशक्तिः क्रियाशक्तिश्चेति। तत्र ज्ञानशक्तिविशिष्टान्तःकरणस्य सुषुप्तौ विनाशः, न तु क्रियाशक्तिविशिष्टस्य इति प्राणाद्यवस्थानमविरुद्धम्। "यदा सुप्तः स्वप्नं न कञ्चन पश्यति, अथास्मिन् प्राण एवैकधा भवति, अथैनं वाक् सर्वैर्नामभिः सहाप्येति," "सता सोम्य तदा सम्पन्नो भवति, स्वमपीतो भवति" इत्यादिश्रुतिरुक्तसुषुप्तौ मानम्।

Or (we may say) the mind has two functions —the function of knowledge and that of activity.

Of these, the mind as possessed of the function of knowledge is destroyed in profound sleep, but not the mind is possessed of the function of activity. Hence the continuity of the vital force etc. is not contradictory. Śruti texts like the following are proofs of the above condition of profound sleep: "When a person is asleep and sees no dreams, he verily becomes one with (Brahman associated with) this vital force. Then the organ of speech with all names merge in It" (*Kau.* IV. 19), "He is then united with Existence, my dear—is merged in his Self" (*Chā.* VI. viii. 1).

प्राकृतप्रलयस्तु कार्यब्रह्मविनाशनिमित्तकः सकलकार्यविनाशः। यदा तु प्रागेवोत्पन्नब्रह्मसाक्षात्कारस्य कार्यब्रह्मणो ब्रह्माण्डाधिकारलक्षणप्रारब्धकर्मसमाप्तौ विदेहकैवल्यात्मिका परा मुक्तिः, तदा तल्लोकवासिनामप्युत्पन्नब्रह्मसाक्षात्काराणां ब्रह्मणा सह विदेहकैवल्यम्।

"ब्रह्मणा सह ते सर्वे सम्प्राप्ते प्रतिसञ्चरे।
परस्यान्ते कृतात्मानः प्रविशन्ति परं पदम्॥"

इति स्मृतेः। एवं स्वलोकवासिभिः सह कार्यब्रह्मणि मुच्यमाने तदधिष्ठितब्रह्माण्ड-तदन्तर्वर्तिनिखिललोक-तदन्तर्वर्तिस्थावरादीनां भौतिकानां भूतानाञ्च प्रकृतौ मायायां लयः, न तु ब्रह्मणि, बाधरूपविनाशस्यैव ब्रह्मनिष्ठत्वात्, अतः प्राकृत इत्युच्यते।

Basic dissolution is the destruction of all

effects consequent on the destruction of Hiraṇyagarbha. (To be explicit:) When Hiraṇyagarbha, who has already[1] had realisation of Brahman, attains, on the termination of his fructifying (*prārabdha*[2]) work in the form of suzerainty of the universe, supreme liberation consisting in isolation characterised by disembodiedness, then those denizens of the world[3] of Hiraṇyagarbha who[4] have realised Brahman, also attain with him isolation characterised by disembodiedness. Witness the Smṛti text, "When, at the end of the lifetime of Hiraṇyagarbha, cosmic dissolution comes, all those who have realised the Self enter with him the supreme state" (*Ku.* I. xii. 269). Thus, when Hiraṇyagarbha together with the inhabitants of his world is liberated, the universe ruled by him, with all its subsidiary worlds[5] and the stationary[6] or other bodies, made up of the elements, that are comprised in them, as also those elements themselves, is merged in *prakṛti* or the cosmic illusion (*māyā*), and not in Brahman—for only destruction in the form of nullification (*bādha*)[7] abides in Brahman.[8] Therefore it is called basic (*prākṛta*).[9]

[[1] Before the dissolution of the universe in the previous cycle.

[2] Lit., 'commenced': that is, that part of one's past work which has already begun to bear fruit by causing the present body. It is exhausted through actual experience of pleasure and pain.

[3] *Satya-loka.*

[4] Not others who have gone there through the mechanical performance of certain rites.
[5] The fourteen worlds enumerated on p. 165.
[6] Such as those of plants.
[7] See p. 60.
[8] As its substratum. See p. 142.
[9] Lit., 'pertaining to *prakṛti*' or the primal material cause of the universe.]

कार्यब्रह्मणो दिवसावसाननिमित्तकः त्रैलोक्यमात्रप्रलयः नैमित्तिकप्रलयः। ब्रह्मदिवसश्चतुर्युगसहस्रपरिमितकालः, "चतुर्युगसहस्राणि ब्रह्मणो दिनमुच्यते" इत्यादिवचनात्। प्रलयकालोऽपि दिवसकालपरिमितः, रात्रिकालस्य दिवसकालतुल्यत्वात्।

The dissolution of only three[1] worlds consequent on the end of a day of Hiraṇyagarbha occasional dissolution. A day of Hiraṇyagarbha is a period measured by four thousand eras (*yuga*[2]), as we have it from such (scriptural) statements as, "A period of four thousand eras is called a day of Brahmā" (*Bṛhannār.* XXXII. 86). The period of dissolution also is as long as the day (of Brahmā), for the duration of a night is equal to that of a day.

[[1] The earth, sky and heaven.
[2] Equivalent to 4,320,000 human years.]

प्राकृतप्रलये नैमित्तिकप्रलये च पुराणवचनानि प्रमाणानि।

"द्विपरार्द्धे त्वतिक्रान्ते ब्रह्मणः परमेष्ठिनः।
तदा प्रकृतयः सप्त कल्पन्ते प्रलयाय हि॥

एष प्राकृतिको राजन् प्रलयो यत्र लीयते।"

इति वचनं प्राकृतप्रलये मानम्।

"एष नैमित्तिकः प्रोक्तः प्रलयो यत्र विश्वसृक्।

शेतेऽनन्तासने नित्यमात्मसात्कृत्य चाखिलम्॥"

इति वचनं नैमित्तिकः प्रलये मानम्।

Regarding basic and ossasional dissolution, the statements of the Purāṇas are proofs. The statement, "When two hundred thousand billion human years comprising the lifetime of Hiraṇyagarbha, the Parameṣṭhin, have passed, the seven (secondary) causes[1] undergo dissolution.[2] This, O King, is basic dissolution, when (every effect) is merged," is a proof of basic dissolution. And the statement, "That is called occasional dissolution when the Creator[3] of the universe, at regular intervals,[4] withdraws the three worlds into himself, and lies[5] on the serpent Ananta as his bed," is a proof of occasional dissolution.

[[1] Entities that are both causes and effects, viz., the cosmic mind, the ego and the five subtle elements.

[2] In the primal *prakṛti*.

[3] Brahmā or Hiraṇyagarbha.

[4] On the approach of every night of his.

[5] As identified with Viṣṇu.]

तुरीयप्रलयस्तु ब्रह्मसाक्षात्कारनिमित्तकः सर्वमोक्षः। स चैकजीववादे युगपदे, नानाजीववादे तु क्रमेण; "सर्व एकीभवन्ति" इत्यादिश्रुतेः।

तत्राद्यास्त्रयोऽपि लयाः कर्मोपरमनिमित्ताः, तुरीयस्तु ज्ञानोदयनिमित्तो लयोऽज्ञानेन सहैवेति विशेषः।

The fourth kind of dissolution is the liberation of all[1] consequent on the realisation of Brahman, According to the doctrine of a single individual self,[2] it is just simultaneous, but according to the doctrine of multiple individual selves,[3] it is gradual. Witness Śruti texts like, "All are united."

Of the above kinds of dissolution the first three[4] are all caused by the cessation[5] of past work,[6] while the fourth kind of dissolution is due to the dawning of knowledge, and it takes place together with the dissolution of nescience iteslf. This is its difference from the others.

[[1] In which there is a destruction of all created things together with their cause, nescience.

[2] In which nescience, which is one, is the limiting adjunct of the self.

[3] In which the different minds are the limiting adjuncts.

[4] Viz., diurnal, basic and occasional.

[5] At the time of one's profound sleep, the passing of Hihanyagarbha, and his falling asleep, respectively.

[6] Of individuals ; but not the cessation of nescience.]

The Order of Cosmic Dissolution

एवं चतुर्विधप्रलयो निरूपितः। तस्येदानीं क्रमो निरूप्यते। भूतानां भौतिकानाञ्च न कारणलयक्रमेण लयः, कारणलयसमये कार्याणामाश्रयमन्तरेणावस्थानानुपपत्तेः, किन्तु सृष्टिक्रमविपरीतक्रमेण ; तत्तत्कार्यनाशे तत्तज्जनकादृष्टनाशस्यैव प्रयोजकतया उपादाननाशस्याप्रयोजकत्वात्।

अन्यथा न्यायमतेऽपि महाप्रलये पृथिवीपरमाणुगतरूपरसादेरविनाशापत्तेः। तथाच पृथिव्या अप्सु, अपां तेजसि, तेजसो वायौ, वायोराकाशे, आकाशस्य जीवाहङ्कारे, तस्य हिरण्यगर्भाहङ्कारे तस्य चाविद्यायाम्—इत्येवंरूप एव प्रलयः। तदुक्तं विष्णुपुराणे—

"जगत्प्रतिष्ठा देवर्षे पृथिव्यप्सु प्रलीयते।
तेजस्यापः प्रलीयन्ते तेजो वायौ प्रलीयते॥
वायुश्च लीयते व्योम्नि तच्चाव्यक्ते प्रलीयते।
अव्यक्तं पुरुषे ब्रह्मन्निष्कले सम्प्रलीयते॥" इति।

एवंविधप्रलयकारणत्वं 'तत्'-पदार्थस्य ब्रह्मणस्तटस्थलक्षणम्।

Thus the four kinds of cosmic dissolution have been described. Now the order of such dissolution is being set forth. The dissolution of the elements and of things made out of them is not according to the order of the dissolution of their causes—for when the causes are dissolved, the effects cannot possibly stay without substratums—but it is in the inverse order to that of projection. For with regard to the destruction of particular effects, the destruction of the particular merits or demerits that caused them is the sole determining factor; hence the destruction of their material causes is not a necessary condition. Otherwise, even according to Nyāya, the colour, taste, etc., belonging to atoms of earth would not be destroyed[1] at cosmic dissolution. So dissolution takes place in the following manner: Earth is merged in water, water in fire, fire in air, air in the ether, the ether in the ego[2] of the individual self, that in the ego of Hiraṇyagarbha, and that, again, in nescience. So it has been said in the *Viṣṇu Purāṇa*,[3] "Earth, which is the support of the world, O divine sage (Nārada), is merged in water, water is merged in fire, fire in air, and air in the ether; this in its turn is merged in the Undifferentiated[4] and the Undifferentiated, O Brahman, in the Supreme Self, which is devoid of parts."

The secondary characteristic[5] of Brahman, the meaning of the word 'That,'[6] is that It is the cause of this kind of dissolution.

[1 Since, according to Nyāya, atoms are eternal.

2 That is, the subtle body.

3 The passage does not seem to occur in the available editions of the book.

4 Nescience.

5 See p. 153.

6 In the dictum, "Thou art That."]

Why the Scriptures Deal with Creation and Meditations

ननु वेदान्तैर्ब्रह्मणि जगत्कारणत्वेन प्रतिपाद्यमाने सति सप्रपञ्चं ब्रह्म स्यात्, अन्यथा सृष्टिवाक्यानामप्रामाण्यापत्तिरिति चेत्, न। नहि सृष्टिवाक्यानां सृष्टौ तात्पर्यम्, किन्तु अद्वये ब्रह्मण्येव। तत्प्रतिपत्तौ कथं सृष्टेरुपयोगः?

इत्थम्—यदि सृष्टिमनुपन्यस्य प्रपञ्चस्य निषेधो ब्रह्मणि प्रतिपाद्येत तदा ब्रह्मणि प्रतिषिद्धस्य प्रपञ्चस्य, वायौ प्रतिषिद्धस्य रूपस्येव, ब्रह्मणोऽन्यत्रावस्थानशङ्कायां न निर्विचिकित्समद्वितीयत्वं प्रतिपादितं स्यात्। ततः सृष्टिवाक्याद् ब्रह्मोपादेयत्वज्ञाने सति, उपादानं विना कार्यस्यान्यत्र सद्भावशङ्कायां निरस्तायां "नेति नेति" इत्यादिना ब्रह्मण्यपि तस्यासत्त्वोपपादनेन प्रपञ्चस्य तुच्छत्वावगमे निरस्तनिखिलद्वैतविभ्रममखण्डं सच्चिदानन्दैकरसं ब्रह्म सिद्धतीति परम्परया सृष्टिवाक्यानामपि अद्वितीये ब्रह्मण्येव तात्पर्यम्। उपासनाप्रकरणपठितसगुणब्रह्मवाक्यानाञ्च उपासनाविध्यपेक्षितगुणारोपमात्रपरत्वम्, न गुणपरत्वम्। निर्गुणप्रकरणपठितानां सगुणवाक्यानान्तु निषेधवाक्यापेक्षितनिषेध्यसमर्पकत्वेन विनियोग इति न किञ्चिदपि वाक्यमद्वितीयब्रह्मप्रतिपादनेन विरुध्यते।

Objection: If Brahman is established by Vedāntic texts as the cause of the universe, then It must be inclusive of the universe, for otherwise the passages dealing with creation would cease to be authoritative.

Reply: No. The passages dealing with creation are not intended to establish creation, but only Brahman, the One without a second. It may be urged: But how does the delineation of creation help to establish It? In the following manner: If, without introducing creation, the universe were negated in Brahman, then, like colour denied in air,[1] the universe might be supposed to exist outside of Brahman, and hence Its indubitable solitariness would not be proved. Therefore, when one has got the idea from the texts delineating creation, that the univrese is the outcome of Brahman, the contigency of an effect existing outside of its material cause is set at rest; and when the universe is known to be insubstantial through the denial of its existence even in Brahman by texts like, "Not this, not this" (*Bṛ.* II. iii. 6), Brahman is established as the indivisible, homogeneous[2] Existence-Knowledge-Bliss Absolute, divested of the phantasm of the entire world of duality.[3] Hence even the texts delineating creation are indirectly intended to establish only Brahman, the One without a second. The passages[4] dealing with the conditioned Brahman that occur in the section relating to contemplation, convey only the *superimposition* of attributes required by the injunctions regarding contemplation,[5] and not the actual presence of such attributes (in Brahman). While the texts[6] dealing with the conditioned Brahman that occur in the section relating to the unconditioned Brahman, are of use as presenting the things to be negated that are required by the passages[7] denying the world. Hence not a single text militates against the establishment[8] of Brahman, the One without a second.

[[1] Colour does not exist in air, but it exists in earth, water and fire.

[2] Devoid of all differences whatsoever, whether within Itself, or from things of the same class, or from things of other classes.

[3] Imagined by ignorant persons.

[4] Such as, "This resplendent Being who is seen inside the sun," etc. (*Chā.* I. vi. 6).

[5] Such as, "One should meditate on the syllable Oṁ, which is designated as *udgītha*" (*Ibid.* I. i. 1).

[6] Such as, "Brahman has only two forms," etc. (*Bṛ.* II. iii. 1).

[7] Such as, "Now therefore the instruction is: Not this, not this," etc. (*Ibid.* II. iii. 6).

[8] By texts like *Chā.* VI. ii. 1. See p. 150.]

Views about Consciousness as God and as the Individual Self

तदेवं स्वरूपतटस्थलक्षणलक्षितं 'तत्'-पदवाच्यमीश्वरचैतन्यं मायाप्रतिबिम्बरूपमिति केचित्। तेषामयमाशयः—जीवपरमेश्वरसाधारणं चैतन्यमात्रं बिम्बम्, तस्यैव बिम्बस्याविद्यात्मिकायां मायायां प्रतिबिम्बमीश्वरचैतन्यम्, अन्तःकरणेषु प्रतिबिम्बं जीवचैतन्यम्, "कार्योपाधिरयं जीवः कारणोपाधिरीश्वरः" इति श्रुतेः। एतन्मते जलाशयगतशरावजलगतसूर्यप्रतिबिम्बयोरिव जीवपरमेश्वरयोर्भेदः। अविद्यात्मकोपाधेर्व्यापकतया तदुपाधिकेश्वरस्यापि व्यापकत्वम्। अन्तःकरणस्य परिच्छिन्नतया तदुपाधिकजीवस्यापि परिच्छिन्नत्वम्।

Some say that the Consciousness called God (*Īśvara*), which is referred to by Its essential and secondary characteristics in the abovementioned manner, and is the significance of the word 'That,'[1] is a reflection in the cosmic illusion. Their idea is this: The Pure Consciousness that is common to both the individual self and God is the thing reflected, and the reflection of that very thing in the cosmic illusion, which is of the nature of nescience, is the Consciousness called God, while the reflection in different minds is the Consciousness called the individual self; for the Śruti says, "This individual self has for its limiting adjunct (the mind, which is) an effect (of nescience), while God has for His limiting adjunct nescience, which is the cause" (*Maitreyī Up.*, 61). According to this view, the difference between God and the individual self is like[2] that between the reflections of the sun in a tank and in the water of a saucer. Since the limiting adjunct consisting of nescience is all-pervading, God, who has that as His limiting adjunct, is also all-pervading, while the mind being limited, the individual self, which has that for its limiting adjunct, is also limited.

[[1] In the dictum, "Thou art That."
[2] That is, it is only apparent, not real.]

एतन्मतेऽविद्याकृतदोषा जीव इव परमेश्वरेऽपि स्युः, उपाधेः प्रतिबिम्बपक्षपातित्वात्, इत्यस्वरसात् बिम्बात्मकमीश्वरचैतन्यमित्यपरे। तेषामयमाशयः—एकमेव चैतन्यं बिम्बत्वाक्रान्तमीश्वरचैतन्यम्, प्रतिबिम्बत्वाक्रान्तं जीव-

चैतन्यम्। बिम्बप्रतिबिम्बकल्पनोपाधिश्चैकजीववादे अविद्या, अनेकजीववादे तु अन्तःकरणान्येव। अविद्यान्तःकरणरूपोपाधिप्रयुक्तो जीवपरभेदः। उपाधिकृतदोषाश्च प्रतिबिम्बे जीव एव वर्तन्ते, न तु बिम्बे परमेश्वरे, उपाधेः प्रतिबिम्बपक्षपातित्वात्। एतन्मते च गगनसूर्यस्य जलादौ भासमानप्रतिबिम्बसूर्यस्येव जीवपरयोर्भेदः।

Others, however, regard this view as unsatisfactory, because according to it the defects[1] caused by nescience would be in God as well as in the individual self, for a limiting adjunct imparts its own character to the reflection. So they say that the Consciousness called God stands for the thing that is reflected.[2] Their idea is this: One and the same Consciousness is the Consciousness called God when it is stamped with the character of the thing reflected, and is the Consciousness called the individual self when it is stamped with the character of a reflection. In this assumption of a thing reflected and its reflection, the limiting adjunct is nescience according to the doctrine of a single individual self, but different minds alone according to that of multiple individual selves. The difference between the individual self and the Supreme Self is due to the limiting adjunct—nescience or minds. The defects caused by the limiting adjunct, however, are in the individual self, which is a reflection, but not in God,[3] who is the thing reflected, for a limiting adjunct tends to influence the reflection. According to this view, the difference between God and the individual self is like that between the sun in the sky and its image reflected in water etc.

[[1] Such as bondage, agency and the experience of pleasure and pain.

[2] And not a reflection.

[3] So this is the advantage of the second view.]

ननु ग्रीवास्थमुखस्य दर्पणप्रदेश इव बिम्बचैतन्यस्य परमेश्वरस्य जीवप्रदेशेऽभावात् तस्य सर्वान्तर्यामित्वं न स्यादिति चेत्, न। साभ्रनक्षत्रस्याकाशस्य जलादौ प्रतिबिम्बितत्वे बिम्बभूतमहाकाशस्यापि जलादिप्रदेशसम्बन्धदर्शनेन परिच्छिन्नबिम्बस्य प्रतिबिम्बदेशासम्बन्धित्वेऽप्यपरिच्छिन्नब्रह्मबिम्बस्य प्रतिबिम्बदेशसम्बन्धाविरोधात्।

Objection: Since God, who is the Consciousness standing for the thing reflected, is absent from the place[1] where the individual self exists, as a face resting on the neck is absent from the place occupied by the mirror, He would not be the Internal Controller of everything.

Reply: Not so. For when the sky with its clouds and stars is reflected in water etc., the all-pervading sky, which is the thing reflected, is also observed to have a connection with the place occupied by the water etc. Therefore, although a limited thing that is reflected may not be connected with the place[2] where the reflection is, there is nothing to prevent the connection of an unlimited thing that is reflected, viz., (the conditioned) Brahman,[4] with the place where the reflection exists.[5]

[[1] Viz., the mind.
[2] The mind.
[3] The individual self.
[4] Whose limiting adjunct, cosmic illusion, is all-pervading.
[5] So the charge of limitation is refuted.]

न च रूपहीनस्य ब्रह्मणो न प्रतिबिम्बसम्भवः, रूपवत एव तथात्वदर्शनात्, इति वाच्यम्; नीरूपस्यापि रूपस्य प्रतिबिम्बदर्शनात्। न च नीरूपस्य द्रव्यस्य प्रतिबिम्बाभावनियमः, आत्मनो द्रव्यत्वाभावस्य उक्तत्वात्।

"एकधा बहुधा चैव दृश्यते जलचन्द्रवत्।"

"यथा ह्ययं ज्योतिरात्मा विवस्वा-
नपो भिन्ना बहुधैकोऽनुगच्छन्।"

इत्यादिवाक्येन ब्रह्मप्रतिबिम्बाभावानुमानस्य बाधितत्वाच्च।

तदेवं 'तत्'-पदार्थो निरूपितः।

It cannot be urged that Brahman, which is colourless, cannot possibly be reflected, since only coloured objects are observed to be so. Because although colour is devoid of any colour,[1] we observe that it is reflected. Nor can it be urged that a colourless *substance* is as a rule devoid of any reflection; for we have already[2] stated that the self is not a substance. And any inference regarding Brahman's not casting a reflection is nullified by scriptural texts like the following: "It is seen as one and as manifold, like the moon reflected in water" (*Amṛtabindu Up.*, 12), and "Just as this luminous mass, the sun, although one, becomes manifold by being reflected in different sheets of water," etc.[3]

So the meaning of the word 'That' has been ascertained in the foregoing manner.

[[1] See note 2 on p. 81.

[2] On p. 80.

[3] Refers to the rest of the verse: "Similarly the shining, birthless Self is made to appear as multiple in different bodies by limiting adjuncts.]

The Meaning of 'Thou': Wakefulness

इदानीं 'त्वम्'-पदार्थो निरूप्यते। एकजीववादेऽविद्याप्रतिबिम्बो जीवः, अनेकजीववादे तु अन्तःकरणप्रतिबिम्बः। स च जाग्रत्स्वप्नसुषुप्तिरूपावस्थात्रयवान्। तत्र जाग्रद्दशा नाम इन्द्रियजन्यज्ञानावस्था, अवस्थान्तरे इन्द्रियाभावात् नातिव्याप्तिः। इन्द्रियजन्यज्ञानञ्चान्तःकरणवृत्तिः, स्वरूपज्ञानस्यानादित्वात्।

Now the meaning of the word 'thou' is being ascertained. Acording to the doctrine of a single individual self, the latter is a reflection (of Brahman) in nescience, while acording to the doctrine of multiple individual selves, it is a reflection (of Brahman) in different minds.[1] It is possessed of the three conditions of wakefulness, dream and profound sleep. Of these, the waking condition is that in which knowledge is obtained through the organs. Since the organs do not function in the other (two) conditions, the definition does not unwarrantedly include them. This knowledge obtained through the organs is a state of the mind,[2] for the knowledge that is the essence of the Self[3] is without a beginning.[4]

[[1] Which accounts for the multiplicity of the selves.
[2] And not Pure Consciousness, which is eternal.
[3] That is, Pure Consciousness.
[4] It is never caused.]

Two Views about the Function of the Mental State

सा चान्तःकरणवृत्तिरावरणाभिभवार्था इत्येकं मतम्। तथाहि—अविद्योपहितचैतन्यस्य जीवत्वपक्षे घटाद्यधिष्ठानचैतन्यस्य जीवरूपतया जीवस्य सर्वदा घटादिभानप्रसक्तौ घटाद्यवच्छिन्नचैतन्यावरकमज्ञानं मूलाविद्यापरतन्त्रमवस्थापदवाच्यमभ्युपगन्तव्यम्। एवं सति न सर्वदा घटादेर्भानप्रसङ्गः, अनावृतचैतन्यसम्बन्धस्यैव भानप्रयोजकत्वात्। तस्य चावरणस्य सदातनत्वे कदाचिदपि घटभानं न स्यादिति तद्भङ्गे वक्तव्ये, तद्भङ्गजनकं न चैतन्यमात्रम्, तद्भासकस्य तदनिवर्तकत्वात्, नापि वृत्त्युपहितं चैतन्यम्, परोक्षस्थलेऽपि तन्निवृत्त्यापत्तेरिति परोक्षव्यावृत्तवृत्तिविशेषस्य, तदुपहितचैतन्यस्य वा, आवरणभञ्जकत्वम्, इति आवरणाभिभवार्था वृत्तिरुच्यते।

One school holds that this mental state serves to remove the covering (off Brahman). To explain: According to the view[1] that the individual self is the Consciousness of which nescience is a limiting adjunct, the Consciousness that is the substratum of a jar etc. not being different[2] from the individual self, the latter would have a constant cognition of the jar etc.[3] To preclude this, one must admit a nescience dependent on the primal nescience, signified by the word 'condition,'[4] which covers the Consciousness limited by the jar etc. In that case there would not be a constant cognition of a jar etc., for only a relation to the Consciousness that is not covered can lead to cognition. Now, if that covering be permanent, there would never be a cognition of the jar. So its break must be admitted. But the cause of the break can neither be Pure Consciousness —for what brings the covering to light[5] cannot be its remover—nor Consciousness that has a mental state[6] for its limiting adjunct, for even in a case of mediate[7] knowledge that covering would be removed.[8] Hence a *particular* state not classed[9] under mediate knowledge, or[10] the Consciousness having such a state for its limiting adjunct, must be the breaker of the covering.[11] So the state is described as sering to remove the covering.

[[1] See the preceding paragraph.

[2] Because its limiting adjunct, nescience, is all-pervading, it too is so, and is therefore one with the Consciousness that is the substratum of a jar.

[3] Which is contrary to fact.

[4] That is, a modification of that nescience.
[5] As the universal revealer.
[6] That is, an unqualified mental state.
[7] That is, non-perceptual cognition, such as inferential knowledge and recollection.
[8] For there also the mental state is present.
[9] This is the specification of the mental state in question.
[10] If the previous alternative is rejected on the ground that the state, being insentient, cannot remove the covering.
[11] So only in perception, where the mental state is in contact with an object, there is a removal of the covering, and not in inference, recollection, etc.]

सम्बन्धार्था वृत्तिरित्यपरं मतम्। तत्राविद्योपाधिकोऽपरिच्छिन्नो जीवः। स च घटादिप्रदेशे विद्यमानोऽपि घटाद्याकारापरोक्षवृत्तिविरहदशायां न घटादिकमवभासयति, घटादिना समं सम्बन्धाभावात्, तत्तदाकारवृत्तिदशायां तु भासयति, तदा सम्बन्धसत्त्वात्।

Another school holds that the mental state serves to establish a connection.[1] According to this view, the individual self, which has nescience for its limiting adjunct, is (really) unlimited. Although it is present at the place occupied by a jar etc., it does not reveal them when there is an absence of a perceptual mental state in the form of the jar etc., for then it is not connected with the latter; but it does reveal them when there is a mental state in the form of those things, for then there is the connection.

[[1] Between Consciousness and objects.]

ननु अविद्योपाधिकस्यापरिच्छिन्नस्य जीवस्य स्वत एव समस्तवस्तुसम्बद्धस्य वृत्तिविरहदशायां सम्बन्धाभावाभिधानमसङ्गतम्, असङ्गत्वदृष्ट्या सम्बन्धाभावाभिधाने च वृत्त्यनन्तरमपि सम्बन्धो न स्यात्, इति चेत्, उच्यते। नहि वृत्तिविरहदशायां जीवस्य घटादिना सह सम्बन्धसामान्यं निषेधामः। किन्तर्हि? घटादिभानप्रयोजकं सम्बन्धविशेषम्। स च सम्बन्धविशेषो विषयस्य जीवचैतन्यस्य च व्यङ्ग्यव्यञ्जकतालक्षणः कादाचित्कस्तत्तदाकारवृत्तिनिबन्धनः। तथाहि—तैजसमन्तःकरणं स्वच्छद्रव्यत्वात् स्वत एव जीवचैतन्याभिव्यञ्जनसमर्थम्। घटादिकस्तु न तथा, अस्वच्छद्रव्यत्वात्। स्वाकारवृत्तिसंयोगदशायान्तु वृत्त्यभिभूतजाड्यधर्मकतया वृत्त्युत्पादितचैतन्याभिव्यञ्जनयोग्यताश्रयतया च वृत्त्युदयान्तरं चैतन्यमभिव्यनक्ति। तदुक्तं विवरणे—"अन्तःकरणं हि स्वस्मिन्निव स्वसंसर्गिण्यपि घटादौ चैतन्याभिव्यक्तियोग्यतामापादयति" इति। दृष्टश्चास्वच्छद्रव्यस्यापि स्वच्छद्रव्यसम्बन्धदशायां प्रतिबिम्बग्राहित्वम्। तथा कुड्यादेर्जलादिसंयोगदशायां मुखादिप्रतिबिम्बग्राहिता। घटादेरभिव्यञ्जकत्वञ्च तत्प्रतिबिम्बग्राहित्वम्, चैतन्यस्याभिव्यक्तत्वञ्च तत्र प्रतिबिम्बितत्वम्।

Objection: The individual self, which has nescience for its limiting adjunct and is unlimited, is naturally connected with everything. So it is absurd to speak of it as having no connection when there is an absence of a mental state; and if in view of its non-attachment[1] it is spoken of as having no connection, then even after the appearance of the mental state there would not be any connection.

Reply: The answer is, we do not deny a general connection of the individual self with a jar etc. when there is an absence of a mental state.

Objection: What, then?

Reply: But we deny that particular connection which leads to the cognition of the jar etc. That particular connection is a contingent relation of revealed and revealer between objects and the Consciousness that is the individual self, which is caused by mental states in the form of those objects. For instance, the luminous mind, being a transparent substance, can by itself[2] manifest[3] the Consciousness that is the individual self, but a jar etc. cannot do so, because they are opaque substances. When, however, they are connected with a mental state of the same form as they, their inertness is overcome by it; and being possessed of a capacity to manifest Consciousnes, imparted by the mental state, they manifest that Consciousness after the appearance of the mental state. So it has been stated in the *Vivarana*, "For the mind imparts to a jar etc. connected with it, as well as to itself, the capacity to manifest Consciousness" (p. 70, l. 13, adapted). It is also observed that even an opaque substance receives reflections when it is connected with a transparent substance; as, a wall, for instance, reflects the face etc. when it is in contact with water and the like. The property of manifestation possessed by a jar etc. is their power of catching a reflection of Consciousness, while the property of being manifested that is possessed by Consciousness is Its being reflected in them.

[[1] As set forth in *Br.* IV. iii. 15 and other Śrutis.
[2] Without the aid of any other thing.
[3] That is, catch the reflection of.]

एवंविधाभिव्यञ्जकत्वसिद्ध्यर्थमेव वृत्तेरपरोक्षस्थले बहिर्निर्गमनाङ्गीकारः। परोक्षस्थले तु वह्न्यादेर्वृत्तिसंसर्गाभावेन चैतन्यानभिव्यञ्जकतया नापरोक्षत्वम्। एतन्मते च विषयाणामपरोक्षत्वं चैतन्याभिव्यञ्जकत्वमिति द्रष्टव्यम्। एवं जीवस्यापरिच्छिन्नत्वेऽपि वृत्तेः सम्बन्धार्थत्वं निरूपितम्।

It is for establishing such property of manifestation that in cases of perception the mental state is admitted to issue outside.[1] But in cases of mediate knowledge,[2] since fire etc. have no connection with the mental state, they cannot manifest Consciousness, and hence they are not immediately known. It should also be noted that according to this view, the perceptibility of objects is their capacity to manifest Consciousness. Thus, even if the individual self be unlimited, it has been demonstrated how the mental state serves to establish a connection.

[[1] See p. 15.
[2] See note 7 on p. 186.]

इदानीं परिच्छिन्नत्वपक्षे सम्बन्धार्थत्वं निरूप्यते। तथाहि—अन्तःकरणोपाधिको जीवः। तस्य न घटाद्युपादानता, घटादिदेशासम्बन्धात्। किंतु ब्रह्मैव घटाद्युपादानम्, तस्य मायोपहितस्य सकलघटाद्यन्वयित्वात्। अत एव ब्रह्मणः सर्वज्ञता। तथाच जीवस्य घटाद्यधिष्ठानब्रह्मचैतन्याभेदमन्तरेण घटाद्यवभासासम्भवे प्राप्ते, तदवभासाय घटाद्यधिष्ठानब्रह्मचैतन्याभेदसिद्ध्यर्थं घटाद्याकारवृत्तिरिष्यते।

Now it is being shown how, even if the individual self be limited, the mental state serves to establish a connection. For instance, the individual self has the mind for its limiting adjunct. It cannot be the material cause of a jar etc., for it has no connection[1] with the place occupied by them.[2] But it is Brahman which is the material cause of the jar etc., for with the cosmic illusion as Its limiting adjunct, It is connected with all jars etc. For this very reason Brahman is omniscient. So, it being impossible for the individual self to reveal[3] a jar etc. except through its oneness with the Consciousness that is Brahman, which is their substratum, mental states in the form of the jar etc. are admitted in order to establish that oneness with the Consciousness that is Brahman, which is their substratum, with a view to making the revelation possible.

[1 Being limited.
2 Whereas the cause and effect must co-exist.
3 Through perception.]

ननु वृत्त्यापि कथं प्रमातृचैतन्यविषयचैतन्ययोरभेदः सम्पाद्यते, घटान्तःकरणरूपोपाधिभेदेन तदवच्छिन्नचैतन्ययोरभेदासम्भवात्, इति चेत्, न। वृत्तेर्बहिर्देशनिर्गमनाङ्गीकारेण वृत्त्यन्तःकरणविषयाणामेकदेशस्थत्वेन तदुपधेयभेदाभावस्य उक्तत्वात्। एवमपरोक्षस्थले वृत्तेर्मतभेदेन विनियोग उपपादितः।

Objection: How can oneness between the Consciousness associated with the subject and that associated with the object be effected even by a mental state, since their limiting adjuncts, viz., the mind and a jar etc., being different, the two Consciousness circumscribed by them cannot be one?

Reply: Not so, for by the administration of the mental state reaching places outside the body it has already been mentioned that the mental state, the mind and the object occupy the same place, and hence the things that have them for their limiting adjuncts are not different from each other.[1] Thus the application of the mental state to a case of perception has been demonstrated according to alternative views.[2]

[1 See p. 16.
2 About the individual self being unlimited or limited.]

Dream and Profound Sleep the Individual Self

इन्द्रियाजन्यविषयगोचरापरोक्षान्तःकरणवृत्त्यवस्था स्वप्नावस्था। जाग्रदवस्थाव्यावृत्त्यर्थम् 'इन्द्रियाजन्ये'ति। अविद्यावृत्तिमत्यां सुषुप्तावतिव्याप्तिवारणाय 'अन्तःकरणे'ति। सुषुप्तिर्नाम अविद्यागोचराविद्यावृत्त्यवस्था। जाग्रत्स्वप्नयोरविद्याकारवृत्तेरन्तःकरणवृत्तित्वान्न तत्रातिव्याप्तिः। अत्र केचिन्मरणमूर्छयोरवस्थान्तरत्वमाहुः, अपरे तु सुषुप्तावेव तयोरन्तर्भावमाहुः। तत्र तयोरवस्थात्रयान्तर्भावबहिर्भावयोः 'त्वं'-पदार्थनिरूपणे उपयोगाभावात् न तत्र प्रयत्यते।

The dream condition[1] is that in which illusory objects are immediately cognised by a mental state that is not caused by the organs.[2] The clause, "That is not caused by the organs," is for excluding the waking condition.[3] In order to guard against the definition unwarrantedly including profound sleep, which has a state of nescience, the word 'mental' has been inserted. Profound sleep is that condition in which a state of nescience has nescience for its object.[4] Since the state resembling[5] nescience in the waking condition and dream[6] is a *mental* state, the definition does not unwarrantedly include them. Regarding this[7] some say that death and swoon are other conditions. Others, however, maintain that they are included in profound sleep. Now as their inclusion in the three conditions or exclusion from them has no bearing on the ascertainment of the meaning of the word 'thou,' no attempt is being made to deal with it.

[[1] Here the author seems to differ from the general view that in dreams there are no mental modifications, but only modifications of nescience.

[2] But by an adventitious defect, viz., sleep.

[3] In which objects are cognised with the help of the organs. See p. 184, top.

[4] A man waking from sleep says, "I slept happily, I knew nothing." This recollection of the natural bliss of the self as also of ignorance is a proof that in profound sleep nescience only functions, not the mind; and the object of that immediate modification of nescience is also nescience.

[5] For example, in the statement, "I do not know a jar." Here the unawareness is apprehended not by a state of nescience, but by a mental state.

[6] Here also the author seems to differ from the accepted view.

[7] Classification of the conditions.]

तस्य मायोपाध्यपेक्षया एकत्वम्, अन्तःकरणोपाध्यपेक्षया च नानात्वं व्यवह्रियते। एतेन जीवस्याणुत्वं प्रत्युक्तम्,

"बुद्धेर्गुणेनात्मगुणेन चैवं
ह्याराग्रमात्रो ह्यवरोऽपि दृष्टः।"

इत्यादौ जीवस्य 'बुद्धि'-शब्दवाच्यान्तःकरणपरिणामोपाधिकस्य परमाणुत्वश्रवणात्।

The individual self[1] is treated as one in respect of its limiting adjunct, nescience,[2] and manifold in respect of its limiting adjuncts, the different minds. By this[3] the atomicity[4] of the individual self is refuted, for in texts like, "Through the attribute[5] of the intellect it is seen to have the size of the point of an awl, and by its own attribute,[6] vaster than anything else, (*Śv.* 7), the Śruti speaks of the individual self as infinitesimal, because that modification of the mind which is signified by the word 'intellect', is its limiting adjunct.[7]

[[1] Which is the meaning of the word 'thou.'

[2] Which is one.

[3] That is, as the manifoldness is but apparent, being merely due to limiting adjuncts.

[4] Held by Rāmānujācārya and others.

[5] That is, subtlety.

[6] Viz., omnipresence.

[7] So the word 'infinitesimal' here means 'subtle,' as the mind is. The last line of the text has got several readings, one of which is **परिमाणोपाधिकपरमाणुत्वश्रवणात्,** meaning, "Because the *size* of the mind, which is signified" etc. In another reading the end portion is **परिमाणश्रवणात्,** in which case the sentence would mean: "The Śruti speaks of the individual self as being of a size that has for its limiting adjunct the size of the mind, signified by the word 'intellect.'"]

स च जीवः स्वयंप्रकाशः, स्वप्नावस्थामधिकृत्य "अत्रायं पुरुषः स्वयं ज्योतिः" इति श्रुतेः। अनुभवरूपश्च, "प्रज्ञानघन एव" इत्यादिश्रुतेः। 'अनुभवामि' इति व्यवहारस्तु वृत्ति प्रतिबिम्बितचैतन्यमादाय उपपद्यते।

एवं 'त्वम्'-पदार्थो निरूपितः।

That individual self is self-effulgent, for regarding its dream condition the Śruti says, "In this state the man himself becomes the light" (*Bṛ.* IV. iii. 9). And it is Knowledge itself,[1] for the Śruti says, "It is Pure Intelligence alone" (*Bṛ.* IV. v. 13). As for the use of the expression, "I know," it is explicable by a reference to the Consciousness reflected in the mental state.

Thus the meaning of the word 'thou' has been ascertained.

[[1] That is, Knowledge Absolute.]

The Identity of the Meaning of 'That' and 'Thou'

अधुना 'तत्-त्वम्'-पदार्थयोरैक्यं महावाक्यप्रतिपाद्यमभिधीयते। ननु "नाहमीश्वरः" इत्यादिप्रत्यक्षेण, किञ्चिज्ज्ञत्वसर्वज्ञत्वादिविरुद्धधर्माश्रयत्वादिलिङ्गेन, "द्वा सुपर्णा" इत्यादिश्रुत्या,

"द्वाविमौ पुरुषौ लोके क्षरश्चाक्षर एव च।
क्षरः सर्वाणि भूतानि कूटस्थोऽक्षर उच्यते॥"

इत्यादिस्मृत्या च जीवपरभेदस्यावगतत्वेन "तत्त्वमस्या"-दिवाक्यम् "आदित्यो यूपः," "यजमानः प्रस्तरः" इत्यादिवाक्यवदुपचरितार्थमेव, इति चेत्, न। भेदप्रत्यक्षस्य सम्भावितकरणदोषस्यासम्भावितदोषवेदजन्यज्ञानेन बाध्यमानत्वात्। अन्यथा चन्द्रगताधिकपरिमाणग्राहिज्योतिःशास्त्रस्य चन्द्रप्रादेशग्राहिप्रत्यक्षेण बाधापत्तेः। पाकरक्ते घटे

"रक्तोऽयम्, न श्यामः" इतिवत् "सविशेषणे हि" इति न्यायेन जीवपरभेदग्राहिप्रत्यक्षस्य विशेषणीभूतधर्मभेदविषयत्वाच्च। अत एव नानुमानमपि प्रमाणम्, आगमविरोधात्, मेरुपाषाणमयत्वानुमानवत्।

Now the identity of the meanings of the words 'That' and 'thou,' which is the signification of the great dictum,[1] is being set forth.

Objection: Since different between the individual self and Brahman is known from such perception as, "I am not God," from (the inference based on) the sign[2] that the self possesses contradictory attributes[3] such as limited knowledge and omniscience, from the Śruti texts, "Two birds of beautiful wings" etc.[4] (*R.* I. clxiv. 11; *Mu.* III. i. 1; *Śv.* IV. 6), and from such Smṛti texts as, "In the world there are these two entities (*puruṣa*)—the mutable and the Immutable; the mutable one comprises all beings,[5] and the changeless (Brahman) is called the Immutable" (*G.* XV. 16)—dictums like, "Thou art That" (*Chā.* VI. viii. 7 ff.), convey only a figurative meaning,[6] like sentences such as, "The sacrificial post is the sun" (*Tai.* Br. II. 1. v. 2), and "The sheaf of *kuśa*[7] grass is the sacrificer" (*Ibid. III.* III. ix. 2, 3).

Reply: No, for the perception of difference, which is likely to be attended with the defects of its instruments,[8] is nullified by the knowledge arising from the Vedas, in which there is no possibility of any defect.[9] Otherwise,[10] astronomy, which observes the great size of the moon, would be nullified by perception, which notices it to be no bigger than a span. Besides, like the perception regarding a jar baked red that it is red, not dark,[11] the perception that cognises a difference between the individual self and God concerns the difference between their qualifying attributes only,[12] on the principle, "In the case of a qualified entity" etc.[13] Hence neither is inference a proof on the matter, for it is contradicted by scriptural evidence, as is the case with the inference about Mount Meru being made of stone.[14]

[1 "Thou art That."

2 The reason or ground for inference.

3 As we know from scriptural testimony.

4 The whole verse runs thus: "Two birds of beautiful wings (the self and Brahman), which are friends and constant companions, perch on the same tree (the body). One of these (the self) eats sweet fruits (enjoys heaven etc.), and the other merely looks on, without eating." Here the self and Brahman are clearly differentiated.

5 The *bodies* of all beings from Hiraṇyagarbha downwards. These are called 'beings,' as the ignorant identify themselves with their bodies.

6 And not identity.

7 *Poa cynosuroides.*

8 The organs such as the eyes.

9 Because they are not of human origin.

10 If perception be given precedence over scriptural testimony simply because it is the first of the means of knowledge.

[11] Where the difference is not in the thing, but in its attributes only.

[12] And not the underlying substance, viz., Pure Consciousness, which is identical.

[13] The whole passage reads thus: "In the case of a qualified entity, if the injunction or prohibition cannot refer to the substantive, then it refers to the qualifying attributes." For example, when a robber turns a saint, we may say, "The robber is dead, the saint is born." Here the difference is not with regard to the identity of the person, but only with regard to his attributes. Similarly, all the difference between the individual self and God is in respect of limited knowledge and omniscience, etc. Divested of the qualifying attributes, the two are identical.

[14] While according to the scriptures it is made of gold. In the face of that, it cannot be inferred to be made of stone simply on the ground of its being a mountain. In matters pertaining to the unseen realm the primacy goes to the scriptures.]

नाप्यागमान्तरविरोधः। तत्परातत्परवाक्ययोस्तत्परवाक्यस्य बलवत्त्वेन लोकसिद्धभेदानुवादि-"द्वा सुपर्णौ"त्यादिवाक्यापेक्षया उपक्रमोपसंहाराद्यवगताद्वैततात्पर्यविशिष्टस्य "तत्त्वमस्या"दिवाक्यस्य प्रबलत्वात्। न च जीवपरैक्ये विरुद्धधर्माश्रयत्वानुपपत्तिः, शीतस्यैव जलस्यौपाधिकौष्ण्याश्रयत्ववत् स्वभावतो निर्गुणस्यैव जीवस्यान्तःकरणाद्युपाधिककर्तृत्वाद्याश्रयत्वप्रतिभासोपपत्तेः। यदि च जलादावौष्ण्यमारोपितम्, तदा प्रकृतेऽपि तुल्यम्। न च सिद्धान्ते कर्तृत्वस्य क्वचिदप्यभावादारोप्यप्रमाहितसंस्काराभावे

कथमारोपः, इति वाच्यम्, लाघवेनारोप्यविषयकसंस्कार-त्वेनैव तस्य हेतुत्वात्। न च प्राथमिकारोपे का गतिः, कर्तृत्वाद्यध्यासप्रवाहस्यानादित्वात्।

Nor is there any conflict with other scriptural texts, for, between a sentence inculcating an identity of the individual self with Brahman and one not doing so, the former is stronger, and hence dictums like, "Thou art That" (*Chā.* VI. viii. 7 ff), which from their introduction, conclusion, etc.,[1] are known to convey non-duality, are stronger than texts as, "Two birds of beautiful wings,"[2] etc., which merely repeat the difference that is already accepted in the world. It cannot be urged that if the individual self be identical with Brahman, its possession of contradictory attributes cannot be explained; for just as (naturally) cold water may (temporarily) possesses heat belonging to its limiting adjunct,[3] similarly, we can understand that the individual self, which is naturally devoid of attributes, may appear to possess agency etc. owing to its limiting adjuncts, such as the mind. If it is said that the heat is superimposed on the water etc., then it is equally the case with the matter at issue. It cannot be questioned how, in the absence of any latent impression left by a valid knowledge of the thing superimposed, there can ever be a superimposition, since according to Vedānta, there is no (real) agency anywhere.[5] Because, on grounds of simplicity, that impression can be a cause[6] as a latent impression[7] regarding the thing superimposed.[8] Nor can it be urged: How to explain the first superimposition? For the stream of superimpositions regarding agency etc. has no beginning.[9]

[[1] The six tests for determining the purport of a scriptural passage, viz., introduction, conclusion, repetition (of the topic at intervals), originality (of the teaching), result (achieved from it), eulogy, and demonstration (through reasoning etc.). For instance, the topic of chapter VI of the *Chāndogya Upaniṣad*, viz., the unity of Brahman, is *introduced* in section ii and *concluded* in the last section. It is *repeated* nine times in the last paragraphs of sections vii—xvi. The unity of Brahman is known only from the Upaniṣads and from no other source (*originality*). It *results* in liberation. It is *eulogised* in the third paragraph of section i as bringing within one's reach things that have not even been thought of. The topic has been *demonstrated* in section i. 4-6 by three illustrations showing that effects are not different from their material causes.

[2] See note 4 on p. 197.

[3] Viz., the element fire, which is mixed up with it.

[4] Viz., agency.

[5] Either in the self or in the mind.

[6] Of the superimposition.

[7] Whether the previous knowledge that leaves it is valid or not.

[8] That is, instead of saying that the latent impression of a *valid* knowledge of agency causes the superimposition, it is simpler to say that *any* latent impression of it, whether valid or invalid, is the cause.

[9] Like the universe of which they are a part, superimpositions are but continually repeating themselves from cycle to cycle.]

तत्र 'तत्त्वम्'-पदवाच्ययोर्विशिष्टयोरैक्यायोगेऽपि लक्ष्य-स्वरूपयोरैक्यमुपपादितमेव। अत एव तत्प्रतिपादक-"तत्त्वमस्या"दिवाक्यानामखण्डार्थत्वम्, "सोऽयम्" इत्यादि-वाक्यवत्। न च कार्यपराणामेव प्रामाण्यम्, "चैत्र, पुत्रस्ते जातः" इत्यादौ सिद्धेऽपि सङ्गतिग्रहात्।

Here,[1] although the qualified entities[2] which are the primary meanings of the words 'thou' and 'That' cannot be identified, yet the identity of their implied meaning,[3] the underlying essence,[4] is conclusively proved.[5] Hence sentences like, "Thou art That," which inculcate that identity, convey a simple notion of identity,[6] like sentences such as, "This is he." It is not that only sentences expressing action have validity,[7] for in the case of sentences like, "Caitra, a son has been born to you," the meanings of the words are apprehended even with regard to statements of fact.[8]

[[1] In the great dictum, "Thou art That."

[2] Viz., the individual self and God, which are possesed of contradictory attributes.

[3] This is stated in accordance with the traditional view. See p. 98. According to the author himself there is no implication in such cases. See p. 100.

[4] Viz., Pure Consciousness.

[5] In this discussion.

[6] See p. 36.

[7] As the Prābhākara school of Mīmāṁsakas maintains.

[8] Which require no activity to bring them about.]

एवं सर्वप्रमाणाविरूद्धं श्रुतिस्मृतीतिहासपुराणप्रतिपाद्यं जीवपरैक्यं वेदान्तशास्त्रस्य विषय इति सिद्धम् ।

इति वेदान्तपरिभाषायां विषयपरिच्छेदः ।

Thus the identity of the individual self and Brahman, which is taught by the Śrutis, Smṛtis, histories and Purāṇas, and is in consonance with the findings of all means of knowledge, is the subject-matter of the Vedānta philosophy.

CHAPTER VIII

THE AIM OF VEDĀNTA

THE AIMS OF LIFE: RELATIVE AND ABSOLUTE BLISS

इदानीं प्रयोजनं निरूप्यते। यदवगतं सत् स्ववृत्तितया इष्यते तत् प्रयोजनम्। तच्च द्विविधम्-मुख्यं गौणञ्चेति। तत्र सुखदुःखाभावौ मुख्ये प्रयोजने, तदन्यतरसाधनं गौणं प्रयोजनम्। सुखञ्च द्विविधम्—सातिशयं निरतिशयञ्चेति। तत्र सातिशयं सुखं विषयानुषङ्गजनितान्तःकरणवृत्तितारतम्यकृतानन्दलेशाविर्भावविशेषः, "एतस्यैवानन्दस्यान्यानि भूतानि मात्रामुपजीवन्ति" इत्यादिश्रुतेः। निरतिशयं सुखञ्च ब्रह्मैव, "आनन्दो ब्रह्मेति व्यजानात्," "विज्ञानमानन्दं ब्रह्म" इत्यादिश्रुतेः।

Now the aim of Vedānta is being described. That which being known is desired to belong to oneself is called an aim. It is of two kinds—primary and secondary. Of these, pleasure and the absence of pain are primary aims, and the means to either of them is the secondary aim. Pleasure is also of two kinds—relative and absolute. Of these, relative pleasure is a particular manifestation of a modicum of bliss caused by difference in the mental state generated by a contact with objects. Witness such Śruti texts as, "Other beings live on a particle of this very bliss" (*Bṛ.* IV. iii. 32). Absolute bliss is Brahman alone. For we have such Śruti texts as, "He knew that Bliss was Brahman" (*Tai.* III. 6), and "Brahman, which is Knowledge and Bliss" (*Bṛ.* III. ix. xxviii. 7).

THE NATURE OF LIBERATION

आनन्दात्मकब्रह्मावाप्तिश्च मोक्षः, शोकनिवृत्तिश्च, "ब्रह्म वेद ब्रह्मैव भवति," "तरति शोकमात्मवित्" इत्यादि-श्रुतेः। न तु लोकान्तरावाप्तिः, तज्जन्यवैषयिकानन्दो वा मोक्षः, तस्य कृतकत्वेनानित्यत्वे मुक्तस्य पुनरावृत्त्यापत्तेः।

The attainment of Brahman, which is Bliss, as also the cessation of grief is liberation; for we have Śruti texts like, "He who knows that (Supreme) Brahman becomes Brahman Itself" (*Mu.* III. ii. 9), and "The knower of the Self transcends grief" (*Chā.* VII. i. 3). Going to another world, or the joy derived from objects consequent on that, is not liberation, for, being a product, it is ephemeral, and this would lead to a return of the liberated.

ननु त्वन्मतेऽप्यानन्दावाप्तेरनर्थनिवृत्तेश्च सादित्वे तुल्यो दोषः, अनादित्वे मोक्षमुद्दिश्य श्रवणादौ प्रवृत्त्यनुपपत्तिरिति चेत्, न, सिद्धस्यैव ब्रह्मस्वरूपस्य मोक्षस्यासिद्धत्वभ्रमेण तत्साधने प्रवृत्त्युपपत्तेः। अनर्थनिवृत्तिरप्यधिष्ठानभूतब्रह्म-स्वरूपतया सिद्धैव। लोकेऽपि प्राप्तप्राप्ति-परिहृतपरिहारयोः

प्रयोजनत्वं दृष्टमेव। यथा हस्तगतविस्मृतसुवर्णादौ "तव हस्ते सुवर्णम्" इत्याप्तोपदेशादप्राप्तमिव प्राप्नोति। यथा वा वलयितचरणायां स्रजि सर्पत्वभ्रमवतः "नायं सर्पः" इत्याप्तवाक्यात् परिहृतस्यैव सर्पस्य परिहारः। एवं प्राप्तस्याप्यानन्दस्य प्राप्तिः, परिहृतस्याप्यनर्थस्य निवृत्तिर्मोक्षः प्रयोजनञ्च।

Objection: Even according to your view, if the attainment of bliss and the cessation of troubles have a beginning, then it is open to the same defect,[1] and if it is without a beginning, then there cannot be any inclination[2] for hearing etc.[3] for the purpose of liberation.

Reply: Not so, for although liberation, which is identical with Brahman, is already achieved, yet, through a mistaken notion about its not being achieved, one can feel inclined to attain it. And the cessation of troubles, since it is identical with its substratum,[4] Brahman, is also a thing already achieved. In the world, too, the attainment of what is already attained and the avoidance of what is already avoided, are patent aims. For instance, with regard to gold that is in one's hand but has been forgotten, the instruction of a trustworthy person saying, "The gold is in your hand," makes one attain it as if it were not already attained. Or when one has mistaken a garland twining round one's leg for a snake, the words of a trustworthy person saying, "This is not a snake," make one get rid of the snake that was already got rid of. Similarly, the attainment of bliss, although it is already attained, and the cessation of troubles, although they are already got rid of, is liberation, and it is the aim (of Vedānta).

[[1] That is, being a product, it will cause the liberated to return.

[2] Since the result is already achieved.

[3] Refers to reflection and meditation.

[4] Everything in the universe, whether positive or negative, is a superimposition on Brahman, and hence has no independent existence of its own.]

स च ज्ञानैकसाध्यः, "तमेव विदित्वाऽतिमृत्युमेति, नान्यः पन्था विद्यतेऽयनाय" इति श्रुतेः, अज्ञाननिवृत्तेः ज्ञानैकसाध्यत्वनियमाच्च। तच्च ज्ञानं ब्रह्मात्मैक्यगोचरम्, "अभयं वै जनक प्राप्तोऽसि," "तदात्मानमेवावेत—अहं ब्रह्मास्मि" इत्यादिश्रुतेः, "तत्त्वमस्यादिवाक्योत्थं ज्ञानं मोक्षस्य साधनम्" इति नारदीयवचनाच्च।

That liberation is achieved only through knowledge, for the Śruti says, "Knowing Him alone one transcends death; there is no other way to follow" (*Śv.* III. 8, VI. 15), and, besides, it is the rule that the cessation of ignorance takes place only through knowledge. That knowledge has for its object the identity of the individual self with Brahman, for the Śruti says, "You have attained fearlessness, O Janaka" (*Bṛ.* IV. ii. 4), and "It knew Itself as: I am Brahman"

(*Ibid.* I. iv. 10), and there is the statement of the *Bṛhannāradīya Purāṇa*, "The means to liberation is the knowledge arising from dictums like: Thou art That" (XXXIII. 66).

TWO VIEWS ABOUT IMMEDIATE KNOWLEDGE

तच्च ज्ञानमपरोक्षरूपम्, परोक्षत्वेऽपरोक्षभ्रमनिवर्तकत्वानुपपत्तेः। तच्चापरोक्षज्ञानं "तत्त्वमस्या"दिवाक्यादिति केचित्, मननिदिध्यासनसंस्कृतान्तःकरणादेवेत्यपरे।

That knowledge, again, is immediate, for were it mediate, it would not be calculated to remove error, which is immediate. According to some,[1] that immediate knowledge arises from dictums like, "Thou art That" (*Chā.* VI. viii. 7 ff). According to others,[2] it arises from the mind itself, purified by reflection and meditation.

[[1] The reference is to Padmapāda, Sureśvara and their followers.

[2] The reference is to Vācaspati Miśra and his school.]

तत्र पूर्वाचार्याणामयमाशयः—संविदापरोक्ष्यं न करणविशेषोत्पत्तिनिबन्धनम्, किन्तु प्रमेयविशेषनिबन्धनम् इत्युपपादितम्। तथाच ब्रह्मणः प्रमातृजीवाभिन्नतया तद्गोचरं शब्दजन्यमपि ज्ञानमपरोक्षम्। अत एव प्रतर्दनाधिकरणे प्रतर्दनं प्रति "प्राणोऽस्मि प्रज्ञात्मा, तं मामायुरमृतमुपास्व" इति इन्द्रप्रोक्तवाक्ये 'प्राण'-शब्दस्य ब्रह्मपरत्वे निश्चिते सति "मामुपास्व" इत्यस्मच्छब्दानुपपत्तिमाशङ्क्य तदुत्तरत्वेन

प्रवृत्ते "शास्त्रदृष्ट्या तूपदेशो वामदेववत्" इत्यत्र सूत्रे शास्त्रीया दृष्टिः शास्त्रदृष्टिः, "तत्त्वमस्या"दिवाक्यजन्यम् "अहं ब्रह्म" इति ज्ञानं 'शास्त्रदृष्टि'-शब्देनोक्तमिति ।

Of these, the teachers of the former school opine as follows: The immediacy of cognition, as has been proved,[1] is due not to its originating through a particular instrument, but to a particular object of knowledge.[2] So Brahman, not being different[3] from the individual self or the subject, the knowledge if It, although produced by words, is immediate. Hence under the topic relating to Pratardana,[4] after it has been decided[5] that the word *Prāṇa,* in the sentence, "I am *Prāṇa,* the intelligent Self; mediate on Me as that and as longevity and immortality" (*Kau.* III. 2), spoken by Indra to Pratardana, refers to Brahman, an objection is raised[6] as to how the use of a form of the word 'I' in "Mediate on Me" is justified. And in the aphorism, "But the instruction is from the scriptural point of view, as in the case of Vāmadeva"[7] which sets about to answer the objection, it is stated that the phrase 'scriptural point of view' means: an attitude that is recommended by the scriptures, that is, the knowledge, "I am Brahman," produced by sentences like, "Thou art That."

[[1] On pp. 19 and 34.

[2] Whether a cognition is immediate or mediate depends not on the organ or mind, but on the nature of the object. When the object is in contact with a

sense organ, perception may arise even from verbal testimony.

[3] That is, since the individual self is really identical with Brahman.

[4] Topic 11, *Br̥.* S. I. i, aphorisms 28-31.

[5] *Ibid.*, aphorism 28.

[6] *Ibid.*, aphorism 29. Because apparently the 'me' refers to Indra, whereas meditation on Brahman alone can be of the highest good to man. The allusion is this: Pratardana, the son of Divodāsa, went to Indra's heaven by dint of his valour in battle. Indra offered him a boon and was requested by him to choose for him one that would be most beneficial to men. Thereupon Indra spoke those words.

[7] *Ibid.*, aphorism 30. Vāmadeva, realising his identity with Brahman, said, "I was the sun, as also Manu" (*Br̥.* I. iv. 10). Here also Indra spoke with that feeling of identity with Brahman.]

अन्येषां त्वेवमाशयः—करणविशेषनिबन्धनमेव ज्ञानानां प्रत्यक्षत्वम्, न विषयविशेषनिबन्धनम्, एकस्मिन्नेव सूक्ष्मवस्तुनि पटुकरणापटुकरणयोः प्रत्यक्षत्वाप्रत्यक्षत्वव्यवहारदर्शनात्। तथाच संवित्साक्षात्त्वे इन्द्रियजन्यत्वस्यैव प्रयोजकतया न शब्दजन्यज्ञानस्यापरोक्षत्वम्। ब्रह्मसाक्षात्कारेऽपि मनननिदिध्यासनसंस्कृतं मन एव करणम्, "मनसैवानुद्रष्टव्यम्" इत्यादिश्रुतेः। मनोऽगम्यत्वश्रुतिश्चासंस्कृतमनोविषया। न चैवं ब्रह्मण औपनिषदत्वानुपपत्तिः, अस्मदुक्तमनसो वेदजन्यज्ञानानन्तरमेव प्रवृत्ततया वेदोपजीवित्वात्; वेदानुपजीविमानान्तरगम्यत्वस्यैव वेदगम्यत्व-

विरोधित्वात्। 'शास्त्रदृष्टि'-सूत्रमपि ब्रह्मविषयकमानस-प्रत्यक्षस्य शास्त्रप्रयोज्यत्वादुपपद्यते। तदुक्तम्—

"'अपि संराधने' सूत्रात् शास्त्रार्थध्यानजा प्रमा।
शास्त्रदृष्टिर्मता, तान्तु वेत्ति वाचस्पतिः परम्॥"

The other school, however, maintains thus: The perceptuality of cognitions depends only on particular instruments, and not on particular objects; for we observe that with regard to one and the same subtle object, the expression 'perceptible' or 'imperceptible' is used by two persons who have a strong or a weak instrument.[1] Hence, since the criterion of the immediacy of cognition is only its being caused by an organ,[2] the knowledge produced by words is not immediate. With regard to the realisation of Brahman also, only the mind purified by reflection and meditation is the instrument, for we have Śruti texts like, "Through the mind alone It is to be realised."[3] And the Śruti texts[4] that speak of Brahman as being inaccessible to the mind, refer to a mind that is not purified. And this does not militate against the fact that Brahman is to be known only from the Upaniṣads,[5] for the mind as described by us proceeds on its inquiry only after it has the knowledge inculcated by the Vedas, and hence it depends on them. What contradicts the fact of Brahman's being known only through the Vedas is the fact of Its being known through other means of knowledge that do not depend on the Vedas. The aphorism relating to the scriptural point of view, too, is justified, because the mental perception of Brahman is based on (knowledge derived from) the scriptures. So it has been said, "The valid knowledge that arises from meditation on the meaning of the (Vedāntic) scriptures is regarded as the scriptural point of view. We know this from the aphorism 'Besides during adoration.'[6] But Vācaspati alone knows it well."[7]

[[1] A man with keen eyes notices things that a man with weak eyes does not. The former would call them visible, and the latter, invisible.

[2] That is, since a cognition is immediate only when it arises through an organ.

[3] *Bṛ.* IV. iv. 19. The prefix *anu* in the verb *anudraṣṭavyam,* translated here simply as 'realised,' suggests that the realisation should be *after* the instruction of the teacher.

[4] Such as, "That which one cannot think of through the mind" (*Kena Up.*, I. 6), and "That from which words come back together with the mind without attaining It" (*Tai.* III. 9).

[5] Cf. *Bṛ.* III. ix. 26.

[6] *Bṛ. S.* III. ii. 24. The whole aphorism runs thus: "Besides (*yogins* see It) during adoration, (as we know) from perception (the Śruti) and inference (the Smṛti)."

[7] *Vedānta-kalpataru.* This is a gloss by Amalānanda Svāmin on Vācaspati Miśra's *Bhāmatī.* See note 3 on p. 1.]

The Means to Realisation: Their Mutual Relation

तच्च ज्ञानं पापक्षयात्, स च कर्मानुष्ठानादिति परम्परया कर्मणां विनियोगः। अत एव "तमेतं वेदानुवचनेन ब्राह्मणा विविदिषन्ति यज्ञेन दानेन तपसाऽनाशकेन" इत्यादिश्रुतिः, "कषाये कर्मभिः पक्वे ततो ज्ञानं प्रवर्तते" इत्यादिस्मृतिश्च सङ्गच्छते।

That knowledge comes from the exhaustion of demerits, and that, again, from the performance of rites. Hence rites are indirectly of use. Therefore Śruti texts like, "The Brāhmaṇas seek to know It through the study of the Vedas, sacrifices, charity, and austerity consisting in a dispassionate enjoyment of sense-objects" (*Bṛ.* IV. iv. 22). and Smṛti texts such as, "When the taint(of the mind) has been burnt by rites, knowledge manifests itself," are appropriate.

एवं श्रवणमनननिदिध्यासनान्यपि ज्ञानसाधनानि, मैत्रेयीब्राह्मणे "आत्मा वा अरे द्रष्टव्यः" इति दर्शनमनूद्य तत्साधनत्वेन "श्रोतव्यो मन्तव्यो निदिध्यासितव्यः" इति श्रवणमनननिदिध्यासनानां विधानात्। श्रवणं नाम वेदान्तानामद्वितीये ब्रह्मणि तात्पर्यावधारणानुकूला मानसी क्रिया। मननं नाम शब्दावधारितेऽर्थे मानान्तरविरोधशङ्कायां तन्निराकरणानुकूलतर्कात्मकज्ञानजनको मानसो व्यापारः। निदिध्यासनं नाम अनादिदुर्वासनया विषयेष्वाकृष्यमाणस्य

चित्तस्य विषयेभ्योऽपकृष्य आत्मविषयकस्थैर्यानुकूलो मानसो व्यापारः।

Similarly, hearing, reflection and meditation also are means to knowledge, since in the section[1] relating to Maitreyī, for the purpose of realisation—introduced in the passage, "The Self indeed, my dear (Maitreyī), should be realised" (*Bṛ.* II. iv. 5; IV. v. 6)—hearing, reflection and meditation are enjoined as means to that in the words, "Is to be heard of, reflected on, and meditated upon" (*Ibid.*). Hearing is a mental activity leading to the conviction that the Vedāntic texts inculcate only Brahman, the One without a second. Reflection is a mental operation producing ratiocinative knowledge that leads to the refutation of any possible contradiction from other sources[2] of knowledge regarding the meaning established by scriptural testimony.[3] Meditation is a mental operation helping to fix the mind on the Self by withdrawing it from objects, when it is drawn towards them by latent evil impressions that have no beginning.[4]

[[1] *Bṛ.* II. iv. and IV. v.
[2] Perception, inference, etc.
[3] Such as, "Thou art That."
[4] Because they are superimposed as a stream on the eternal self, it is impossible to trace their origin.]

तत्र निदिध्यासनं ब्रह्मसाक्षात्कारे साक्षात् कारणम्, "ते ध्यानयोगानुगता अपश्यन्, देवात्मशक्तिं स्वगुणैर्निगूढाम्"

इत्यादिश्रुतेः। निदिध्यासने च मननं हेतुः, अकृतमननस्यार्थदार्ढ्याभावेन तद्विषयकनिदिध्यासनायोगात्। मनने च श्रवणं हेतुः, श्रवणाभावे तात्पर्यानिश्चयेन शाब्दज्ञानाभावेन श्रुतार्थविषयकयुक्तत्वायुक्तत्वनिश्चयानुकूलमननायोगात्। एतानि त्रीण्यपि ज्ञानोत्पत्तौ कारणानीति केचिदाचार्या ऊचिरे।

Of these, meditation is the direct cause of the realisation of Brahman, for we have Śruti texts like, "Following the *yoga* of meditation, they visualised that power,[1] which is identical with the Supreme Being, and is hidden by its own ingredients (*guṇas*)" (*Śv.* I. 3). Reflection is a cause of meditation, because it is not possible for a person who has not reflected to meditate on the meaning of what has been heard of, for he lacks a conviction about it. And hearing is a cause of reflection, because in the absence of hearing, the intention (of a passage) cannot be ascertained, and consequently no verbal comprehension can take place, with the result that there cannot be reflection leading to a certitude about the reasonableness or otherwise of the meaning of what has been heard of. Some teachers[2] have said that all the three are causes of the origination of knowledge.

[[1] The cosmic illusion.
[2] The reference is to Vācaspati Miśra.]

अपरे तु श्रवणं प्रधानम्, मनननिदिध्यासनयोस्तु श्रवणात् पराचीनयोरपि श्रवणफलब्रह्मदर्शननिर्वर्तकतया

आरादुपकारकतयाऽङ्गत्वमित्याहुः। तदप्यङ्गत्वं न तार्तीय-शेषत्वरूपम्, तस्य श्रुत्याद्यन्यतमप्रमाणगम्यस्य प्रकृते श्रुत्याद्यभावेऽसम्भवात्। तथाहि "व्रीहिभिर्यजेत," "दध्ना जुहोति" इत्यादाविव मनननिदिध्यासनयोरङ्गत्वे न काचित् तृतीया श्रुतिरस्ति। नापि "बर्हिर्देवसदनं दामि" इत्यादि-मन्त्राणां बर्हिःखण्डनप्रकाशनसामर्थ्यवत् किञ्चिल्लिङ्गमस्ति। नापि प्रदेशान्तरपठितस्य प्रवर्ग्यस्य "अग्निष्टोमे प्रवृणक्ति" इति वाक्यवत् श्रवणानुवादेन मनननिदिध्यासनविनियोजकं किञ्चिद्वाक्यमस्ति। नापि "दर्शपूर्णमासाभ्यां स्वर्गकामो यजेत" इति वाक्यावगतफलसाधनताकदर्शपूर्णमासप्रकरणे प्रयाजादीनामिव फलसाधनत्वेनावगतस्य श्रवणस्य प्रकरणे मनननिदिध्यासनयोराम्नानम्।

Others,[1] however, maintain that hearing is the principal cause, while reflection and meditation, although they are subsequent to hearing.[2] serve to usher the realisation of Brahman, which is the result of hearing, and therefore, being directly helpful,[3] are subsidiary factors. This susidiariness, too, does not consist in their being parts of the kind discussed in the third chapter of the *Pūrva-Mīmāṁsā-Sūtras*,[4] for the latter, being known from one or other of the (six) tests such as direct enunciation (*śruti*), cannot fit in with the topic under discussion, since direct enunciation etc. are absent here. For instance, there is no third case-ending to show that reflection and meditation are parts (of hearing), as in the case of passages like, "One should sacrifice with rice grains," and "One should sacrifice with curd." Nor is there any indication, such as the capacity of sacred texts like, "I cut thee, O *kuśa* grass, who art the seat of the gods" (*Maitrāyaṇī Saṁhitā* I. i. 2, i. 9), to express the cutting of the *kuśa* grass.[5] Nor is there any supplementary statement directing[6] the use of reflection and meditation as a corollary to hearing (already enjoined), like the statement, "One should perform the Pravarga rite in the Agniṣṭoma sacrifice," with regard to the Pravarga, mentioned in a different place. Nor[7] are reflection and meditation mentioned by the Śruti in a context relating to hearing, which is known to be a means to the result,[8] as the Prayāja[9] sacrifices etc. are mentioned[10] in a context relating to the new- and full-moon sacrifices, which are known to be means to the result (heaven) from the sentence, "One who desires heaven should perform the new- and full-moon sacrifices."

[[1] The reference is to the author of the *Vivaraṇa*.

[2] And hence nearer to the result.

[3] As contributing directly to the result, and not by improving the accessories only.

[4] See note 1 on p. 89.

[5] Although there is no specific direction to that effect, it is clear from this sentence.

[6] Which might make them parts of hearing.

[7] This deals with the third item, context.

[8] The reasilisation of the highest truth, viz., the identity of the self with Brahman.

[9] A sacrifice performed before certain main sacrifices. See note 5 on p. 105.

[10] To satisfy the expectancy about the *modus operandi* of the new- and full-moon sacrifices.]

ननु 'द्रष्टव्यः' इति दर्शनानुवादेन श्रवणे विहिते सति फलवत्तया श्रवणप्रकरणे तत्सन्निधावाम्नातयोर्मननिदिध्यासनयोः प्रयाजन्यायेन प्रकरणादेवाङ्गतेति चेत्, न, "ते ध्यानयोगानुगता अपश्यन्" इत्यादिश्रुत्यन्तरे ध्यानस्य दर्शनसाधनत्वेनावगतस्य अङ्गाकाङ्क्षायां प्रयाजन्यायेन श्रवणमननयोरेवाङ्गत्वापत्तेः। क्रमसमाख्ये च दूरनिरस्ते।

Objection: Since as a corollary to realisation, introduced in the words, "Is to be realised" (*Bṛ.* II. iv. 5, IV. v. 6), hearing is enjoined, and since it is possessed of a result,[1] reflection and meditation, which are mentioned in a context relating to hearing in proximity to it, should from the context itself be parts[2] of that, on the analogy of the Prayāja sacrifices.

Reply: No, because from another Śruti text, "Following the *yoga* of meditation they visualised," etc. (Śv. I. 3), we know that meditation is a means to realisation, and an expectancy being raised regarding its parts,[3] it is hearing and reflection that would be treated as those parts,[4] on the analogy of the Prayāja sacrifices. As for order[5] and derivation,[6] they are entirely out of account.[7]

[[1] Viz., realisation.

[2] As satisfying the expectancy about how to do the hearing.

[3] Constituting the process of meditation.

[4] Instead of reflection and meditation forming parts of hearing.

[5] Parallel position. This also helps us to ascertain the relation of whole and part between two things, for example, a certain sacrifice and a particular sacred text, each occupying an identical place in two parallel sereis.

[6] Which also helps us to fix this relation.

[7] Because there is no question of parallelism with another series, nor is the derivation of the words in question a guide to their mutual relationship.]

किञ्च प्रयाजादिष्वङ्गत्वविचारः सप्रयोजनः। पूर्वपक्षे विकृतिषु न प्रयाजाद्यनुष्ठानम्; सिद्धान्ते तु तत्रापि तदनुष्ठानमिति। प्रकृते तु श्रवणं न कस्यचित् प्रकृतिः, येन मनननिदिध्यासनयोस्तत्राप्यनुष्ठानमङ्गत्वविचारफलं भवेत्। तस्मान्न तार्तीयशेषत्वं मनननिदिध्यासनयोः, किन्तु तथा घटादिकार्ये मृत्पिण्डादीनां प्रधानकारणता, चक्रादीनां सहकारिकारणतेति प्राधान्याप्राधान्यव्यपदेशः, तथा श्रवण-मनननिदिध्यासनानामपीति मन्तव्यम्।

Besides, in the case of the Prayāja and other sacrifices, a discussion on their relationship as a part of something else fulfils a purpose, viz., that according to the *prima facie* view[1] the Prajāja etc. are not to be performed in the variant[2] sacrifices, but that according to the decision, even there they should be performed. In the passage under discussion, however, hearing does not stand for the typical rite with regard to anything, in which case the performance of reflection and meditation even in the latter[3] might be the result of a discussion on the question of their relationship as parts of something. Therefore we must understand that reflection and meditation are not parts of hearing in the manner discussed in third chapter of the *Pūrva-Mīmāṁsā-Sūtras*, but just as with regard to an effect such as a jar, we speak of the relative importance of its causes, saying that the lump of clay, for instance, is the principal cause, and the wheel etc. are auxiliary causes, similarly with regard to hearing, reflection and meditation also.[4]

[[1] Which holds that the Prayāja etc. are not parts of the new- and full-moon sacrifices.

[2] Such as the sacrifice to the sun. See note 7 on p. 92.

[3] That is, some variant function.

[4] That is, hearing is the principal cause and the other two auxiliary causes of the realisation of one's identity with Brahman.]

सूचितश्चैतद्विवरणाचार्यैः—"शक्तितात्पर्यविशिष्टशब्दाव-धारणं प्रमेयावगमं प्रत्यव्यवधानेन कारणं भवति, प्रमाणस्य प्रमेयावगमं प्रत्यव्यवधानात्। मनननिदिध्यासने तु चित्तस्य प्रत्यगात्मप्रवणतासंस्कारपरिनिष्पन्न - तदेकाग्रवृत्तिकार्यद्वारेण ब्रह्मानुभवहेतुतां प्रतिपद्येते इति फलं प्रत्यव्यवहितकारणस्य

शक्तितात्पर्यविशिष्ट-शब्दावधारणस्य व्यवहिते मनननिदिध्यासने तदङ्गे अङ्गीक्रियते" इति ।

This has also been indicated by the author[1] of the *Vivaraṇa* in the following passage: "The comprehension[2] (of the meanings) of words[3] that are possessed of significance and intention[4] is the immediate cause of a cognition of the object to be known, for a means of knowledge is the immediate antecedent[5] to the knowledge of objects. But reflection and meditation become causes of the realisation of Brahman through a concentrated state of the mind with regard to the Supreme Self[6]—an effect accomplished by the latent impressions produced by a tendency[7] of the mind towards It. Hence with regard to the comprehension of words possessing significance and intention, which is the immediate cause of the result,[8] reflection and meditation, which are farther removed,[9] are admitted to be its parts"[10] (V.S.S., p. 104).

[[1] See note 3 on p. 1.

[2] *Comprehension*..............*intention*—All this stands for hearing.

[3] Such as 'thou' and 'That' occurring in the Upaniṣads.

[4] The import of a Vedāntic dictum like, "Thou art That."

[5] A cause is an invariable and immediate antecedent.

[6] Same as Brahman.

[7] That is, a more or less intermittent effort at concentration.

[8] The comprehension of the meaning of dictums indicating the identity of the self with Brahman.

[9] From the result than the comprehension mentioned above, that is, hearing.

[10] That is, auxiliary causes of the comprehension of the identity of the self with Brahman.]

AIDS TO LIBERATION

श्रवणादिषु च मुमुक्षूणामधिकारः, काम्ये कर्मणि फलकामस्याधिकारित्वात्। मुमुक्षायां च नित्यानित्यवस्तु-विवेकस्येहामुत्रार्थफलभोगविरागस्य शमदमोपरतितितिक्षा-समाधानश्रद्धानाञ्च विनियोगः। अन्तरिन्द्रियनिग्रहः शमः। बहिरिन्द्रियनिग्रहो दमः। विक्षेपाभाव उपरतिः। शीतोष्णादिद्वन्द्वसहनं तितिक्षा। चित्तैकाग्र्यं समाधानम्। गुरुवेदान्तवाक्येषु विश्वासः श्रद्धा।

It is aspirants after liberation who are qualified for hearing etc., for (only) one who desires (finite) results is qualified for optional rites. To stimulate a desire for liberation, the discrimination between eternal and transitory things,[1] a dispassion for the enjoyment of sense-objects and their result[2] here and hereafter, calmness, self control, self-withdrawal, fortitude, concentration and faith are of use. Calmness is control of the mind. Self-control is mastery over the senses. Self-withdrawal is the absence of distractions. Fortitude is the bearing of the pairs of opposites such as cold and heat. Concentration is the one-pointedness of the mind. Faith is believing in the words of the teacher and Vedānta.

[[1] Only Brahman is eternal; all else is transitory.
[2] Viz., pleasure.]

अत्र 'उपरम'-शब्देन सन्न्यासोऽभिधीयते ; तथाच सन्न्यासिनामेब श्रवणादावधिकारः, इति केचित्। अपरे तु 'उपरम'-शब्दस्य सन्न्यासवाचकत्वाभावात् , विक्षेपाभाव-मात्रस्य गृहस्थेष्वपि सम्भवात्, जनकादेरपि ब्रह्मविचारस्य श्रूयमाणत्वात् , सर्वाश्रमसाधारणं श्रवणादिविधानमित्याहुः ।

Here some say that the word 'self-withdrawal' means renunciation,[1] so that only monks are qualified for hearing etc. Others, however, maintain that the injunction about hearing etc. is common to all the orders[2] of life, because the word 'self-withdrawal' never signifies renunciation, and a mere absence of distractions is possible even in the case of householders,[3] and also because even Janaka and others are reported to have held discussions on Brahman.

[[1] *Sannyāsa* or giving up the world.
[2] Viz.; those of the student, householder, hermit and monk.
[3] Not monks alone.]

The Goal of Meditation on the Conditioned and the Unconditioned Brahman

सगुणोपासनमपि चित्तैकाग्रयद्वारा निर्विशेषब्रह्मसाक्षात्-कारहेतुः। तदुक्तम् —

"निर्विशेषं परं ब्रह्म साक्षात्कर्तुमनीश्वराः ।
ये मन्दास्तेऽनुकम्प्यन्ते सविशेषनिरूपणैः ॥
वशीकृते मनस्येषां सगुणब्रह्मशीलनात् ।
तदेवाविर्भवेत् साक्षादपेतोपाधिकल्पनम् ॥"

इति । सगुणोपासकानाञ्च अर्चिरादिमार्गेण ब्रह्मलोकगतानां तत्रैव श्रवणाद्युत्पन्नतत्त्वसाक्षात्काराणां ब्रह्मणा सह मोक्षः । कर्मिणान्तु धूमादिमार्गेण पितृलोकं गतानामुपभोगेन कर्मक्षये सति पूर्वकृतसुकृतदुष्कृतानुसारेण ब्रह्मादिस्थावरान्तेषु पुनरुत्पत्तिः । तथाच श्रुतिः—"रमणीयचरणा रमणीयां योनिमापद्यन्ते, कपूयचरणाः कपूयां योनिमापद्यन्ते" इति । प्रतिषिद्धानुष्ठायिनां तु रौरवादिनरकविशेषेषु तत्तत्पापोचित-तीव्रदुःखमनुभूय श्वशूकरादितिर्यग्योनिषु स्थावरादिषु चोत्पत्तिः, इत्यलं प्रसङ्गागतप्रपञ्चेन ।

Meditation on the conditioned Brahman is also a cause of the realisation of the unconditioned Brahman through the concentration of the mind. So it has been said, "Those dull-witted persons who are unable to realise the unconditioned Supreme Brahman are done a favour by the delineation of the conditioned Brahman. When their minds are brought under control by the practice (of meditation) on the conditioned Brahman, that very unconditioned Brahman, divested of the superimposition of limiting adjuncts directly manifests Itself."[1]

Those who meditate on the conditioned Brahman go by the path of light etc.[2] to the world of Hiraṇyagarbha, and attaining there itself a realisation of the Truth by means of hearing etc., they are liebrated along with Hiraṇyagarba.[3] Ritualists,[4] however, go by the path of smoke etc.[5] to the world[6] of the manes, and when their past work has been exhausted through fruition, they are reborn, according to their past good or bad deeds, in bodies beginning with the of Hiraṇyagarbha down to those of plants. Witness the Śruti, "Those who lead good lives attain agreeable births, while those who lead impious lives attain evil births" (*Chā.* V. x. 7, adapted). But those who do forbidden acts, suffer excruciating pain appropriate to their particular sins, in hells such as the Raurava, and are then born in the bodies of lower animals such as dogs and swine, or in plant bodies etc. It is needless to dilate on this incidental matter.

[[1] *Vedānta-kalpataru*, verses 1-2, on *Bṛ.* S. I. i. 20.

[2] That is, the northern route or the path of the gods, in which the deities identified with light, the day, the bright fortnight, the six months of the sun's northward journey, the year, the world of the gods, air, the sun, the moon and lightning, as also Varuṇa (the god of water), Indra and Prajāpati, serve as successive guides, the last three only helping the superhuman being who takes charge of the travellers from the deity of lightning and conducts them to the *Satya-loka*.

[3] See p. 170.

[4] Who mechanically perform scriptural rites, works of public utility and charity.

[5] That is, the southern route or the path of the manes, in which the deities identified with smoke, the night, the dark fortnight, the six months of the sun's southward journey, the world of the manes and the sky, successively guide the travellers to the moon, where they serve the gods and have a limited measure of enjoyment.

[6] To be more precise, the moon.]

निर्गुणब्रह्मसाक्षात्कारवतस्तु न लोकान्तरगमनम्, "न तस्य प्राणा उत्क्रामन्ति" इति श्रुतेः, किन्तु यावत्प्रारब्ध-कर्मक्षयं सुखदुःखे अनुभूय पश्चादपवृज्यते।

One who has realised the unconditioned Brahman, however, never goes to any other world, for the Śruti says, "His vital forces do not depart" (*Bṛ.* IV. iv. 6); but experiencing pleasure and pain till his fructifying[1] work is exhausted, he is afterwards liberated.

[[1] See note 2 on p. 170.]

Fructifying and Accumulated Work

ननु "क्षीयन्ते चास्य कर्माणि तस्मिन् दृष्टे परावरे" इत्यादिश्रुत्या, "ज्ञानाग्निः सर्वकर्माणि भस्मसात् कुरुते तथा" इत्यादिस्मृत्या च ज्ञानस्य सकलकर्मक्षयहेतुत्वनिश्चये सति प्रारब्धकर्मावस्थानमनुपपन्नमिति चेत्, न। "तस्य तावदेव चिरं यावन्न विमोक्ष्ये, अथ सम्पत्स्ये" इत्यादिश्रुत्या, "नाभुक्तं क्षीयते कर्म" इत्यादिस्मृत्या चोत्पादितकार्यकर्मव्यतिरिक्तानां सञ्चितकर्मणामेव ज्ञानविनाश्यत्वावगमात्।

Objection: Since from such Śruti texts as, "And his actions are destroyed when He who is both high and low is seen" (*Mu.* II. ii. 8), and from such Smṛti texts as, "So does the fire of knowledge burn to ashes all actions" (*G.* IV. 37), knowledge is definitely known to be the cause of the destruction of all actions, the survival of the fructifying work does not stand to reason.

Reply: Not so; for from such Śruti texts as, "The delay in his case is only till he is freed from the body; after this he is one with Brahman" (*Chā.* VI. xiv. 2), and from such Smṛti texts as, "Work is not exhausted without fruition" (*Bṛhannār.* XXIX. 76), we know that only accumulated actions that are other than those which have already commenced their effects,[1] are destroyed by knowledge.

[[1] Which is the meaning of the word *prārabdha.*]

सञ्चितं द्विविधम्—सुकृतं दुष्कृतञ्च। तथाच श्रुतिः—"तस्य पुत्रा दायमुपयन्ति, सुहृदः साधुकृत्याम्, द्विषन्तः पापकृत्याम्" इति।

ननु ब्रह्मज्ञानान्मूलाज्ञाननिवृत्तौ तत्कार्यप्रारब्धकर्मणोऽपि निवृत्तेः कथं ज्ञानिनां देहधारणमुपपद्यते इति चेत्, न, अप्रतिबद्धज्ञानस्यैवाज्ञाननिवर्तकतया प्रारब्धकर्मरूप-प्रतिबन्धकदशायामज्ञाननिवृत्तेरनङ्गीकारात्।

Accumulated work is of two kinds, consisting of good deeds and bad deeds. Witness the Śruti,

"His sons inherit his legacies, friends his good deeds, and enemies his bad deeds.[1]"

Objection : With the cessation of primal nescience through the realisation of Brahman, its effect, viz., fructifying work, also ceases. So how can one account for the continunity of bodies of men of realisation ?

Reply : Not so, for since it is unobstructed knowledge that removes nescience, so long as the obstacle of fructifying work persists, the cessation of nescience is not admitted to take place.

[[1] That is, their results.]

Is Liberation Simultaneous for All ?

नन्वेवमपि तत्त्वज्ञानादादेकस्य मुक्तौ सर्वमुक्तिः स्यात्, अविद्याया एकत्वेन तन्निवृत्तौ क्वचिदपि संसारायोगादिति चेत्, न, इष्टापत्तेरित्येके। अपरे तु एतद्दोषपरिहारायैव "इन्द्रो मायाभिः" इति बहुवचनश्रुत्यनुगृहीतमविद्यायानानात्वमङ्गीकर्तव्यमित्याहुः। अन्ये तु एकैवाविद्या, तस्याश्चाविद्याया जीवभेदेन ब्रह्मस्वरूपावरणशक्तयो नाना ; तथाच यस्य ब्रह्मज्ञानं तस्य ब्रह्मस्वरूपावरणशक्तिविशिष्टाविद्यानाशः, न त्वन्यं प्रति, इत्युपगमात् नैकमुक्तौ सर्वमुक्तिः। अत अव "यावदधिकारमवस्थितिराधिकारिकाणाम्" इत्यस्मिन्नधिकरणे अधिकारिपुरुषाणामुत्पन्नतत्त्वज्ञानानामिन्द्रादीनां देहधारणानुपपत्तिमाशङ्क्य अधिकारापादकप्रारब्धकर्मसमाप्त्य-

नन्तरं विदेहकैवल्यमिति सिद्धान्तितम्। तदुक्तमाचार्यवाचस्पतिमिश्रैः—

"उपासनादिसंसिद्धितोषितेश्वरचोदितम्।
अधिकारं समाप्यैते प्रविशन्ति परं पदम्॥"

इति। एतच्चैकमुक्तो सर्वमुक्तिरिति पक्षे नोपपद्यते। तस्मादेकाविद्यापक्षेऽपि प्रतिजीवमावरणभेदोपगमेन व्यवस्थोपपादनीया।

तदेवं ब्रह्मज्ञानान्मोक्षः। स चानर्थनिवृत्तिर्निरतिशयब्रह्मानन्दावाप्तिश्चेति सिद्धं प्रयोजनम्।

इति वेदान्तपरिभाषायां प्रयोजनपरिच्छेदः।

Objection: Even in that case, when one person is liberated through the realisation of Truth, all would be liberated, for since nescience is one, when that ceases, transmigration can never exist for anybody.

Reply: It is no harm, for some say they welcome this objection. Others, however, just to avoid this objection, say that nescience must be admitted to be manifold, as is supported by the use of the plural in the Śruti text, "The Supreme Lord through His powers of cosmic illusion,"[1] etc. Still others maintain that nescience is but one, yet its powers that cover the true nature of Brahman are manifold according to different individual selves. So for one who has realised Brahman, there is destruction of nescience that is possessed of the power to cover Brahman, but not with regard to others. From the above viewpoint, the liberation of one would not lead to the liberation of all. Therefore, under the topic covered by the aphorism, "Those who hold particular authorities live as long as their authority lasts" (*Bṛ S.* III. iii. 31), a doubt is raised as to how persons like Indra, who hold particular positions and who have attained a realisation of Truth, can continue in their bodies, and the conclusion reached on the point is that they attain absolute isolation characterised by disembodiedness after finishing the fructifying work that led them to the particular position. So it has been said by Ācārya Vācaspati Miśra, "After finishing the authority conferred on them by God, who was pleased with their perfection in contemplation etc., they attain the supreme state."[2] This does not fit in with the view that the liberation of one leads to the liberation of all. Therefore, even according to the view that nescience is one, the distinction (between the bound and the liberated) is to be explained by the admission of a different covering (due to nescience) for every individual self.

So this kind of realisation of Brahman leads to liberation, which is the cessation of troubles and the attainment of the absolute bliss of Brahman. Thus the aim of Vedānta (liberation) has been established.

[[1] *Ṛ.* VI. xlvii. 18. See p. 39.
[2] Verse in the *Bhāmatī* on the above aphorism.]

GLOSSARY

(Arranged according to the Sanskrit alphabet)

akhandopādhi: unanalysable characteristic
atīvyāpti: too wide application
atīndriya: imperceptible
atyantābhāva: absolute non-existence
adhikaraṇa: (1) substratum; (2) topic
adhiṣṭhāna: substratum
adhyāsa: superimposition
anavasthā: *regressus in infinitum*
anirvacanīya: indescribable, logically indefinable
anupapatti: inexplicability
anupalambha: non-apprehension
anubhava: experience
anumāna: inference (the instrument)
anumiti: inferential knowledge
anuyogin: support, substratum
anuvāda: restatement
anuvyavasāya: perception of a cognition, apperception
antaḥ-karaṇa: the internal organ, mind
anyathā-khyāti: error, taking one thing for another
anyathāsiddha: superfluous
anyonyābhāva: mutual non-existence
anvaya: (1) (method of) agreement; (2) logical connection
anvaya-vyatirekin: having both similar and contrary instances
aparokṣa: (1) immediate; (2) perceptual
apūrva: (1) the unseen result; (2) original

apramā: invalid knowledge, error
abhyupagama: (1) admission; (2) tentative admission
arthavāda: corroborative statement
arthāpatti: presumption
alaukika: extraordinary
avacchedaka: determining characteristic
avacchinna: limited or determined
avayava: aggregate, whole
Avayavin: Aggregate, whole
avidyā: nescience
avyāpti: too narrow application
asiddha: unfounded
ākāṁkṣā: expectancy
ākāśa: ether
āgama: verbal or scriptural testimony
āpta: a trustworthy person
āropya: the thing superimposed
āśraya: basis, substratum
āsatti: contiguity
indriya: organ
iṣṭa: desirable
upacāra: metaphor
upamāna: comparison (the instrument)
upamiti: knowledge based on comparison
upasthiti: knowledge
upahita: possessed of a limiting adjunct
upādāna: material cause
upādhi: (1) a general property other than the generic attribute (*jātī*); (2) limiting adjunct; (3) condition
kapāla: one-half of a jar, or potsherd
kāraṇatā: causality
kṛti: volition

klṛpta: prescribed, necessarily to be accepted
kevalānvayin: having no contrary instance, universally present
kevala-vyatirekin: having no similar instance
guṇa: (1) quality, (2) ingredient, (3) merit
gaurava: cumbrousness
graha: apprehension
cit: Pure Consciousness
citta: the recollective aspect of the mind
caitanya: Pure Consciousness
jāti: generic attribute
jīva: individual self
jñāna-lakṣaṇa: based on knowledge
tarka: argument, *reductio ad absurdum*
tātparya: intention
tādātmya: identity
tejas: fire, light
deśa: space, place
dravya: substance
dharma: (1) attribute; (2) righteousness
dharmin: something possessing an attribute
naya: system
nigamana: conclusion
nirvikalpa: indeterminate
pakṣa: subject, that in or about which something is inferred.
pakṣa-dharmatā: presence in the subject
pada: (1) word; (2) status
padārtha: (1) category; (2) the thing signified by a word
paramāṇu: atom
paramparā-sambandha: indirect relation

parāmarśa: consideration, the knowledge that a subordinate concomitant of the thing to be inferred is in the subject.
pariṇāma: transformation, actual change
parokṣa: mediate
pāramārthika: absolute
puruṣa: (1) man; (2) person; (3) soul
puruṣārtha: human end
prakaraṇa: context
prakāra: feature in knowledge, corresponding to the adjectival part of its object
prakṛti: (1) Nature; (2) typical (sacrifice)
pradhvaṁsābhāva: non-existence as destruction
pratiyogin: (1) counterpositive, that which is negated; (2) that which rests on something else; (3) that which corresponds to something
pratyakṣa: (1) perception (the instrument); (2) perceptual knowledge
pratyabhijñā: recognition
pratyāsatti: connection, especially between a sense-organ and its object
pramā: valid knowledge
pramāṇa: instrument of valid knowledge
pramātṛ: subject or knower
prameya: object of valid knowledge
prayojaka: (1) criterion or deciding factor; (2) corroborative argument; (3) cause
pravṛtti: effort
prāgabhāva: previous non-existence or potential existence
prātibhāsika: illusory
bādha: (1) contradiction, nullification; (2) incongruity

bādhita: contradicted, nullified
buddhi: (1) intellect; (2) cognition
bhāna: cognition
bhāva: (1) positive entity; (2) existence
bhūta: element (such as earth)
mahat-tattva: cosmic intellect
māya: cosmic illusion
yogyatā: (1) consistency; (2) capacity
rūpa: (1) colour; (2) form
lakṣaṇa: definition, characteristic
lakṣaṇā: implication, secondary meaning
lāghava: the law of simplicity or parsimony
liṅga: (1) sign, reason; (2) indication
laukika: ordinary, conventional
vijñāna: knowledge
vipakṣa: contrary instance
viruddha: contradictory
vivarta: apparent change
viśiṣṭa-buddhi: (1) cognition of a qualified entity; (2) qualified knowledge
viśeṣaṇa: qualifying attribute
viśeṣya: substantive
viṣaya: object
visaṁvādin: unsuccessful
vṛtti: (1) mental state; (2) existence; (3) existent; (4) reference
vaiśiṣṭya: relatedness
vyakti: individual
vyatireka: (method of) difference
vyatireka-vyāpti: negative invariable concomitance
vyadhikaraṇa: not abiding in the substratum of a thing, extraneous
vyavahāra: use, convention
vyāpaka: inclusive
vyāpāra: operation, intermediate cause

vyāpti: invariable concomitance
vyāpya: subordinate concomitant
vyāvartaka: that which generates the idea of distinction
vyāvahārika: conventional, relatively real
vyāvṛtta: excluded
śakti: (1) inherent power; (2) significance
śabda: (1) sound; (2) word; (3) verbal testimony
śābda-bodha: verbal comprehension
śruti: (1) revealed knowledge, the Vedas; (2) direct enunciation
saṅkara: cross division
saṁyoga: conjunction
saṁvādin: successful
saṁsāra: transmigratory existence
saṁskāra: latent impression
sannikarṣa: see *pratyāsatti*
sapakṣa: similar instance
samavāya: inherence
samavāyi-kāraṇa: inherent cause
samaveta: inherent
samānādhikaraṇa: having a common substratum, co-existent
savikalpa: determinate; consisting of a substantive, a qualifying attribute and a relation between the two
sahacāra: co-existence
sākṣātkāra: realisation
sākṣin: witness
sādharmya: similarity
sādhya: the thing to be inferred
sāmagrī: totality of causes
siddha: established, proved
smṛti: (1) recollection; (2) sacred literature based on the Vedas
hetu: reason or ground for inference

INDEX